Lose Your Mother

Lose Your Mother

A Journey Along the

Atlantic Slave Route

SAIDIYA HARTMAN

FARRAR, STRAUS AND GIROUX

NEW YORK

FARRAR, STRAUS AND GIROUX
19 Union Square West, New York 10003

Library of Congress Cataloging-in-Publication Data
Hartman, Saidiya V.
    Lose your mother : a journey along the Atlantic slave route / Saidiya Hartman.— 1st ed.
        p.   cm.
    ISBN-13: 978-0-374-27082-7 (hardcover : alk. paper)
    ISBN-10: 0-374-27082-1 (hardcover : alk. paper)
      1. Ghana—Description and travel.   2. Hartman, Saidiya V.—Travel—Ghana.
    3. Slave trade—Ghana—History.   4. Historic sites—Ghana.
    5. Ghana—History, Local.   I. Title.

DT510.2.H375   2006
306.3´6209667—dc22

                                                                    2006029407

Designed by Cassandra J. Pappas

www.fsgbooks.com

1   3   5   7   9   10   8   6   4   2

To

Samuel and Kasia

CONTENTS

LIST OF ILLUSTRATIONS

Lose Your Mother

Prologue:
The Path of Strangers

As I DISEMBARKED from the bus in Elmina, I heard it. It was sharp and clear, as it rang in the air, and clattered in my ear making me recoil. *Obruni.* A stranger. A foreigner from across the sea. Three children gathered at the bus station shouted it, giggling as it erupted from their mouths, tickled to have spotted some extraterrestrial fallen to earth in Ghana. They summoned me, *"obruni, obruni,"* as if it were a form of *akwaaba* (welcome), reserved just for me. As the words weaved their way through the crowd and landed on me, I imagined myself in their eyes: an alien tightly wrapped in the skin of a blue rain slicker, the big head bursting from its navy pod.

My appearance confirmed it: I was the proverbial outsider. Who else sported vinyl in the tropics? My customs belonged to another country: my too-fast gait best suited to navigating the streets of Manhattan, my unfashionable German walking shoes, my unruly tufts twisted into two French braids, fuzzy and unfurling in the humid air. Old and new worlds stamped my face, a blend of peoples and nations and masters and slaves long forgotten. In the jumble of my features, no certain line of origin could be traced. Clearly, I was not Fanti, or Ashanti, or Ewe, or Ga.

Then I started to hear it everywhere. It was the buzz in the market. It was the shorthand my new Ghanaian friends used to describe me to their old friends. *Obruni* lurked like an undertone in the hustle of street peddlers. People said it casually in my face, until I sucked my teeth and said "ehh!" informing the speaker that first, I knew what the word meant, and second, I didn't relish the label.

But then I learned to accept it. After all, I was a stranger from across the sea. A black face didn't make me kin. Even when otherwise undetected, I was betrayed when I opened my mouth and heard my father's Brooklyn brogue rippling across the surface of my studied speech, wreaking havoc with the regimented syntax enforced by my mother the grammarian, whose scrupulous speech was a way of masking her southern origins and blending into New York. My direct way of speaking sounded sharp-edged and angular when compared to the tactful evasion and obliging indirection of the local English idiom. The brisk clip of my speech, flattened vowels, and sounds trapped in the dome of my mouth, expiring from lack of air, branded me the foreigner.

I was the stranger in the village, a wandering seed bereft of the possibility of taking root. Behind my back people whispered, *dua ho mmire*: a mushroom that grows on the tree has no deep soil. Everyone avoided the word "slave," but we all knew who was who. As a "slave baby," I represented what most chose to avoid: the catastrophe that was our past, and the lives exchanged for India cloth, Venetian beads, cowrie shells, guns, and rum. And what was forbidden to discuss: the matter of someone's origins.

Obruni forced me to acknowledge that I didn't belong anyplace. The domain of the stranger is always an elusive *elsewhere*. I was born in another country, where I also felt like an alien and which in part determined why I had come to Ghana. I had grown weary of being stateless. Secretly I wanted to belong somewhere or, at least, I wanted a convenient explanation of why I felt like a stranger.

As a child, when I was angry with my mother and father, I'd conjure up glorious imaginary parents who'd rescue me from the awful people forcing me to call them Mom and Dad. I often imagined that the singer Johnny Hartman was my father since we shared the same last name. Whenever my dad played his Coltrane albums, I listened for Johnny Hartman's lovely wistful voice. If I didn't think too hard about why he had abandoned me, I could find succor in this fiction of origins. The sting of *obruni* allowed for no such fiction.

I complained to an expatriate friend living in Accra that I had never felt as much a stranger as I did in Ghana. He muttered, "uh-huh," and then he asked, "When you go to Chicago, do you expect black folks there to welcome you because you're from New York? Well, why should it be any different here?"

THE MOST UNIVERSAL DEFINITION of the slave is a stranger. Torn from kin and community, exiled from one's country, dishonored and violated, the slave defines the position of the outsider. She is the perpetual outcast, the coerced migrant, the foreigner, the shamefaced child in the lineage. Contrary to popular belief, Africans did not sell their brothers and sisters into slavery. They sold strangers: those outside the web of kin and clan relationships, nonmembers of the polity, foreigners and barbarians at the outskirts of their country, and lawbreakers expelled from society. In order to betray your race, you had first to imagine yourself as one. The language of race developed in the modern period and in the context of the slave trade.

The very term "slavery" derived from the word "Slav," because Eastern Europeans were the slaves of the medieval world. At the beginning of modernity, slavery declined in Europe as it expanded in Africa, although as late as the seventeenth and eighteenth centuries, it was still possible to purchase "white" slaves—English, Spanish, and Portuguese captives in the Mediterranean ports of North Africa. The Iberians can be credited, according to one historian, "for restricting bondage, for the first time in history to peoples of African descent." It was not until the sixteenth and seventeenth centuries that the line between the slave and the free separated Africans and Europeans and hardened into a color line.

For Europeans, race established a hierarchy of human life, determined which persons were expendable, and selected the bodies that could be transformed into commodities. For those chained in the lower decks of a slave ship, race was both a death sentence and the language of solidarity. The vision of an African continental family or a sable race standing shoulder to shoulder was born by captives, exiles, and orphans and in the aftermath of the Atlantic slave trade. Racial solidarity was expressed in the language of kinship because it both evidenced the wound and attempted to heal it. The slave and the ex-slave wanted what had been severed: kin. Those in the diaspora translated the story of race into one of love and betrayal.

I HAD COME TO GHANA in search of strangers. The first time for a few weeks in the summer of 1996 as a tourist interested in the slave forts hunkered along the coast and the second time for a year beginning in the fall of 1997 as a Fulbright Scholar affiliated with the National Museum of Ghana. Ghana was as likely a place as any to begin my journey, because I wasn't seeking the ancestral village but the barracoon. As both a professor conducting research on slavery and a descendant of the enslaved, I was desperate to reclaim the dead, that is, to reckon with the lives undone and obliterated in the making of human commodities.

I wanted to engage the past, knowing that its perils and dangers still threatened and that even now lives hung in the balance. Slavery had established a measure of man and a ranking of life and worth that has yet to be undone. If slavery persists as an issue in the political life of black America, it is not because of an antiquarian obsession with bygone days or the burden of a too-long memory, but because black lives are still imperiled and devalued by a racial calculus and a political arithmetic that were entrenched centuries ago. This is the afterlife of slavery—skewed life chances, limited access to health and education, premature death, incarceration, and impoverishment. I, too, am the afterlife of slavery.

Nine slave routes traversed Ghana. In following the trail of captives from the hinterland to the Atlantic coast, I intended to retrace the process by which lives were destroyed and slaves born. I stepped into the path of more than seven hundred thousand captives, passing through the coastal merchant societies that acted as middlemen and brokers in the slave trade, the inland warrior aristocracies that captured people and supplied slaves to the coast, and the northern societies that were raided and plundered. I visited the European forts and storehouses on the three-hundred-mile stretch of the littoral from Beyin to Keta, the slave markets established by strong inland states that raided their enemies and subordinates and profited from the trade, and the fortified towns and pillaged communities of the hinterland that provided the steady flow of captives.

I chose Ghana because it possessed more dungeons, prisons, and slave pens than any other country in West Africa—tight dark cells buried underground, barred cavernous cells, narrow cylindrical cells, dank cells, makeshift cells. In the rush for gold and slaves that began at the end of the fifteenth century, the Portuguese, English, Dutch, French, Danes, Swedes, and Brandenburgers (Germans) built fifty permanent outposts, forts, and castles designed to ensure their place in the Africa trade. In these dungeons, storerooms, and holding cells, slaves were imprisoned until transported across the Atlantic.

Neither blood nor belonging accounted for my presence in Ghana, only the path of strangers impelled toward the sea. There were no survivors of my lineage or far-flung relatives of whom I had come in search, no places and people before slavery that I could trace. My family trail disappeared in the second decade of the nineteenth century.

Unlike Alex Haley, who embraced the sprawling clans of Juffure as his own, grafted his family into the community's genealogy, and was feted as the lost son returned, I traveled to Ghana in search of the expendable and the defeated. I had not come to marvel at the wonders of African civilization or to be made proud by the royal court of Asante, or to admire the great states that harvested captives and sold them as slaves. I was not wistful for aristocratic origins. Instead I would seek the commoners, the unwilling and coerced migrants who created a new culture in the hostile world of the Americas and who fashioned themselves again, making possibility out of dispossession.

By the time the captives arrived on the coast, often after trekking hundreds of miles, passed through the hands of African and European traders, and boarded the slaver, they were strangers. In Ghana, it is said that a stranger is like water running over the ground after a rainstorm: it soon dries up and leaves behind no traces. When the children of Elmina christened me a stranger, they called me by my ancestors' name.

"STRANGER" IS THE X that stands in for a proper name. It is the place-holder for the missing, the mark of the passage, the scar between native and citizen. It is both an end and a beginning. It announces the disappearance of the known world and the antipathy of the new one. And the longing and the loss redolent in the label were as much my inheritance as they were that of the enslaved.

Unwilling to accept the pain of this, I had tried to undo the past and reinvent myself. In a gesture of self-making intended to obliterate my parents' hold upon me and immolate the daughter they hoped for rather than the one I was, I changed my name. I abandoned Valarie. She was the princess my mother wanted me to be, all silk and taffeta and sugar and spice. She was the pampered girl my mother would have been had she grown up in her father's house. Valarie wasn't a family name but one she had chosen for me to assuage the shame of being Dr. Dinkins's outside daughter. Valarie was a name weighted with the yearning for cotillions and store-bought dresses and summers at the lake. It was a gilded name, all golden on the outside, all rawness and rage on the inside. It erased the poor black girl my mother was ashamed to be.

So in my sophomore year in college, I adopted the name Saidiya. I asserted my African heritage to free myself from my mother's grand designs. Saidiya liberated me from parental disapproval and pruned the bourgeois branches of my genealogy. It didn't matter that I had been rejected first. My name established my solidarity with the people, extirpated all evidence of upstanding Negroes and their striving bastard heirs, and confirmed my place in the company of poor black girls—Tamikas, Roqueshas, and Shanequas. Most of all, it dashed my mother's hopes. I had found it in an African names book; it means "helper."

At the time, I didn't realize that my attempt to rewrite the past would be as thwarted as was my mother's. Saidiya was also a fiction of someone

I would never be—a girl unsullied by the stain of slavery and inherited disappointment. Nor did I know then that Swahili was a language steeped in mercantilism and slave trading and disseminated through commercial relations among Arab, African, and Portuguese merchants. The ugly history of elites and commoners and masters and slaves I had tried to expunge with the adoption of an authentic name was thus unwittingly enshrined.

I realized too late that the breach of the Atlantic could not be remedied by a name and that the routes traveled by strangers were as close to a *mother country* as I would come. Images of kin trampled underfoot and lost along the way, abandoned dwellings repossessed by the earth, and towns vanished from sight and banished from memory were all that I could ever hope to claim. And I set out on the slave route, which was both an existent territory with objective coordinates and the figurative realm of an imagined past, determined to do exactly this.

IT WAS MY GREAT-GRANDFATHER MOSES, my mother's grandfather, who initiated me on this journey. On a hazy summer morning my brother and I set out with Poppa to learn about our people. The summer of 1974 would be the last time we visited Montgomery, Alabama, for anything other than a brief four-day trip, and Poppa, sensing this, introduced us to our past. Peter and I had outgrown the boundaries of Underwood Street and tired of the local kids who, in turn, had grown weary of us and too many sentences beginning "In New York," which lorded the wonders of our world over the restrictions of theirs—really good Chinese food, the roller coaster at Coney Island, knishes, fire hydrants like geysers crashing on sweltering asphalt streets, and the one-hour mass where we were allowed to wear jeans and Sister Madonna played the guitar, instead of the all-day trial of Morning Pilgrim Baptist Church, where you were pinched if you nodded off and had to wear dresses and tights and jackets and ties, no matter how hot it was.

Poppa took us on a tour of the rural outskirts of Montgomery County, where our people had lived before moving into town. As we drove through the monochromatic brown stretch of farmland broken only by dull grazing cows, Poppa would stick his hand out the window at regular intervals and declare, "Land used to be owned by black folks." Now agribusiness owned everything as far as the eye could see.

Looking at all the land worked by us but that was no longer ours triggered Poppa's memory. No doubt he remembered *his* grandfather, whose land had been stolen by a white neighbor upon his death, forcing his wife and children off the property. White neighbors had poisoned his well and killed his farm animals, trying to drive him off the land, but only after his death did they succeed in evicting his family and taking his property with a fraudulent deed. In the middle of explaining how black farmers lost it all—to night riders, banks, and the government—Poppa drifted into a story about slavery, because for men like Poppa and my great-great-great-grandfather to be landless was to be a slave. He called slavery times *the dark days*.

What I knew about slavery up until that afternoon with Poppa had been pretty basic. Of course I knew black people had been enslaved and that I was descended from slaves, but slavery was vague and faraway to me, like the embarrassing incidents adults loved to share with you about some incredulous thing you had done as a toddler but of which you had no memory. It wasn't that you suspected them of making it up as much as it concerned some earlier incarnation of yourself that was not really you. Slavery felt like that too, something that was part of me but not me at the same time. It had never been concrete before, not something as palpable as my great-grandfather in his starched cotton shirt sitting next to me in a brown Ford, or a parched red clay country road, or a horse trader from Tennessee, or the name of a girl, not much younger than me, who had been chattel.

Slavery was never mentioned at my school, Queen of All Saints, although I learned about Little Black Sambo from my fourth-grade teacher, Mrs. Conroy, whose lilting Irish tones mollified offense. When I wore Afro-puffs, she called me an African princess, provoking the derisive laughter of my classmates, black and white alike. Nor was slavery discussed at the Black Power summer camp where, unbeknownst to my parents who recognized only that the camp was free and within walking distance from our house, counselors forbade us to apologize to white people, where I wore T-shirts embossed with revolutionary Swahili slogans, the meanings of which I could never remember. The counselors taught us to disdain property, perform the Black Power handshake, and march in strict formation, but they never mentioned the Middle Passage or chattel persons.

As we drove through the countryside, Poppa told us his mother and grandmother had been slaves. His grandmother Ellen was born in Tennessee around 1820. She was a nursemaid for a horse and mule trader. As a house slave, she was spared the onerous work of the field, dressed better than the hands, dined on crumbs and leftovers, and traveled with her owners. Yet the relative advantage she might have enjoyed when compared with other slaves didn't prevent her from being sold when her owner discovered himself in a "situation."

Ellen had accompanied her master and his family on a trip to Alabama, where he went to sell a parcel of horses. Something went wrong in Alabama and she was sold, along with the horses. Maybe an unlucky hand at cards or outstanding debts or quick cash were what went wrong, at least for Ellen. In Tennessee, she might have had children of her own because nursemaids were often wet nurses who suckled their master's children. If she was lucky her mother might have lived with the family too. If she had children or a mother or a man back in Tennessee, then she was separated from them without a good-bye.

Poppa's mother, Ella, was born in Alabama and still a girl when slavery ended. He said less about her than about his grandmother, maybe because his grandmother raised him or maybe because speaking of his mother made him feel like the grief-stricken fifteen-year-old he had been in 1907 when she died. He preferred to stick to the essential facts—birth, death, and emancipation.

Sometime in 1865, a Union soldier approached Ella in the middle of her chores. "A soldier rode up to my ma and told her she was free." The starkness of Ella's story stunned me. Her life consisted of two essential facts—slavery and freedom juxtaposed to mark the beginning and end of the chronicle. But this was what slavery did: it stripped your history to bare facts and precious details.

I don't know if it was the bare bones of Ella's story or the hopefulness and despair that lurked in Poppa's words as he recounted it, as if he were weighing the promise of freedom against the vast stretches of stolen land before him, that made me eager to know more than what Poppa remembered or wanted to share. Peter and I listened, silent. We didn't know what to say.

Poppa didn't remember any kin before his grandmother, who smoked a corncob pipe. He had inherited his love of pipes from her. It was one of the things I adored about him. He always smelled sweet like the maple tobacco smoke rising from his pipe. What he knew about our family ended with his grandmother Ellen. He remembered no other names. When he spoke of these things, I saw how the sadness and anger of not knowing his people distorted the soft lines of Poppa's face. It surprised me; he had always seemed invincible, strapping, six foot two, and handsome, even at eighty-five. I had seen this ache in others too. At a barbecue at my grandmother's, two of her cousins nearly came to blows disputing a grandfather's name. I was still too young then to recognize the same feelings inside me. But I wondered about my great-great-great-grandmother's mother, as well as all the others who had been forgotten.

If Poppa's mother or grandmother shared any details about their lives in slavery, he didn't share them with my brother and me. No doubt he was unwilling to disclose what he considered unspeakable. Still, he shared more with my brother and me than he had with my mother. Even now, he liked to call her "little girl." When I returned home and asked her if Poppa had ever spoken to her about slavery or her great-grandmother Ella, the girl on the road, she replied, "When I was growing up we didn't talk of such things." Her great-grandmother had died before she was born, so my mother recalled nothing about her, not even her name.

At twelve I became obsessed with the maternal great-great-grandmother I had never known, endlessly constructing and rearranging the scene: her unease as the soldier advanced toward her, or the soldier on horseback looming over her and the smile inching across her face as she digested his words, or the peal of laughter trailing behind her as she turned upon her heels, or the war between disbelief and wonder that overcame Ella as she bolted toward her mother. Mulling over the details Poppa had shared with me, I tried to fill in the blank spaces of the story, but I never succeeded.

Since that afternoon with my great-grandfather, I had been looking for relatives whose only proof of existence was fragments of stories and names that repeated themselves across generations.

Unlike friends who possessed a great trove of family photographs, I had no idea what my great-grandmother looked like or even my grandaunts when they were girls. All these things were gone; some of the photographs were given as tokens to dead relatives and buried with them; others were lost. The images I possessed of them were drawn from memory and imagination. My aunt Mosella, whose name was itself a memorial to my great-grandfather Moses and his mother Ella, once described a photograph taken of her mother and my great-great-grandmother Polly, whom everyone called Big Momma. In the photograph, her mother, Lou, was wearing a ruffled dress with bloomers and seated on Big Momma's lap. She didn't remember what my great-great-grandmother wore but only reechoed my mother's description of her: she was a big-boned woman with a round face the color of dark chocolate.

Big Momma had never spoken of her life in slavery, nor had Ellen or Ella. Poppa could fill in only the bare outlines of their lives. The gaps and

silences of my family were not unusual: slavery made the past a mystery, unknown and unspeakable.

THE TALES OF THE PAST that my mother had been willing to share were all about Jim Crow. She had grown up in a segregated world where essentially she was barred from childhood from parks and swimming pools and malt shops. Her reminiscences were replete with proscriptions; the simplest needs, whether for a drink of water or to use the bathroom, were regulated by the color line.

My father's stories about racism were few. He remembered being called nigger for the first time as an enlisted man in the Air Force in Alabama, and he barely escaped being court-martialed after striking a white corporal. But I never heard him utter the words "slave" or "slavery." I knew even less about my paternal kin. My father and his family did not hanker after unnamed ancestors or wonder what might have been. Their losses were too immediate. My grandparents had left Curaçao, a thirty-five-mile stretch of arid land adrift in the Caribbean Sea, vowing to make good in New York and to return home. But as the decades passed, they convinced themselves that it was still too soon, or that the money wasn't right yet, or that it would be easier to leave the following year.

Not ready to admit the defeat of their permanent estrangement, they held steadfast to the belief in American opportunity. It was a word they uttered to stave off fear; it consoled them on bad days; it reminded them why they were in the States rather than at home. Opportunity—it was intoned as if it was the consolation they required, as if it repelled prejudice, warded off failure, remedied isolation, and quieted the ache of yearning. It shrouded the past and set their gaze solely on the future. The money sent home didn't assuage the anger of mothers nursing abandonment or teenage children anticipating a life in the States they would never have. Nostalgia or regret could kill you in a place like America, so they banked only on tomorrow.

At the same time, they blamed America for everything that went wrong. America was the benediction and the curse. It was weather so frigid it brought you to tears. It was the high price of coal. It was your son's insolence. It was your daughters' refusal to speak Papiamento. America was the cause of every complaint and the excuse for every foul deed.

When it became clear that they would never return home, my grandparents erected a wall of half-truths and silence between themselves and the past. They parceled time, lopping off the past as if it were an extra appendage, as if they could dispose of the feelings connecting them to the world before this one and banish the dreams they had always imagined as the route back. In time, they decided the present was all they could bear. They died in the States with their green cards as the only proof that they had once belonged elsewhere.

Unlike my grandparents, I thought the past was a country to which I could return. I refused the lesson of their lives, which in my arrogance I had misunderstood as defeat. I believed that I would succeed in accomplishing what my grandparents had not; to me this meant tumbling the barricade between *then* and *now*, liberating my grandmother and grandfather from the small, small world of Park Place, and revisiting a history that began long before Brooklyn. So I embarked on my journey, no doubt as blindly as they had on theirs, and in search of people who left behind no traces.

I HAPPENED UPON my maternal great-great-grandmother in a volume of slave testimony from Alabama, while doing research for my dissertation. I felt joyous at having discovered her in the dusty tiers of the Yale library. (Not Ella the girl on the road, but my great-grandmother Minnie's mother, Polly.) When asked what she remembered about slavery, she replied, "Not a thing." I was crushed. I knew this wasn't true. I recognized that a host of good reasons explained my great-great-grandmother's reluctance to talk about slavery with a white interviewer in Dixie in the age of Jim Crow. But her silence stirred my own questions about memory and slavery: What is it we choose to remember about the past and what is it we will to forget? Did my great-great-grandmother believe that forgetting provided the possibility of a new life? Was nothing to be gained by focusing on the past? Were the words she refused to share what I should remember? Was the experience of slavery best represented by all the stories

I would never know? Were gaps and silences and empty rooms the substance of my history? If ruin was my sole inheritance and the only certainty the impossibility of recovering the stories of the enslaved, did this make my history tantamount to mourning? Or worse, was it a melancholia I would never be able to overcome?

"I do not know my father." "I have lost my mother." "My children are scattered in every direction." These were common refrains in the testimony. As important were the silences and evasions, matters cryptically encoded as "the worst things yet" or the "dark days," which exceeded the routine violence of slavery—whippings, humiliation, and separation from kin—and identified abuses that were beyond description: excremental punishments, sexual violation, and tortures rivaling anything the Marquis de Sade had imagined. Alongside the terrible things one had survived was also the shame of having survived it. Remembering warred with the will to forget.

My graduate training hadn't prepared me to tell the stories of those who had left no record of their lives and whose biography consisted of the terrible things said about them or done to them. I was determined to fill in the blank spaces of the historical record and to represent the lives of those deemed unworthy of remembering, but how does one write a story about an encounter with nothing?

Years later when looking through the Alabama testimony, I was unable to find her. There was an Ella Thomas in the volume. Had I confused one great-great-grandmother with another? I reviewed my preliminary notes, desperately searched for the interview I had never copied, scoured five volumes, the two from Alabama and the adjacent ones, but there was no Minnie or Polly or anyone with a name similar, nor did I find the paragraph stamped in my memory: the words filling less than half the page, the address on Clark Street, the remarks about her appearance, all of which were typed by a machine in need of a new ribbon. It was as if I had conjured her up. Was my hunger for the past so great that I was now encountering ghosts? Had my need for an entrance into history played tricks on me, mocked my scholarly diligence, and exposed me as a girl blinded by mother loss?

The few traces of my great-grandmother had disappeared right before my eyes. This incident turned out to be representative. It served as my introduction to the slipperiness and elusiveness of slavery's archive.

The archive contained what you would expect: the manifests of slavers; ledger books of trade goods; inventories of foodstuffs; bills of sale; itemized lists of bodies alive, infirm, and dead; captains' logs; planters' diaries. The account of commercial transactions was as near as I came to the enslaved. In reading the annual reports of trading companies and the letters that traveled from London and Amsterdam to the trade outposts on the West African coast, I searched for the traces of the destroyed. In every line item, I saw a grave. Commodities, cargo, and things don't lend themselves to representation, at least not easily. The archive dictates what can be said about the past and the kinds of stories that can be told about the persons cataloged, embalmed, and sealed away in box files and folios. To read the archive is to enter a mortuary; it permits one final viewing and allows for a last glimpse of persons about to disappear into the slave hold.

I ARRIVED IN Ghana intent upon finding the remnants of those who had vanished. It's hard to explain what propels a quixotic mission, or why you miss people you don't even know, or why skepticism doesn't lessen longing. The simplest answer is that I wanted to bring the past closer. I wanted to understand how the ordeal of slavery began. I wanted to comprehend how a boy came to be worth three yards of cotton cloth and a bottle of rum or a woman equivalent to a basketful of cowries. I wanted to cross the boundary that separated kin from stranger. I wanted to tell the story of the commoners—the people made the fodder of the slave trade and pushed into remote and desolate regions to escape captivity.

If I had hoped to skirt the sense of being a stranger in the world by coming to Ghana, then disappointment awaited me. And I had suspected as much before I arrived. Being a stranger concerns not only matters of familiarity, belonging, and exclusion but as well involves a particular relation to the past. If the past is another country, then I am its citizen. I am the relic of an experience most preferred not to remember, as if the sheer will to forget could settle or decide the matter of history. I am a reminder that twelve million crossed the Atlantic Ocean and the past is not yet over. I am the progeny of the captives. I am the vestige of the dead. And history is how the secular world attends to the dead.

ONE

Afrotopia

"NO MATTER HOW BIG a stranger's eyes, they cannot see." I don't think Stella, the housekeeper at the Marcus Garvey Guest House, was the person I first heard use these words to describe the proverbial blindness of Westerners, but she might as well have been. I credit her with my initiation. The judgment stung as much the first month as it did ten months later. It was as if these words were always floating about in my head, just waiting for the right occasion. Now it's impossible for me to recall that first evening without them.

The Marcus Garvey Guest House was in precipitous decline. When Stella opened the door to the room that would be mine, I hoped my disappointment wasn't too obvious. I didn't want to appear the spoiled American. Looking at the dingy yellowed walls and the brown water stains that seeped across the ceiling and the green carpet stiff with dirt, I felt the first pang of homesickness and realized that a week at the guesthouse was going to be a long time. The room was sweltering and the air was thick with mildew. A colleague at the National Museum had chosen the guesthouse because it was a bargain for Accra. It was only forty dollars a night, one-third the price of the average two-star hotel. So I would have to stick it out until my too expensive flat in Osu, a trendy commercial district of Accra with a sprawl of stores, restaurants, bars, Internet cafés, and discotheques, was ready at the end of the week.

Stella turned on the overhead fan, which churned the stale air but brought no comfort, retrieved a small stack of threadbare towels from the corner bureau and placed them on the bed, pointed out the bathroom down the hall, and then excused herself for the night. The room made me uneasy, so I turned up all the lights and delayed getting into bed. I was writing in my journal about the squalor of the guesthouse and Marcus Garvey's faith in Africa's redemption and wondering if I shared his optimism when I dozed off in the overstuffed chair.

"Turn off the lights! Turn off the lights!" Stella screamed as she burst into my room and the door slammed into the wall. She was naked except for a towel wrapped around her, which barely covered her breasts and privates. The terror on her face made me obey. I jumped out of the chair, turned off the lamps on the nightstands, and ran to the corner to shut off the overhead light. Before I had the chance to ask what was going on, she flew out of the room and pulled the door behind her. Then I heard the firecrackers or what I first thought were firecrackers. It was pitch-black outside. All the exterior lights of the guesthouse had been cut off. I peered from behind the heavy gold curtains and saw soldiers and jeeps and armored tanks moving along the streets of the capital. Oh, my God. A coup. My knees began to tremble and then urine rushed down my legs.

There had been a series of coups in Ghana. In 1966, Colonel Kotoka and Lieutenant General Afrifa had deposed Kwame Nkrumah; there were coups again in 1972, 1979, 1981, 1982, and 1983. Five military governments and three civilian governments had ruled the country since independence. Ghana's current president, Jerry Rawlings, had been a flight lieutenant in the Air Force when he seized the state through a military revolt on December 31, 1981; he had staged the last successful coup. (He had since been elected in 1992 and again in 1996.) In sub-Saharan Africa, more than seventy leaders of state had been overthrown by the armed forces. It was how the state changed hands. Soldiers decided who held the reins of power.

I fumbled around in the darkness until I found my money belt and passport, which I quickly strapped beneath my skirt, hoping that three hundred dollars and a few thousand more in American Express traveler's checks would be enough to buy my way out of trouble, thwart a rapist, and make my way to the airport. Maybe the soldiers would leave me alone because I was an American. God, please let me survive this night, I prayed, and I promise I will leave Ghana on the first available flight. I blockaded the door with a chair and put on running shoes so I would be able to flee if and when I needed to. As I listened to the tanks rolling through the streets, I began to cry. What was I doing here?

For more than an hour I listened to the sounds of vehicles rumbling along the road and the boots of soldiers striking the pavement and the volley of commands and the crack and pop of exploding shells. Where was Stella? I knew she lived with her children in a small building on the grounds of the DuBois Center complex, which included the guesthouse, but I didn't know exactly where. I should have followed her. I knew she was too frightened to come back for me.

I turned on the radio, but all I could find was static, except for a prerecorded program on the Voice of America Radio about Jackie Robinson breaking the color bar in baseball.

I had to use the bathroom, but I was too scared to venture down the hallway, so I peed (that is, I tried to) in an empty water bottle. Fear had stripped away the veneer of civility.

An hour before sunrise, the street quieted. I crawled over to the window and peered out from behind the drapes. The road was empty. All the soldiers were gone. I stretched out on the bed and waited for daylight.

Pots banging in the kitchen woke me up. I heard Stella's voice and ran out.

"Is it over? Is it safe to leave?"

"Yes, it's finished."

"Is Rawlings still the president?"

"Yes, Rawlings is the president."

"The coup failed?"

Stella looked at me blankly and then she laughed. "The house next door catch fire. I had to cut all the lights, so we wouldn't burn too."

"Did the soldiers set the house on fire?"

"There was no coup."

"But I saw the soldiers on the road."

"The army barracks are near here, just a little ways down Military Road. They practice their maneuvers at night."

She laughed again. And her nine-year-old daughter Abena snickered at the *obruni* talking foolishness to her mother.

When I moved out of the guesthouse at the end of the week, I doubted whether my way of seeing things had any footing in reality. Daily conversations with Stella painted a dire picture of Accra, which was quite different from the city I had come to know during a four-week visit the previous summer. The Accra I remembered was always saturated in the golden-rose color of sunset. When the taxi pulled away from the guesthouse I could not tell if the grim expression on Stella's face was intended to issue one last warning.

THE APARTMENT IN OSU was less than a mile from Christiansborg Castle. Even with the fort in clear sight, it was hard to picture the slave routes and pathways hidden beneath the concrete pavements and the tar roads of the city and terminating at the shore. The seat of government was housed in what had been a Danish slave-trading post and then the headquarters of British colonial administration. Before the heels of parliamentarians clicked against the polished floors of the castle, captives restrained with neck rings and iron clamps were imprisoned inside the garrison until Danish, English, Portuguese, and French slave ships transported them to the Americas. Guns, brandy, cowries, and gold decided their fate, ensured their disappearance, and dictated that they be forgotten. Centuries later, this state of oblivion has yet to be remedied.

Aban is the Akan word for "castle." It is how Ghanaians refer to the government and how they perceive it: as a fortress and a foreign entity protected by great white walls. Even Kwame Nkrumah, the great anti-imperialist, had chosen the castle as his presidential residence, appropriating the symbol of colonial authority as his own and, at the same time, distancing himself from its corruption by building a new edifice for the Parliament. "The old slave castle had become the proud seat of the new rulers," writes Ayi Kwei Armah, "the blind children of slavery themselves."

The specter of captives glistening with palm oil and stripped of every-thing except the neck collars and chains connecting one to the other or of ships' captains prying open the mouths of slaves to inspect their teeth, palming their genitals for signs of disease, and readying their flesh for the brand did not encumber the daily workings of the state. The brutality of the past had been exorcised with the demise of colonialism—at least this was the position espoused by the new statesmen. The monumentality of the castle gave heft to the assertion and grandeur to the fledgling post-colonial state. The old days had ended and the era of freedom had ar-rived. And after all, at this late date, what claim could slaves, factors, and merchants have on the seat of government? Why diminish the glory of

nationhood with mention of an ugly past? Independence had done away with all of that. The uncanny feeling that the new days were too much like the old ones plagued only dissidents, intellectuals, and the poor.

In Accra, the landscape of anticolonialism was everywhere indicated by roundabouts named after freedom fighters and slain martyrs and boulevards endowed with the totemic power of ideals like liberation, independence, and autonomy. The city propped up thwarted and grand schemes of an Africa for Africans at home and abroad. I had been living in Accra for a month before I realized that few ever called the streets by these grand names. They were hollow ideals to most people, who had never committed the names to memory and who plotted their course through the city with a map patterned out of contempt for the official-dom of the state, nostalgia for the bad old days of colonialism, and the desire to name the world in their own terms. I quickly learned when ask-ing for directions that the street names inscribed on maps with unequivo-cal certainty were virtually useless. As far as I could tell, not one taxi driver in Accra could find his way to African Liberation Square, but almost all knew the location of the U.S. Information Service, the American and British embassies, and KLM. The drivers joked that the only change in forty years of independence was the name of the place. In getting around the city, few were mindful of the signs of slavery or independence.

In my daily trek from Osu to the University of Ghana in Legon, which was a twenty- to thirty-minute excursion by taxi, I began to map the city in my own terms. I identified the street on which I lived as Volta River Club Street, because the club was adjacent to the apartment building and no other street markers existed. My signposts were Not Independence Avenue and Obruni Road and Beggar's Corner and Shitty Lane. In a month I had become as indifferent to the elusive glory of the age of inde-pendence as everyone else in Accra. I passed through Thomas Sankara Circle every afternoon on the way home, oblivious to his dream of erad-icating poverty, hunger, and illiteracy and unaware of the ten million trees he intended to plant in the sahel to contain the spread of the desert, mend the ravages of slavery and colonialism, and right the balance among hu-mans, nature, and society. I was not bolstered by his words, which I had first read as a graduate student: "We must have the courage to invent the future. All that comes from man's imagination is realizable," or sobered by them: "We are backed up against the wall in our destitution like bald and mangy dogs whose lamentations and cries disturb the quiet peace of the manufacturers and merchants of misery." On the anniversary of Sankara's assassination, I didn't respect his memory with a moment of silence or think of the makeshift grave in which his body had been dumped or shed a tear because another path to Utopia had been blocked. These grand visions and beautiful promises were the ruins of another age and as remote and distant from my present as the dream of forty acres and a mule. So I hurried up Osu Road as blind to the future Sankara had envisioned as every other beleaguered pedestrian.

I MET MARY ELLEN RAY at Kwatson's, the neighborhood grocery store, which catered to the taste of homesick foreign nationals and charged exorbitant prices for the comforts of milk and cheese from Holland, Ceres juice, three kinds of nori, expensive tins of wasabi and smoked oysters, French bread, and Planter's cashews. We acknowledged one another with a tentative hello. There were enough African Americans in Accra to cultivate a polite indifference when we encountered one another. The reasons we were in Ghana could be summed up with a glance: the gerontocracy, those over-sixty-five men and women who had been invited to Ghana by President Nkrumah because of their skills as engineers, physicians, educators, and contractors were settled in upscale enclaves like Labone or Cantonments. They kept their distance from the steady wave of new arrivals and the ideologues. The less senior branch of the well-to-do were employed by international corporations and aid organizations; a few were entrepreneurs. They were rarely seen outside their gated compounds and air-conditioned SUVs. The visiting scholars, artists, and journalists lacked the comforts of air-conditioned vehicles and drivers and spacious, lovely homes and lived in the borderland between rich foreigners and middle-class Ghanaians, paying *obruni* prices for rent and everything else but not receiving the quality of goods and services that the powerful commanded and that Ghanaians exacted. The young ones

bedecked in jeans, shorts, T-shirts, and cowrie shell necklaces were exchange students and Peace Corp volunteers. Sometimes we nodded in
recognition when we passed one another; at other times, it was more convenient to avert your gaze and not call attention to the fact that you too
were a stranger.

Mary Ellen was an attractive woman in her sixties with luminous, sad
brown eyes, a mischievous smile, and the unmistakable comportment of a
bohemian. There was no trace of the matron about her, and her unre-
strained brunette dreadlocks, magenta tank top, and linen shorts flouted
the sartorial regulations for female modesty; either she relished being a
bad girl or she simply didn't gave a damn what people thought. All of
which made me instantly admire her. She had been living in Ghana with
her husband, John, for well over a decade. Mary Ellen was a technical
writer and John a sculptor and photographer. We discovered we were
neighbors. She lived near the Fulbright compound (virtually all of the
tenants of the Kwatchie family were Fulbright scholars) and invited me
over to dinner the following evening.

Mary Ellen and John lived only five blocks away from me, but finding
their house was tricky. The concrete sidewalks and asphalt streets didn't
extend beyond the main artery of Osu. Cars moved carefully on these
roads, not out of concern for the goats, chickens, and pedestrians with
whom they shared it but because of the large potholes. Only the poor
walked, which was the majority of the city's million and a half dwellers.
The neighborhood consisted of squat apartment buildings, modest middle-
class homes, and one-room cinder-block dwellings populated by a dozen
or more inhabitants who rotated hours in order to sleep. I asked a pair of
teenage boys hanging out in front of a convenience store if they knew the
American couple, and they escorted me to the Rays' front door.

John Ray was a slender, handsome man with dark, piercing eyes that
made you falter and a mouth set in a fixed expression of disapproval. He
was fiercely intelligent and self-educated, so he had little patience for most
academics, whom he could think circles around and whom he found te-
dious. When I said hello, I saw he was trying to decide whether I was
painfully dull or only moderately so. Interesting wasn't on the list of
possibilities.

When I told John about my project on slavery, he asked, "Why Ghana? There are no archives here. There is nothing to discover that Wilks and Van Dantzig and McCaskie haven't already written about."

"I know where the archives are. I've been to the British Museum, the Public Records Office in Kew, the Bodleian Library at Oxford, and to the National Archives in Accra."

John smiled, pleased that I could bite if pushed. He was a cantankerous type who didn't hold back his opinions, even if they hurt your feelings. He didn't care.

"I'm interested in the popular memory of slavery. My plan is to retrace the slave route."

"Which one?" John asked.

I hadn't accepted Mary Ellen's dinner invitation to prove I wasn't a fool to an old man I had never seen before this evening, so I ignored John and sipped the lukewarm beer Mary Ellen had placed in front of me.

"There were nine major slave routes in Ghana," John replied, answering his own question. "Every step you take in Ghana crosses the trail of slaves. It's not hard to find a slave route. It's the freedom trail you should be looking for."

"Have you been to Elmina and Cape Coast yet?" Mary Ellen asked, trying to compensate for John's summary dismissal and to rescue the flagging conversation.

"Yes, on my first trip here in 1996," I said. "I plan to spend a few weeks there at the end of October. I can't believe how long it has taken me to get settled."

"In Ghana, one has to go and come, go and come, go and come, before you can get a damned thing done," said Mary Ellen.

"I know that now," I said. "Last summer it seemed like paradise. But living here it feels more like hell."

Mary Ellen raised her bottle of beer in a toast and said, "It just may be, my dear."

"Mercenary soldiers, thieves, refugees, prostitutes, broke soldiers, corrupt policemen, and the desperate hard-pressed enough to try anything are out there on Osu Road too," John said. "Remember that, Professor. Keep your eyes open. Read the signs. People are still being bought

and sold in Ghana. People will sell their soul for five thousand cedis."
(Two thousand cedis was the equivalent of one U.S. dollar.)

Depending upon how he said it, "professor" sounded like a diminutive or a synonym for idiot. I was growing irritated.

"Another beer?" Mary Ellen asked as she cleared the empty bottles. I nodded my head. She didn't ask John but placed another beer before him. I suspected they had begun drinking before I arrived.

"Did your mother raise a fool?" John asked me after taking a swig.

"What?"

"Did your mother raise a fool?"

"No."

"Well, then don't act like one. Accra is no different than New York. So follow your instinct and don't let anyone make you a fool. I can't stand watching folks from the States come here and lose the sense they were born with. The Ghanaians will take your head."

"Take my head?"

"When a chief died, they would make sacrifice." John pulled his fingers across his throat. "Slaves and servants and wives were killed so they could accompany the chief as they had during his lifetime. Now 'taking heads' means ripping somebody off. They say hustling black Americans is like stealing candy from a baby. The *obruni* even thanks you when you do it."

"I guess I must be headless, then. I'm paying five hundred and fifty dollars a month in rent. That's almost as much as graduate students pay in Berkeley, and I'm not living as well."

"Don't complain too much," John said in a tone of reproach. "You're still sitting pretty compared to most. Do you know how many families could live on your Fulbright fellowship?"

"John, that's not the point," said Mary Ellen. She extended her arm and patted the top of my hand in a gesture that I might have mistaken for maternal if it hadn't seemed so perfunctory. "My dear, you are being chopped. That's how they welcome you home."

"And calling you a white person," I added.

"Don't think of every black person here as your brother and sister,"

John cautioned. "As long as you remember that you won't be taken advantage of, at least not too badly."

"Welcome to the motherland," Mary Ellen added with a bitter laugh. "This is what it means to be a black American in Africa."

"Not all of it——" sputtered John.

Mary Ellen interrupted him. "I'm sick of it. John, he doesn't care. He wants to die here."

"Where else can I go, Mary Ellen? Where else? You tell me," John said.

"We can go to Cuba."

John sucked his teeth and turned his head in frustration. "I'm too old to try a new country." The despair unloosed by these words engulfed him, and his thin frame sagged under its weight. He excused himself and headed down the hall toward the bathroom.

"I won't die here, John," shouted Mary Ellen to his back. "Not in a place where people will spit on my grave." She turned to me. "You know they hate us, or haven't you figured that out yet?"

MARY ELLEN WAS NO LONGER WILLING to call herself an African American. "I've been here too long to call myself anything except a black American," she confided. "That is what feels true." For Mary Ellen, there was no longer a future in being an *African* American, only the burden of history and disappointment.

What connection had endured *after* four centuries of dispossession? The question of *before* was no less vexed since there was no collective or Pan-African identity that preexisted the disaster of the slave trade. Were desire and imagination enough to bridge the rift of the Atlantic? The nightly conversations I had with Mary Ellen and John made me doubt it.

My research made me even more pessimistic. Each afternoon I went to the university library and read about the role of African merchants and royals in the Atlantic slave trade. Yellow Post-its scribbled with all the ugly details plastered the cover of my laptop. Ghana, or the Gold Coast as it was called until 1957, had been entangled with the West for at least five centuries, and the buying and selling of slaves had been central to this association. The slave trade required that a class of expendable people be created. The big men of Africa and Europe proved themselves suited to the task. The sentence I recalled most vividly was one written by Walter Rodney: "There was in existence a fundamental class contradiction between the ruling nobility and the commoners; and the ruling classes joined hands with the Europeans in exploiting the African masses—a not unfamiliar situation on the African continent today."

These words made me think hard about the Africa in "African American." Was it the Africa of royals and great states or the Africa of disposable commoners? Which Africa was it that we claimed? There was not one Africa. There never had been. Was Africa merely a cipher for a lost country no one could any longer name? Was it the remedy for our homelessness or an opportunity to turn our backs to the hostile country we called home? Or was there a future in Africa too? There was still the chance that all the poverty, death, and suffering would come to an end. There was still the chance that the manufacturers of misery would be toppled and the empires derailed. There was still the chance that Sankara's dream of a White House in Harlem might be realized. As long as I believed this, I could still call myself an African American.

ON THE DAY BEFORE I left for Elmina, which is about one hundred miles west of Accra on the curved shoreline that forms the Gulf of Guinea, I suffered my first migraine. All the terrible details of the slave trade thundered in my head and I spent the day battling nausea. I drank ginger ale, pressed a cold compress against my forehead, shut all the blinds, and hid from the world in my dark bedroom. Nothing helped. I wasn't able to dislodge the atrocities committed in wars of capture and slave raids: the elderly and infirm slaughtered by the conquering army, infants murdered by bashing their heads against trees, pregnant women disemboweled with a lance, girls raped, and young men buried in anthills and thrown onto pyres and burned alive. Nor could I clear my head of what one historian had described as the trail of bleached bones that led from the hinterland to the sea. Or forget the disobedient wives who were sold under the pretext of witchcraft, the quarrelsome young men who were sentenced to slavery for being troublemakers, and the ever-growing list of petty infractions punishable by slavery that cost many commoners their lives. Desperate situations and bad luck exacted their toll as well: famished children were sold by their parents so that they might live, the indigent offered themselves as slaves to escape poverty and hunger, nieces and nephews were corralled in barracoons and packed in slavers because of their uncles' unpaid debt. Varied circumstances funneled persons into the market and transformed them into commodities. Yet the outcome of theft and exchange was identical: the slave was born.

For every slave who had arrived in the Americas, at least one and perhaps as many as five persons died in wars of capture, on the trek to the coast, imprisoned in barracoons, lingering in the belly of a ship, or crossing the Atlantic. Death also awaited them in pesthouses, cane fields, and the quarters. Historians still debate whether twelve million or sixty million had been sentenced to death to meet the demands of the transatlantic commerce in black bodies.

Impossible to fathom was that all this death had been incidental to the acquisition of profit and to the rise of capitalism. Today we might describe it as collateral damage. The unavoidable losses created in pursuit of the greater objective. Death wasn't a goal of its own but just a by-product of commerce, which has had the lasting effect of making negligible all the millions of lives lost. Incidental death occurs when life has no normative value, when no humans are involved, when the population is, in effect, seen as already dead. Unlike the concentration camp, the gulag, and the killing field, which had as their intended end the extermination of a population, the Atlantic trade created millions of corpses, but as a corollary to the making of commodities. To my eyes this lack of intention didn't diminish the crime of slavery but from the vantage of judges, juries, and insurers exonerated the culpable agents. In effect, it made it easier for a trader to countenance yet another dead black body or for a captain to dump a shipload of captives into the sea in order to collect the insurance, since it wasn't possible to kill cargo or to murder a thing already denied life. Death was simply a part of the workings of the trade.

When my headache finally subsided, I decided to walk to the ocean to sort out the jumble of painful facts and awful details that I had worked so diligently to learn. I needed to see the Atlantic, which was where I reckoned with the dead, the men and women and children who were all but invisible in most of the history written about the slave trade; academics had continued to quarrel about how many slaves packed per ton constituted "tight packing" and a deliberate policy of accepting high mortality, estimate rates of cargo productivity in the slave trade versus the other kinds of commodity trade, and quantify the gains and losses of the slave trade with algebraic formulas that obscured the disaster: Deck Area $=$ Constant $\times$ (Tonnage) $\frac{2}{3}$. The ocean never failed to remind me of the losses, and its roar echoed the anguish of the dead.

I could get access to the shore a few blocks away from my apartment. I was slightly apprehensive about going to the beach alone but decided to do so anyway. There was a small path to the beach on the other side of Labadi Road. The walkway was surrounded by a small settlement of shanties. The rickety houses had been assembled from discarded shipment containers and cardboard boxes and stray pieces of wood and were topped with corrugated tin roofs. I felt like an interloper walking through the community as women washed their children and fanned small coal fires for the evening meal. Poor people couldn't afford gates to keep trespassers out. I looked straight ahead and kept my eyes fixed on the rocky outcrops and dunes, avoiding what I suspected were quizzical and irritated glances. I pretended not to notice the stench and quickened my pace. The closer I got to the sea, the worse the smell, which reeked of things dead and rotten. Many of the streets of Accra were lined with open sewers, and poor neighborhoods were often without toilet facilities, but this was more intense than usual. I knew there was no plumbing in these dwellings, but was there an outhouse nearby? Had the community latrine overflowed? When I reached the dunes I noticed a little swamp that had been created by sewage pipes emptying onto the beach. A group of children were playing near the fetid pool, and one boy created ripples on its surface with his small arc of urine. The black water allowed no reflection of their hovering faces.

The children looked at me, curious as to what I was doing here, in a zone of Accra that people like me entered only by accident. I don't know why I continued to approach the beach in light of all of this, but I did. The ocean was a few yards away, but it was impossible to smell the sea. Atop the dune I could see Christiansborg Castle and the little fishing village that sat on the other side of it. I had taken a few steps toward the beach when I noticed the men hunkered down on their heels and scattered across the dune. The men squatting in irregular rows looked like mushrooms sprouting from the sand. It took me a minute before I realized what they were doing. Stupid *obruni*! I was embarrassed more for myself than for them. For weeks I couldn't shake the vision of men defecating with their backs to the statehouse.

"Don't lie when you go back home. Everyone goes home and tells lies." It was the only thing John ever asked of me. I didn't promise him that I would tell the truth. Nearly two months in Ghana had already made the truth too difficult. Telling the truth risked fueling the racism that could see Africa only through the Kurtzian lens of horror, warring tribes, filth, pestilence, famine, and AIDS. Telling the truth risked savaging the dreams of those who might never travel to Africa but still imagined soil on which they would be embraced. Telling the truth risked sullying the love of romantics who kissed the ground as soon as they landed in mother Africa, not caring that it was the tarmac of the airport.

"We have to stop bullshitting about Africa. The naïveté that allows folks to believe they are returning home or entering paradise when they come here has to be destroyed," John said. I nodded in silent agreement. It was as far as I could commit myself. As I drank the beer Mary Ellen placed in my hand, I wondered how Ghana would look in my eyes by the end of the year. Would I love it, or would I never want to return?

The country in which you disembark is never the country of which you have dreamed. The disappointment was inevitable. What place in the world could sate four hundred years of yearning for a home? Was it foolish to long for a territory in which you could risk imagining a future that didn't replicate the defeats of the present?

In 1787 Prince Hall didn't believe so when he petitioned the General Court of Massachusetts, along with seventy-three other black men, requesting that the state repatriate its black residents because he thought it doubtful that they would ever experience anything other than racism and inequality in the white man's country. In our native country, he wrote, "We shall live among our equals and be more comfortable and happy, than we can be in our present situation; and at the same time, may have a prospect of usefulness to our brethren there." By the nineteenth century, the Africa envisioned by blacks in the Americas had everything to do with a future in which our subjection would end and the race would be redeemed. Nearly a century and a half later, in 1951, when William Patterson, the national executive secretary of the Civil Rights Congress, and Paul Robeson presented a petition to the UN charging the United States with genocide against the Negro people, they too conceded that black folks in the United States were without a state to protect their human rights. An entire people, the petition stated, were "not only unprotected by their government but the object of government inspired violence."

IN 1957, Ghana's independence was a beacon of freedom to the civil rights movement and Nkrumah, the liberator of black people worldwide. Not only did black Americans identify with the anticolonial struggle, they believed that their future too depended upon its victory. An article published in the *Chicago Defender* in February 1957 declared: "Some day black men from Ghana may stand before the U.N. and plead the case for American Negroes and be the cause for their winning complete equality . . . The free people of Ghana may be able to strike the last of the shackles from their brothers in America." The *Amsterdam News* expressed a similar sentiment: "The independence of Ghana breaks another link in the powerful chain that . . . enchained the black man . . . It is not so much a question of color that we rejoice over Ghana as it is a question of freedom."

African Americans had flocked to Ghana in the fifties and sixties. They came running away from Jim Crow, the Cold War, the backseat of the bus, a trail of slain leaders, spent dreams, and what they called, euphemistically, second-class citizenship. They knew either you were a citizen or you were not. They knew the outhouse wasn't the parlor.

John came to Ghana for the first time during the early sixties. He said it was hard to determine which was greater: the love of mother Africa or hatred of the United States. George Jackson, writing his father from a cell in Soledad Prison, imagined that he would crawl back from the grave of solitary confinement. "I'll see Ghana yet," he declared.

The architects and laborers of the Pan-Africanist dream had arrived in these first waves. They were comrades in the Black International. It was an age of possibility, when it seemed that as soon as tomorrow the legacy of slavery and colonialism would be overthrown. Richard Wright had visited the Gold Coast in 1953 and written a powerful account of the struggle for independence. In 1957, Martin Luther King, Jr., Ralph Bunche, Adam Clayton Powell, Jr., A. Philip Randolph, and Horace Mann (at the request of Nkrumah and against the expressed wishes of the U.S. State Department) had traveled to Ghana for the celebration of its independence. King, upon seeing the Black Star replace the Union Jack as the flag of the nation and listening to the audience of half a million people shout, "Freedom! Freedom!" began to weep.

An apocryphal story captures the bittersweet quality of these tears. Vice President Nixon, who attended the ceremonies as the head of the U.S. delegation, asked a group of jubilant men, "How does it feel to be free?" "We don't know," they replied. "We're from Alabama."

These early journeys had been auspicious. African Americans crossed the Atlantic in droves to do something momentous—to participate in an international movement for freedom and democracy and to build a black nation. Nkrumah solicited Africans and those of African descent from Cairo to Cape Town and from Harlem to Havana to build the new nation. He envisioned a United States of Africa that would embrace those exiled in the Americas among its citizens. When he had been a student at Lincoln University, Nkrumah experienced firsthand the assault of Jim Crow. On a trip to Washington, D.C., he was refused a glass of water at a restaurant in the bus station. When Nkrumah explained that he was very thirsty, the waiter pointed to a spittoon and said, "You can drink there."

Nkrumah believed the independence of Ghana meant nothing unless all Africans were free. Black émigrés shared that dream. They came from the United States, the Caribbean, Brazil, and the United Kingdom, as well as other countries in Africa still fighting against colonialism and apartheid. George Padmore, the Trinidadian intellectual who had presided over the sixth Pan-Africanist Congress in Manchester, England, in 1945 (where Nkrumah and Kenyatta pledged to defeat imperialism and abolish the poverty and servitude of Africa), was Nkrumah's adviser on African affairs. Padmore organized the first meeting of Independent Africa's Heads of State and the first All African Peoples Congress. W.E.B. DuBois spent his last days working diligently on the *Encyclopedia Africana*, a comprehensive reference to the black world. Shirley Graham Du Bois established Ghana Television. Drs. Robert and Sara Lee were the first black dentists in the country. Robert Lee had become friends with Kwame Nkrumah while they were both students at Lincoln University. Carlos Allston laid the power lines that helped illuminate the fledgling nation. Julian Mayfield wrote for the *Ghana Evening News*. Anna Livia Corderia opened the first women's clinic at the Military Hospital. Malcolm X visited and lectured in Ghana in an effort to build the Organization of Afro-American Unity. Frantz Fanon wrote a large part of *The Wretched of the Earth* while in Ghana. Maryse Condé taught French at the Institute for Ideological Training. Tom Feelings, Ted Pointiflet, Frank Lacey, and John Ray taught school and trained young Ghanaian artists. Sylvia Boone acted as a cultural ambassador, always schooling new arrivals that "the single key to seeing Africa as it is, not as a reflection of the bogus stories you have been told [was] to think of every African you meet as a person just like yourself, with the same needs and desires, hopes and dreams." None of which prevented her from describing Accra as a "dream come true, for here is a city in a country that is *black* up and down."

With all the conceit and ardor of youth, a small group dubbed themselves the Revolutionist Returnees. The Ghanaians called them the Afros, short for Afro-Americans. They arrived with what Maya Angelou described as a "terrible yearning to be accepted," to pitch in their lot with Ghanaians, and to undertake the hard labor of nation building. They wanted their talents to be used. The lucky ones enjoyed the privilege of serving the bourgeoning black republic; the ones waiting tried to be patient and reassured themselves that as the months stretched out they weren't being idle.

I envied them. In the sixties it was still possible to believe that the past could be left behind because it appeared as though the future, finally, had arrived; whereas in my age the impress of racism and colonialism seemed nearly indestructible. Mine was not the age of romance. The Eden of Ghana had vanished long before I ever arrived.

INDEPENDENCE WAS A short century. It lasted for as little as two months in the Congo and less than a decade in Ghana. In 1966, the police and the armed forces overthrew the government of Kwame Nkrumah and the goodwill evaporated. The dream of an age after colonialism, after racism, after capitalism, which had provided the bridge across the Atlantic for the émigrés, fell to pieces. African Americans were no longer welcome. They were accused of betraying Nkrumah and of being in cahoots with the CIA, which had engineered the coup. They were accused of blindly loving the old autocrat—who had by then engineered a one-party state and declared himself president for life. The political opponents of the *Osagyefo*, the Redeemer, who after the coup were now the leaders of the country, distrusted the Afros because they had been religiously loyal to Nkrumah. The Afros adored him because of his unwavering commitment to the freedom of black people worldwide. The Ghanaians criticized him for his dictatorial style and inattention to domestic matters. The British-educated elite and the conservative middle classes were hostile to Nkrumah's socialist revolution, and they resented his attacks on traditional forms of caste and privilege. As Nkrumah tried to embrace the world, he lost the home front. Upon hearing the news that Nkrumah had been overthrown, African Americans wept as Ghanaians rejoiced and danced in the street.

The émigrés had no illusions about their status, according to Leslie Lacy: "We were tolerated out of sufferance of Nkrumah, and if they could kill him at eight o'clock, our fate would be his at eight-thirty." Ghanaians resented the Afros for occupying positions that were rightfully theirs, having the president's ear, and presuming to know what was best for Africa. Most African Americans fled voluntarily. A handful were deported. The military officers who forced them from their homes and abandoned them at the Togo border cursed them and called them strangers. The Afros expressed their chagrin in the language of ex-slaves: "They sold us once and they will sell us again."

A small community remained and stuck it out, weathering more coups and food shortages. Typically those who stayed were married to Ghanaians or were the rich ones who owned businesses and were insulated by wealth or were the stateless ones who were unable to erase the image of a fourteen-year-old boy's bloated corpse dredged from the Mississippi, or four dead little girls buried in the rubble of a church in Birmingham, or Malcolm's slumped figure on the floor of the Audubon Ballroom, or Martin's body on a hotel balcony in Memphis, or the bullet-shattered bodies of Fred Hampton and Mark Clark.

MY ARRIVAL IN GHANA was not auspicious. Mine was an age not of dreaming but of disenchantment. I grew up in the aftermath of African independence and the civil rights and Black Power struggles, and like many of my generation I was pessimistic about my prospects at home and abroad. I came of age in the demise of liberation movements and after the visionaries had been assassinated. Marcus Garvey's vision of an Africa for Africans on the continent and in the diaspora was a theme, which in college I chanted and danced to in the music of Bob Marley and the Wailers, Steel Pulse, and Third World, but dared not believe. It belonged to the Old Garveyites who assembled every August in Mount Morris Park to celebrate Garvey's birthday and who wore their United Negro Improvement Association uniforms no less proudly half a century later. Every year I was there with them, the skeptic among the faithful.

The dream belonged to the émigrés, whose "horizon of hope" was the historical debris of my present. The revolutionaries had come to Ghana believing they could be made anew, reborn as the African men and women they would have been had their ancestors not been stolen four hundred years ago. Every revolution promises to stop all the old clocks, jettison the old entailments, and institute a new order. They left the States hoping to leave slavery behind too. America had made them, but Ghana would remake them. They had faith that the breach of the Middle Passage could be mended and orphaned children returned to their rightful homes.

The émigrés had wanted to belong to a country of the future. Who wouldn't yearn for a place where the color line didn't exist and black bodies were never broken on the rack or found hanging from trees or expiring at the end of a police officer's gun or wasting away in a cell on death row? What orphan had not yearned for a mother country or a free territory? What bastard had not desired the family name or, better yet, longed for a new naming of things? Why not dream of a country that might love you in return and in which your skin wasn't a prison? Desire was as reliable as any map when you were searching for the Promised Land or trying to find the path to Utopia or imagining the United States of Africa.

The dreams that defined their horizon no longer defined mine. The narrative of liberation had ceased to be a blueprint for the future. The decisive break the revolutionaries had hoped to institute between the past and the present failed. The old forms of tyranny, which they had endeavored to defeat, were resuscitated and the despots lived long and vigorous lives. The freedom dreams had been routed and driven underground.

I knew that no matter how far from home I traveled, I would never be able to leave my past behind. I would never be able to imagine being the kind of person who had not been made and marked by slavery. I was black and a history of terror had produced that identity. Terror was "captivity without the possibility of flight," inescapable violence, precarious life. There was no going back to a time or place before slavery, and going beyond it no doubt would entail nothing less momentous than yet another revolution.

While the Afros were far too intelligent to believe the past could be forgotten, they definitely wanted their distance from slavery and colonialism. They valued history to the extent that it aided the task of liberation. So it was more common for them to disparage the slave mentality than to claim the slave. They preferred romance to tragedy. In trying to reverse the course of history, eradicate the degradation of slavery and colonialism, and vindicate the race, they looked to the great civilizations of ancient Africa. The restoration of a noble past would provide the bridge to a radiant future. African Americans weren't the only ones who desired a monumental history and hungered for a grand narrative. Nkrumah also indulged this vision of a splendid royal past. In changing the name of the Gold Coast to Ghana, which had been an ancient kingdom at the edge of the desert and a seat of civilization more than a thousand years ago when Europe was still in the Dark Ages, Nkrumah "conjured up the image of a New Jerusalem." And even his enemies considered him a messiah. Redemption and resurrection infused the language of African nationalism. The new era was to incarnate the best features of antiquity and to create "the golden city of our heart's desire."

WHAT HAD ATTRACTED the émigrés to Ghana were this vision of a new life and the promise of rebirth; what attracted me were the ruins of the old one. They were intent upon constructing a new society; I was intent upon tracing an itinerary of destruction from the coast to the savanna. They went to be healed. I went to excavate a wound. The expatri-

ates crossed the Atlantic to break the chains of slavery, and I did so doubting that I would ever be free of them.

There was nothing exceptional about me. My predecessors had been the most gifted men and women of their generation. The political exiles of the late fifties and sixties possessed pedigrees much more impressive than my own. They had participated in freedom struggles around the globe. They understood they were actors on the stage of world history. I always have felt at a distance from the events of my time, and I have never believed that the balance of power hung upon any act of mine.

There was nothing exceptional about my journey. Any tourist with the willingness and the cash could retrace as many slave routes as her heart desired. But there was something particular, perhaps even peculiar, about it. My generation was the first that came here with the dungeon as our prime destination, unlike the scores of black tourists who, motivated by Alex Haley's *Roots*, had traveled to Ghana and other parts of West Africa to reclaim their African patrimony. For me, the rupture was the story. Whatever bridges I might build were as much the reminder of my separation as my connection. The holding cell had supplanted the ancestral village. The slave trade loomed larger for me than any memory of a glorious African past or sense of belonging in the present.

I was struck by this difference when I read Maya Angelou's memoir about her residence in Ghana. She steadfastly avoided Cape Coast and Elmina castles. As she described it, if she succeeded in keeping the ugly history of slavery at a distance, then perhaps she could be something more than a stranger, perhaps she could pass for being a young Ghanaian woman: "I didn't want to remember that I was an American. For the first time since my arrival I was very nearly home . . . I drove into Cape Coast before I thought of the gruesome castle and out of its environs before the ghosts of slavery caught me. Perhaps their attempts had been half-hearted. After all, in Dunkwa, although I let a lie speak for me, I had proved that one of their descendants, at least one, could just briefly return to Africa, and that despite cruel betrayals, bitter ocean voyages and hurtful centuries, we were still recognizable." A lie was the price of kinship, which as the émigrés discovered was much less inclusive or elastic than they had anticipated. Kinship was as much about exclusion as affiliation. As it turned out, eluding the slave past was the prerequisite to belonging.

I was not trying to dodge the ghosts of slavery but to confront them. To what end? was the only question. John said there was no point to it. There was nothing new to be discovered. He and Mary Ellen had refused the invitation to accompany me on the journey from Accra to Elmina, which was a three-hour excursion on the State Transport Bus. I had not wanted to travel to Elmina alone. Small towns always made me uncomfortable and a bit claustrophobic. I preferred the crowded sidewalks and traffic of Osu, where I could move almost unnoticed among the stream of foreigners and affluent Ghanaians entering and exiting the shops along Osu Road.

John and Mary Ellen had visited the castle once and had never felt the need to return. John resented the way Ghanaians had made the slave trade into their new hustle. He called them slavery pimps and joked, "Man, they sold me once, now I have to pay to return. I won't pay-o."

I pressed him about it. "You know more about the history of black people than I do, so why are you so disinterested in slavery?"

"It's the exercise of freedom that matters," he said. This sounded idealistic to me. Freedom and slavery had always been tethered, and freedom was more than a state of mind or exercise of the will. He knew this as well as I did, especially when he was in his cups. Whenever he was drunk, Mary Ellen would say, "We're losing my husband," as if to assure herself that the belligerent man tottering through the living room wasn't the same man she had married. As of late, hardly a night passed without her uttering these words. I too learned to make excuses. As I grew to love John and Mary Ellen, I pretended not to see the pain and isolation of their exile, not to notice what living in Ghana had cost them.

The unrealized dreams of two continents had embittered John. Resentment and loneliness were the proof of his statelessness. When he was in his cups, he said all the things that were too painful to admit when he was sober.

"You don't know anything about defeat!" John yelled at me the evening before I departed for Elmina. I had been talking about the despair of the post–civil rights age and wondering if it was the same kind of despair Ghanaians had experienced in the aftermath of independence. I recently had read Ayi Kwei Armah's *The Beautyful Ones Are Not Yet Born*, a novel about the disillusionment that followed in the wake of decolonization. I was surprised that it had all seemed so familiar: the betrayal of freedom and the sickening despair and aching emptiness experienced after the beauty of the first days of independence had passed.

"What do you know, Professor? Soon the Europeans will own all of it again. Do you think slavery is just some old buildings and dead folks?" John demanded, trying to control his slurred speech. "No, it's when other people decide whether you live or die."

John's eyes were on me and he was assessing all my shortcomings with his stern gaze. He was contemptuous of most of the African Americans in Ghana. Would I turn out to be no better than the rest of them? John often spoke as if the expatriates who had returned to the States had betrayed him personally. They had abandoned the dream and been rewarded with university chairs, fat salaries, and celebrity, while he labored in the trenches and pieced together an existence. They claimed to love Ghana but stayed at the Golden Tulip, one of Accra's five-star hotels, when they visited. They loved Ghana from a comfortable distance. John resented the privileged black visitors almost as much as did the Ghanaians, perhaps more, because he knew them better. He knew exactly how full of shit they were. That night I represented all of them.

"Do you know what it feels like to be living in a place for nearly twenty years, scraping to get by and still being treated like a foreigner?" But he was a foreigner. He hadn't found home, he was stranded. There was no question John hoped to answer in the dungeon, because like many exiles he no longer hoped for anything.

It was the opposite for me. I was willing to enter the dungeon again and again and encounter the disaster anew, as if the Portuguese were still in transit, as if the sugar crops had yet to be planted in Brazil, as if the first slave had yet to be exiled, because, at this late date, I was still hoping for a different outcome. I was convinced that even now lives hung in the balance. My own as much as anyone else's.

Like John, I was stateless too. I had never been at home in the world. It was a sensibility I had inherited sitting on my great-grandfather's knee in Morning Pilgrim Baptist Church as he implored in his scratchy baritone voice along with the other congregants, "Lord, I'm going home, / No more toils, no more care, / No more grief to bear." Even as a child I perceived the gravity of these words and I knew they contained an appeal as well as a complaint. Abandoned by all but God, song after song declared. It was a feeling that seemed too ancient for my thirty-six years, but I came by it honestly. I was trying to get to the bottom of it, and for me it began in a holding cell.

An old storehouse built by white men had everything to do with who I was in the world, or at least it had no less to do with it than did the great kingdom of Asante or a shortsighted plan, hatched by a Dominican friar, for saving the "Indians." Whether I could pass for a young Ghanaian woman could not redress my losses, settle the questions that plagued me, or bring me any comfort. It was a desire whose moment had passed. The questions before me—What was the afterlife of slavery and when might it be eradicated? What was the future of the ex-slave?—could not be answered by deciding whether or to what degree I could blend into African society.

In any case, by the time I landed in Ghana, the slogan "Africa for Africans at home and abroad" had been out of favor for at least three decades. In 1999, a measure to grant African Americans Ghanaian citizenship was defeated. No one seemed to be waiting any longer for the hour of Africa's redemption. Disenchantment prevailed. On radio talk shows Ghanaians debated whether they had been better off under colonialism. The structural adjustment programs and debtor country initiatives orchestrated by the World Bank and the International Monetary Fund were the new slavery. Ghana didn't even print its own currency. It was manufactured in Europe and paid for with U.S. dollars. Pan-Africanism had yielded to the dashed hopes of neocolonialism and postcolonialism and African socialism (which Nkrumah defined as the traditional spirit of African humanism and communalism refashioned for the modern world), had been ambushed by the West and bankrupted by African dictators and kleptocrats, all of whom had made a travesty of independence.

I had come to Ghana too late and with too few talents. I couldn't electrify the country or construct a dam or build houses or clear a road or run a television station or design an urban water system or tend to the sick or improve the sanitation system or revitalize the economy or cancel the debt. No one had invited me. I was just another stranger, an academic from the States conducting research on slavery, which, in most people's eyes, made me about as indispensable as a heater in the tropics. There were a handful of African Americans who were useful; I wasn't one of them. I found myself, like most members of the small community of nearly one thousand African-American expatriates, living on the periphery of Ghanaian society. It was a lonely existence even after I had grown accustomed to living *in country*. "When you really *really* realize you are not African," one expatriate admitted, "it's the loneliest moment of your life, and if you can withstand that, you can make it here. It goes on being lonely, and it's how you adjust yourself to that loneliness that matters, not how you adjust to Africa."

WHEN I LANDED at Accra's Kotoka Airport, I had come looking for the underground, not Utopia. Even so, the dreams of the émigrés were a part of my inheritance, which I couldn't entirely shake loose, no matter how hard I tried. Utopia had left its traces in my disappointment, and in the pang of desire that reminded me something was missing, something had been lost. The self-forgetfulness of belonging would never be mine. No matter where I went, I'd always be a stranger lurking outside the house. And this interminable condition—"the abstract nakedness of being nothing but human," to borrow the words of Hannah Arendt—was nowhere more apparent than in Ghana. And the futures envisioned by Nkrumah and King and eclipsed by assassins, military coups, and the CIA never seemed more distant.

Utopias always have entailed disappointments and failures. They cast a harsh light on the limits of our imagination, underscore our shortsightedness, and replicate the disasters of the world we seek to escape. Utopia never turns out to be the perfect society. Look hard enough and you'll find the underworld occupied by drudges, inferiors, conscripts, and prisoners. Look long enough and you'll identify the winners and losers, the big men and small boys, the royals and the slaves, the owners and the owned. You'll see the African elites and nobles fashioning themselves after Europe's kings and the captives trailing behind them in tow. You'll discern the disease of royalty beneath the visage of eternal glory. You'll witness the dream of freedom crash and burn.

No better demonstration of the missed opportunities and the tragic disappointments of Utopia could be found than in the work of its sixteenth-century architect Thomas More. He had imagined a commonwealth where all the necessities of life were provided for, where the comforts were abundant and experienced by all, where the land easily supported the people, where greed had been eliminated, where money had been abolished, where the idle crowd of gentlemen and nobles had been eradicated, and where all true pleasures were encouraged. No one wanted for the necessities of life, no one lived off the labor of others, and no one bared his head or bent his knee before another. But even in Utopia there were slaves laboring in chains. They were assigned the foul and degraded labor suited only to those bereft of the dignity and compassion of free men. The lowest rung wore shackles, albeit of gold, which was associated with pollution, excrement, and dishonor: "From gold and silver they make chamber pots and all the humblest vessels for use everywhere, not only in the common halls but in private homes also. Moreover they employ the same metals to make the chain and solid fetters which they put on their slaves."

The utopian equation of gold, filth, and slavery also resonated in Ghana. There was an Akan saying: *Atantanie nti ye to odonko*—We buy a slave because of filthy work. What better illustration of the degradation of gold than its capacity to transform persons into things; what better example of its offensive character than the excremental conditions of the barracoon; what better sign of its mutability than the "black gold" of the slave trade. Before Sigmund Freud detailed the symbolic affinities between gold and excrement, African royals were stockpiling their gold in privies and selling slaves for chamber pots. And European traders were transforming humans into waste and back again through the exchange of gold.

Kinishi wo wu shua, kumo e nan wu ebin gba: The eye that sees gold will see excrement too. So it is said in the heartland of slavery where people knew firsthand the scent of the slave hold. Karl Marx didn't put it any better when he described the genesis of capital, which came into the world "dripping from head to toe, from every pore, with blood and dirt." He didn't mention excrement, but he should have. Mounds of waste were also the testament of pillage and exchange. The reek of trading forts and slave ships identified the presence of merchant capital and human commodities on the West African coast, as the foul odor of toilet beaches and open sewers marked the end of "the beauty of the first days," or the shortfall of independence.

The smell hung in a black cloud over Accra. When I breathed deeply I swore I could discern the sulfurous odor of things dead and decaying. Utopia could not be separated from this rottenness. For the dream of a *black country* was born in slave pens and barracoons and holding cells. When the path home disappeared, when misfortune wore a white face, when dark skin guaranteed perpetual servitude, the prison house of race was born. And so too was the yearning for the black promised land and the ten million trees that would repel the enemy's advance and stand in for all of those gone and forgotten.

Markets and Martyrs

WHEN THE BUS DEPOSITED ME at the lorry park in Elmina, I refused to heed the voice telling me, "There is nothing here for you."

Except for the castle, no visible signs of slavery remained. All about me, the commerce of everyday life proceeded in its banal course. A jagged row of blue kiosks, home to lottery agents, seamstresses, chop bars, and makeshift stores, looped around the Benya River. The banks of the river swarmed with people: market women installed behind their stands traded Dutch print fabric, Lever Brothers soap, secondhand *obruni* clothes, iridescent lipsticks, and cut-rate nail polish. Others, less optimistic about the prospects of a sale, stretched out on straw mats, babies curled beside them, hidden behind black bricks of *kenkey* (fermented cornmeal wrapped in a plantain leaf). Shoppers haggled for better prices, hoping to return home with a few cedis in their pockets. Clerks, unsullied in their oxford shirts and ties, exited chop bars and strolled to their offices. Tourists drenched with perspiration scuttled en masse to the slave dungeon. Schoolchildren swept through the streets in their brown uniforms like clouds of dust. Street hawkers offered oranges, groundnuts, and toilet paper, piercing the air with their yelps. Adolescent girls, haloed by hair burnt the color of sienna from cheap perms, sold small bags of cold water for fifty cedis. Children played guilefully, having abandoned their errands. Entrepreneurs, technocrats, and fashionable wives snaked through the crowd armored in the icy world of air-conditioned Pajeros and Land Rovers and untouched by the sweat and dust of the outside. Tro-tros crammed with passengers rushed through the streets, indifferent to the swarms of ambling pedestrians.

I recoiled from the whirl of life spinning about me and threatening to pull me under. It had been more than a year since I had first visited Elmina, and the town I pictured barely resembled the one spread out before me. I had remembered the town as a graveyard, so I was disturbed by the greetings shouted back and forth between market women and the peals of laughter, which interrupted conversations in languages I could not understand. The smell of grilled plantains and the astringent odor of sweat breaking through the white veneer of bath powder made the air pungent and sweet and heavy. Waves of heat rose from the bodies of lovely black and tawny complexioned girls who were vigorous and alive and who would bear even more life. It was to my eyes a terrible beauty. It didn't seem right that this prodigal and teeming display of life brushed against the walls of a slave warehouse and failed to notice it.

I would have preferred mourners with disheartened faces and bowed heads and the pallor of sadness coloring the town. Or at least something Gothic: bloodstained ruins, human skulls scattered like cobblestones in the street, the castle draped in black crepe. Instead I found myself immersed in the prosaic conduct of everyday life—the petty negotiations, squabbles, and contested transactions key to good bargaining. The orchestrated dance between buyer and seller replayed endlessly in the sea of makeshift stands.

FOR CENTURIES, Elmina had been famed for its thriving trade. In the Middle Ages, merchants crossed the Sahara loaded with textiles and salt, which they exchanged for gold on the coast. Malian cavalry units raided the farmlands of the forest and transported thousands of captives southward. With these slaves they purchased bags of gold dust and sacks filled with nuggets. By the fifteenth century, the news of the Akan gold fields had spread in the ports of Andalusia and Portugal. European sailors and merchants listened eagerly to rumors of naked people with fists bulging with gold and eager to trade it for old clothes and other trifles. Twice-told tales goaded adventurers, entrepreneurs, and seamen to traverse the Atlantic.

When the Portuguese arrived, they called the area "Mina de Ouro" or "El Mina" after the gold mines of which they had come in search. From the fifteenth century onward, three hundred miles of the Guinea coast were referred to as "the Mine" and centuries of common use made a proper name of Europe's exploits. The Portuguese landed hungry for gold and eager to find its source. They exchanged textiles, used garments, metal hardware, shells and beads, wine, and slaves for gold, which filled the treasury of Portugal's kings with the greatest supply of this precious metal that Europe had ever known. The gold obtained from the Akan financed the Portuguese slaving efforts in Benin and Kongo, the first major sources of slaves in the Atlantic trade.

When the Europeans arrived in Guinea, the land of the blacks, "there was no servile class simply waiting to be shipped." Raids and kidnapping inaugurated Europe's trafficking in African slaves. Over the span of a few decades, commercial agreements forged between Europe's merchant princes and Africa's royals commenced the transatlantic slave trade proper and established the protocols of theft, kidnapping, and war.

The Afro-European trade in slaves did not begin in Ghana as it did elsewhere with Africans selling slaves and Europeans buying them. It began with Europeans selling slaves and Africans buying them. The Portuguese started out as middlemen in the internal slave trade. They kidnapped and purchased slaves from Kongo and Benin and sold them on the Gold Coast. For each slave sold to African merchants and royals, the Portuguese received three to six ounces of gold. Slaves fetched better prices on the Gold Coast than they did in Lisbon. The gold transported from El Mina spurred the traffic in slaves and rewarded the Portuguese with the premier place in the Atlantic slave trade for its first two centuries.

By 1600, the Portuguese had enslaved and exported nearly half a million Africans. In the first century and a half of the trade, the majority of slaves were shipped to the Atlantic islands and to Europe. By 1700, two million Africans had been captured, seized, and sold as slaves to European traders from all nations.

The Gold Coast entered the slave trade as an exporter of slaves at the end of the seventeenth century. In 1637 the Dutch commandeered Elmina Castle, and a few decades later the Atlantic slave trade shifted into high gear. The selling of slaves had become more lucrative than the gold trade because of the demand for labor in the plantation economy of the Americas. By the end of eighteenth century, there were sixty slave markets in Ghana. The merchants and royals of Elmina, like those of other major coastal towns, acted as intermediaries in the Atlantic slave trade. Elmina was a gateway between the African hinterland, the entrepôts of Western Europe, and the plantations of the New World.

Elmina was a boomtown with inns, dancing houses, gambling dens, brothels, artisan guilds, merchant-broker firms, and wealthy sprawling compounds. Rich men, criminals, rogues, skilled laborers, prostitutes, and growing numbers of the poor resided in the coastal settlement. The population consisted of nearly twenty thousand residents. The town had been as large then as it was now. As the numbers of captives taken from the coast increased to the tens of thousands, the population of Elmina declined rapidly. A smallpox epidemic, the harsh governorship of the director general of the Dutch West India Company, and the instability, wars, and skirmishes endemic to the trade prompted many of the town's residents to relocate elsewhere and at a safe distance from the dangers of the coast. While the royals and merchants benefited from the traffic in slaves, the commoners experienced only its chaos and dangers. This state of emergency made traveling on public roadways unsafe and the threat of captivity unremitting. By the first decades of the eighteenth century, according to the Dutch governor of Elmina, the settlement had become a ghost town and the Gold Coast a slave coast. Over the course of the eighteenth century, the population of the town expanded and contracted in response to the vagaries of the slave trade.

The storerooms of Elmina, which had once held bolts of cloth, copper and porcelain basins, kegs of liquor, brass bracelets, and other trade goods, filled with captives. The majority of them were seized from the north and sold on the coast by African brokers to European traders. Ships crowded the harbor in wait of human cargo. By the first decade of the eighteenth century, large wooden cargo vessels of two hundred tons anchored offshore were commonplace sights. The boats resembled wooden houses with wings because of their great flying sails. Canoes carried small lots of slaves from the shore to the ships. Hundreds of captives were packed between the decks. The stink of sweat and waste and disease thickened as the cargo was completed. The reek of slavers could be detected five miles off the coast.

The townspeople would have grown accustomed to the stench. Watching the canoes ferry the slaves offshore, some might have wondered why none who boarded those ships were ever seen again, and the curious might have speculated about what happened to them in the countries across the water. No doubt there were those who preferred not to think about them at all.

TAKING IN THE FESTIVAL of color and sound before me, what I found troubling was that the scars of slavery were no more apparent in

Elmina than in Boston or Rhode Island or Charleston (or Lisbon or Bristol or Nantes). Only the blessings of the slave trade remained, according to the town's residents, by which they meant their modernity. The Atlantic slave trade had introduced them to literacy and Christianity, and of this they were very proud. Images of Jesus abounded, as if salvation rather than secondhand goods were for sale. The Son of God wearing his crown of thorns illustrated kiosks, and "Blood of the Lamb" and "Jesus Saves" christened open-air beauty shops. Propagating and luminous, the many heads of Jesus encircled the town, overseeing exchange and pledging deliverance. A defiant driver emblazoned his van, "Try. Let God rest." A lone kiosk was adorned with hagiographic portraits of Tupac and Biggie Smalls; the hip-hop saints vied with the Son of God for devotees.

For the ever-increasing throngs of Pentecostals, Christ promised a future unencumbered by history; he was the antidote to recollection. Nothing could have been more at odds with my own desire than the aspiration of the faithful to enter the world anew, to be born again cleansed of the past. What we shared was the wish to resurrect the dead. I wanted to redeem the enslaved and they wanted to give the repentant a new life. The congregants were steadfast in their belief, whereas I wavered and doubted. My pessimism was stronger than my longing. In my heart I knew my losses were irreparable.

I scanned the town, hungry for a detail or trace of the hundreds of thousands of persons deported from the Gold Coast. I tried to imagine how many sacked villages and abandoned dwellings and destroyed families and orphaned children made up this number. But I was unable to translate a string of zeros into human figures or to hear the clamor of slaves assembled on the beach or to catch a whiff of their fear as they stood before the ocean. I tried to calculate how long it would have taken to embrace each one and whisper good-bye. If each farewell took as long as a minute, it would have added up to seven hundred and seventy-seven days, a little over two years, which didn't seem like enough time. Besides, there had been no one to see them off and say I love you and we will never forget you. These words were of no use now.

The old town surrounding the market had changed little in two centuries, except of course that there were no small lots of slaves for sale. The stone houses on Liverpool Street and Buitenrust Lane, in which Dutch traders cohabited with their "local wives," were lined up along the road, robust and stationed like sentinels. Fort St. Jago, nestled on the hill, still overlooked the town. Elmina Castle sprawled on the rocky point of the peninsula. The Atlantic roared as it approached and recoiled beneath the underbelly of the castle. The intimacy of civilization and barbarism was everywhere apparent in the castle's dazzling vastness, architectural prowess, and unabashed monumentality.

The castle appeared inviolate, which made me want to deface it, to inflict damage commensurate with the wreckage of the slave trade. I would have preferred to find Elmina Castle in a heap of stones. I would have preferred a Jacobin bloodbath: the captors trounced, their throats slit, and their heads planted on pikes along the beach and a band of slaves celebrating their ruin; or the soldiers poisoned by the very same slave women who washed their clothes, prepared their meals, and fellated them; or the castle set ablaze by the mixed-race offspring of the Portuguese governor.

Now it was too late for retribution. The director general of the Dutch West India Company hadn't resided there since the nineteenth century. The Portuguese were ousted almost four hundred years ago. The Akan royals and merchants were dead. The captives had been scattered. Those I wanted to harm were not within my reach. Those I wanted to rescue were gone. The banks, shipping companies, insurers, nation-states, manufacturers, and ports still thrived, but they were too powerful for any blow or kick or complaint of mine to make them cry out in pain or wish they were dead.

FROM THE SMALL BRIDGE spanning the Benya River and connecting Elmina Castle to the town, I couldn't quite see the yard where the Portuguese corralled their captives and where the Dutch branded the human property of the Dutch West India Company. The perimeter wall of the castle blocked any view of the courtyard, but this didn't stop me from looking. Nor did the river stench of dried fish and human waste drive me from the overpass.

People strode past me wiping their drenched brows with madras handkerchiefs, walking determinedly but with sparse and conservative steps designed to avoid any undue expenditure of energy in the oppressive midday heat. Most failed to notice me and simply pushed past, shuffling onward in an elusive quest for shade. A few heads turned, curious about why I was standing frozen in the middle of traffic and allowing myself to be trounced by the sun's harsh rays. I couldn't imagine that anyone wondered why I was here or what held my attention in the distance. Glances tempered with disdain, amusement, and pity: another American here to cry about what happened so long ago. The polite ones waited until they were a few feet away before angling their heads back; others, bolder, stared nakedly. A woman muttered to her friend in English for my benefit, "Americans come here to cry but they don't leave their money behind."

An octogenarian brushed by me as I loitered on the bridge. He walked a few steps ahead of me, then turned around and asked, "Is it negro or nigra?" The old man's words fell upon me like a hail of stones, stinging and accusatory, openly decrying what could be skirted in a gaze—the isolation of my implacable grief and the unbridgeable gulf between stranger and kin. I caught myself before Brooklyn rushed from my mouth in a string of profanity. I looked at the man's face; either he was sincere or he was crazy, so I settled for returning his gaze with a stony stare that I hoped translated into a polite "Don't fuck with me."

Chance encounters in the street made plain the difference between how I saw myself and how I was seen by others. In my estimation, I was the aggrieved; to others I was a privileged American and as such was required to perform regular acts of penance. My ignorance regularly collided with that of passers-by. To my hoary inquisitor I was an oddity. "Who and what are you?" was what the old man wanted to know. His curiosity was counterbalanced by detachment, and for this reason his assessment of me was more judicious than my assessment of him. My first thought was *old fool*.

I doubted he had ever wasted an afternoon daydreaming about my arrival, whereas I had dreamed of living in Ghana since I was in college. I had imagined a world less racist than the one from which I came. I had longed for a country in which my inheritance would amount to more than dispossession and in which I would no longer feel like a problem. Three months in Ghana were enough to disabuse me of these notions. People might call me the white man, but no one treated me as one. In supermarkets and banks, I grew accustomed to clerks and tellers calling white people to the front of the line, to the rude way Syrian and Lebanese storeowners treated their black customers, to there being one set of rules for white people and another for blacks. Black life was even more expendable in Africa than in the United States; only the particulars varied.

I was already angry, so it was not surprising I heard the old man's question as fighting words. His clear doubts about my identity dashed whatever hopes I had of losing myself in a sea of black faces and experiencing the intimacy and anonymity of the crowd. When I calmed down, I realized that he was only trying to name me, to figure out exactly who I was, which he was smart enough to know was not something that he could take for granted. After all, I was a stranger. His words acknowledged what we didn't share—a common identity. I had been named in another place and under disparate circumstances. I was a mystery, so the only assumption he made about me was lodged in the form of a question.

In truth I knew no more about the old man than he knew about me. As a boy he might have attended the blackface minstrel and vaudeville shows staged in Cape Coast by traveling actors inspired by Al Jolson and heard the word "nigger" for the first time in a "plantation song"; or his father might have used that word or a similar one when he told him stories about the black troops from Barbados and Jamaica who had helped the British defeat the Asante empire (in a war that has been described as a case of chickens coming home to roost); or "nigger" might have been the only word he could discern in the X-rated gansta rap that played uncensored on Ghana radio, precisely because no one could make out the words of the explicit lyrics; or he might have picked up the word "nigger" from the reruns of *Roots*, which were regularly aired on Ghana TV; or a friend of his who had studied at Lincoln University might have told him this was what black people were called in the United States; or he might have overheard a group of boisterous Americans in town bandying the word back and forth like a term of endearment, or complaining bitterly that they didn't expect to be treated like niggers here.

It dawned on me that the man's question explained why I was standing on a bridge and gawking at a castle. Negro or nigra—it tethered me to the past. I lost my footing in the world swirling about me: the shoppers plodding their way through the labyrinth of the market, the manifold faces of Jesus, the mottled sea of umbrellas shading market women. Everything regressed, and archaic forms assumed their place. I mistook a market woman selling dead *obruni* clothes for a sixteenth-century *feitor de roupa velha* (factor of used clothing). One era settled upon another. The apparitions of slaves and sovereigns hovered above the town.

THE PORTUGUESE BUILT Elmina Castle in 1482. Ten years before Columbus stumbled onto Hispañola and professed to discover it, the trade post and military fortification was erected. It was the first durable European edifice constructed in sub-Saharan Africa. Clearly the Portuguese had intended to put down stakes. Things didn't turn out as they expected—they never found the goldfields of which they had come in search—but they resided in Elmina for 150 years before the Dutch expelled them from the fort.

It would be tempting to say that in 1482 the handwriting was already on the wall. It would be easy to trace a straight line from then to now, as if the twelve million who arrived in the Americas, or the millions who were slaughtered in war; left for dead on the trail; killed by dysentery, cholera, and dehydration; or dumped in the Atlantic were sentenced to their fate when the ground was broken for the castle. In hindsight it would appear as if the demise of centuries could be foreseen in the exchange of gifts and promises between a Portuguese captain and an Akan viceroy.

In an apocalyptic account of history, the end is inevitable and destruction can be traced to the most innocuous and routine beginnings, like the exchange of salutations and vows of love on the Atlantic coast. The certitude of hindsight gives the demise an inevitable cast. But there were no black clouds casting a shadow on the Portuguese when they arrived, nor were storms brewing on the horizon. The heavens did not weep. All the omens that might have betrayed something terrible about to happen failed to appear or went unnoticed. Who knew then the price to be paid for love? Who knew the cost of naming the world anew? Who could have imagined the worlds destroyed by the horse and the musket, or the death reaped by luxury goods, or that sugar, coffee, and tobacco would transform three continents? It was not possible to foresee the Portuguese royal insignia scored along the West African coast as far south as Angola or to anticipate the crucifix branded onto the breasts and arms of captives. Nor could anyone have known that the gold revenue earned from El Mina would enable the Portuguese to become the masters of the slave trade in its first two centuries. So is it fair to blame two men meeting one late afternoon on a beach in Guinea for more than forty thousand slaving voyages that transported nearly twelve million Africans to the Americas?

Deciding the matter of cause and effect is, by necessity, belated; causality is the benefit of retrospection. One apprehends the signs of an inevitable demise only in hindsight. It is like trying to figure out when things began to change in a failed relationship: are the signs visible only after things have ended badly, or were the signs always there and you just failed to heed them? Only in looking back can the course from now to then be traced; or can we say, "Ah, this is how it began"; or weigh contingency and necessity, chance and causality; or wonder if the seemingly inexorable character of events was little more than the collective force of circumstance, accident, and caprice.

The randomness and contingency of history nonetheless produces two classes, winners and losers. Like men at a gaming table, over the course of time the gap between these groups will become bigger and bigger. The exchange of vows of love and friendship between two men one afternoon in 1482, albeit a kind of fiction, was one of the many occasions in the early modern period that set in motion a new order. Chance events engendered a racial global order so intractable that it now appears fated.

The record of the encounter between Europe and Africa is a litany of stories about events that never happened. Myth is the threshold of

history. On the slave route, it is no different. It all begins with apocryphal tales of knights and princes, with searches for Utopia, quests for fabled kingdoms, visions of the Garden and premonitions of the Fall. The "land of the negroes," wrote a Portuguese chronicler, seemed "a gracious fruit garden ordained for the sole end of their delight." As late as the eighteenth century, Europeans still imagined Africa as paradise or Eden. Not even Marx was able to resist the language of the Garden when recounting the violence that inaugurated modernity. In his essay on primitive accumulation, he described the scene of the Fall, which in his account was triggered not by the plucking of the apple but by the commercial hunting of black skins.

Two men meeting on the Guinea coast was yet another myth of beginning. Imagination created the event by endowing one afternoon with undue significance. Gods and kings appointed the central players. Cartographers drew the imaginary places. The royal scribes of Portugal authored the written account, so it began with Diego de Azambuja at the helm of his ship.

ON JANUARY 19, 1482, ten caravels and two transports loaded with four hundred tons of timber, bricks, tiles, stone, and mortar, and with a small pinnace in tow, set anchor off the coast of Guinea. Diego de Azambuja, the captain of the expedition, espied the landscape and recorded its features: the stark headlands, red cliffs, small bays, and the river winding through the town and slicing it in half. Surveying the coast, he decided on the best location for the trading fort: the narrow peninsula at the mouth of the river. It was an ideal spot, protected by the bay, the river, and the rocky shore, and offered suitable defense from enemies.

When Azambuja landed on the beach, six hundred men and a handful of women accompanied him. Among this company were the not yet legendary Bartolomeu Dias and Christopher Columbus, and the nameless—an army of soldiers, artisans, manual laborers, impoverished dreamers, exiled convicts, slaves, and prostitutes. The captain and his officers laid claim to the territory with the symbols of their sovereign and God, planting the royal insignia in the landscape and hoisting a banner with the royal escutcheons. With this elaborate ceremony, they took possession of *terra nullius*, no-man's-land; the following day they requested permission to do so.

Decked out for his meeting with the Akan statesman, Captain Azambuja cut a striking figure clothed in a jerkin of silk brocade with a golden collar of precious stones. The men posted at his side were also dressed in silk to impress "King" Caramansa with the riches of Portugal, although it was the riches of Guinea, the famed goldfields, that Azambuja and his men hoped to command. Through the mouthpiece of his black slave, who in all likelihood had been seized from Mina years earlier, Azambuja explained the purpose of his mission, which was to build a storehouse in Mina for the king of Portugal. *Fala de preto*, black man's speech or slave Portuguese, was the language of diplomacy; it bore little resemblance to the courtly language and embellished speech represented in the royal chronicles.

The captain began his remarks by declaring his love and that of his king: "The knowledge that the King, his Lord, had of Caramanca's [*sic*] desire to serve him well, as he had striven to show by the rapid lading of his ships when they arrived in that part; and because these things proceeded from love, the King wished to repay them with love, which would be more advantageous than his [Azambuja's], for it was love for the salvation of his soul, the most precious thing that man had, because it gave life, knowledge, and reason, which distinguished man from beast."

To which Caramansa replied: "Friends who met occasionally remained better friends than if they were neighbors." According to the royal chronicle, "He did not speak thus to disobey the commands of the

King of Portugal, but for the benefit of the peace and trade he desired to have with those who might come to that port . . . with peace between them, his people would be more willing to hear of God, whom he wished them to know."

Azambuja convinced Caramansa to change his mind, whether with threats or a flurry of sweet words is anyone's guess. The two men reached an accord. In exchange for love, salvation, and rent, Azambuja gained permission to build a storehouse for the lord of his country. At least that was the story told in the royal chronicle, a story that established Portugal's rights of occupation and deterred other European princes from commanding title to Mina. But the captain and the viceroy were just stand-ins for a greater set of social forces—emergent maritime technologies, merchant capital, competing trade interests, and divergent political stratagems.

Even the king's scribes disagreed as to exactly what happened on the beach that afternoon in 1482. It is impossible to know whether Caramansa granted the Portuguese permission to build the fort or if they proceeded to build without it, since beneath the silk brocade of Azambuja and his men were hidden firearms in case of need. If the bargain had been rejected and the gift of God spurned by "idolaters," then presumably the force of arms would have achieved what "love speech" failed to accomplish. Needless to say, love had many expressions. Once the settlement had been completed, a portion of Elmina was torched to protect trade and establish peace firmly. Love was the language of dominion, and its offspring were men and women in chains.

SOON AFTER THE fort was erected, the courtyard began to fill with slaves. Every fifty or so days, a ship loaded with slaves arrived at the fort. The slaves disembarked in small groups of one to two hundred. Between five hundred and one thousand slaves passed through the fort each year. By 1540, anywhere between ten thousand and twenty thousand slaves had been confined within its gates.

A handful worked inside the garrison, mostly girls and women assigned to the soldiers for their personal use; the rest (anywhere from one hundred to one hundred fifty slaves) were chained in the courtyard in wait of buyers. Some hunkered against the walls of the fort, others skulked about as far as the ropes and chains would allow. The women sat curled and slump shouldered, aware of their nakedness because of the gaze and groping of soldiers. The children's eyes darted about nervously with the fear plain on their faces.

Caravels had ferried the captives from the Slave Rivers of Benin and the ports of Kongo to Elmina. In a single expedition to the Slave Rivers, the Portuguese sometimes returned to the fort with as many as four hundred captives. Most of those taken from Benin were girls and women between the ages of ten and twenty. The *oba* (king) of Benin had restricted the sale of men and boys and eventually prohibited it. Each woman seized by the Portuguese had her right arm seared with the cross.

Locked away in the courtyard were also the ones stolen from Kongo. Prisoners of war taken by marauding armies; artisans, farmers, healers, weavers, fishermen, and metalworkers captured in raids on their towns and villages; undesirables, criminals, and troublemakers sentenced to slavery; and students, the sons of Kongolese nobles, kidnapped in São

Tomé on their journey to seminary in Lisbon, all shared the same fate. Kongo was a Christian kingdom. The *mani-Congo* (king) Dom Affonso had converted to Catholicism in 1490. The spread of Christianity among royals and nobles and the commerce in slaves proceeded apace, since the royal converts tied their fortunes to the slave trade.

The ubiquitous crucifix had spearheaded the great numbers of captives headed to the slave ports.

IN HONOR OF the patron saint of Portugal and their newly discovered African El Dorado, the Portuguese bestowed the storehouse with the name O Castellano de São Jorge or São Jorge de Mina, Saint George of the Mine. Like the hallowed and melodious names of slave ships—*Christ the Redeemer, Amistad, Blessed, John Evangelist, The Lord Our Savior, Recovery, Trinity*—so too the saintly eponym of Elmina Castle, São Jorge, announced the sacred errand commenced on the Guinea coast.

A religious crusade against infidels—*ad propagandam fidem* (for the propagation of the faith)—had inaugurated the slave trade forty years earlier on the upper Guinea coast. In 1444, the Portuguese had seized two hundred thirty-five captives in a raid for chattel.

Upon catching sight of the village of "Moors," the soldiers attacked, crying out, "Saint George," their patron and protector, and, "Portugal." The royal chronicle depicted the rout as booty gained with the Lord's blessings: The Portuguese attacked the villagers, "killing them, and seizing as many as they could. There you would have seen mothers forsaking their children, husbands abandoning their wives, each person trying to escape as best they could. And some drowned themselves in the water; others tried to hide in their huts; others, hoping they would escape, hid their children among the sea grasses where later they were discovered. And in the end our Lord God, who rewards every good deed, decided that, for their labors undertaken in his service, they should gain a victory of their enemies that day."

Saint George had many faces: martyr, proselytizer, celibate, submitter, procreator, soldier, and heretic. The villagers of the Rio de Oro experienced the avenging knight and the carnage conducted in the name of *our Lord God*.

The Age of Discovery required a man of arms, and George fit the bill. The conquering knight personified civilization pitted against beastly antagonists and monstrous races. The dragon slayer mounted on his steed antedated the charge: "Exterminate all the brutes." It would be hard to imagine a better representative of the Portuguese errand or a saint more suitable to the task.

Saint George was also a martyr among martyrs. Most saints endured one particular torture to evidence their faith. But the hapless George suffered virtually all the tortures known. Saint Sebastian's body pierced with arrows and Saint Agatha's slashed breast and Saint Peter's crucifixion paled in comparison.

In Palestine, Saint George was imprisoned. He was tortured with iron spikes, scourged, and his skull was crushed. In Persia, he was poisoned by the king's magician. In Nubia, an eyewitness averred that he was tortured

for seven years and killed four times. First, he was roasted over a flaming pit, but he was resurrected. Then his body was divided in two by a double-bladed saw, but again he defeated death. Next he was dismembered, but angels assembled his body parts and pieced him back together, and last he was boiled in a cauldron of oil. In Greece, he was bound to a post and his flesh lacerated with rakes and burned with a flaming torch.

The trial of saints and the anguish of martyrs would be put to the test in the holding cells of the castle and beyond. Did Saint George also provide an emblem for the suffering of slaves or a vision of life resurrected? In the Gold Coast, his ears were cut off and then he was put to death. In São Tomé, he was drowned in the sea. In Dahomey, he was decapitated. In Kongo, he was asphyxiated in a barracoon. In Santo Domingo, boiling sugarcane was poured on his head and withered the flesh on his body. In Barbados, he was flogged with a seven-headed whip. In Cuba, he was filled with gunpowder and blown up with a match. In St. John, he was burned at the stake, sawed in half, and impaled. In Maryland, he was hanged and decapitated. In Georgia, he was covered with sugar and buried in an anthill. In Curaçao, his face was scorched and his head cut off and

placed on a pole for the amusement of vultures. In Surinam, they cut off his hands and crushed his head with a sledgehammer. In Trinidad, he was dismembered and his body parts were thrown into the Atlantic. In Brazil, his ears were chopped off and a dagger buried in his back, his putrefied head displayed in the central square. In Panama, a sword disemboweled him. In Lima, he was paraded through the streets, beaten with the lash, and his wounds were washed with urine and rum. In Jamaica, he was force-fed excrement and burned on a pyre. In Grenada, he was shoved into a kiln and roasted. In Paramaribo, they cut his Achilles tendon and amputated his right leg. In Virginia, he was skinned. In Texas, his feet were bound and he was dragged through the streets by a horse. In New York, he was beaten with cudgels and hanged from a lamppost. In North Carolina, they burned him with torches and threw his body into quicklime. In Mississippi, he was cut to pieces on a wheel of blades. In Washington, D.C., he was mounted like a beast of burden and driven to death. In Alabama, he was tied to a cross, scourged by flaming torches, and beaten with chains. In Louisiana, his belly was sliced open and his entrails spilled out.

In the face of such torments, some allowed themselves to dream that the defeated might rise and the world be transformed. Broken bones, severed appendages, and charred limbs didn't stop them from swearing oaths to destroy their enemies, or rejoicing that they were going home, or taunting their masters, "You can roast me today, but can't tomorrow."

THE SIGNS AND SYMBOLS of Saint George's world were firsthand knowledge to the slaves imprisoned in the fort. The crucifix and a cursory baptism had ushered them into slavery. In the horrible trials endured by saints, there is, at least, the gift of consolation provided by faith affirmed and the promise of being liberated from the stench of the grave. But no solace can be found in the death of the slave, no higher ground can be located, no perspective can be found from which death serves a greater good or becomes anything other than what it is. The slaves corralled in the yard of the castle experienced the death of slaves—they lived and breathed, but they were dead in the social world of men. They were "commodities in the hands of merchants and use-goods and patrimony in the hands of buyers." Seized from home, sold in the market, and severed from kin, the slave was for all intents and purposes dead, no less so than had he been killed in combat. No less so than had she never belonged to the world.

The dead were reborn as new identities were foisted upon them. But what the slaves knew intimately was that "neither death nor rebirth was glorious"; rather, they were part and parcel of the life of the commodity. Slavery annulled lives, transforming men and women into dead matter, and then resuscitated them for servitude. Toiling away in the aftermath of death could only be a curse, not a miracle, and Saint George was the exterminating angel.

The lives awaiting them after Elmina were to be spent excavating gold in the mines of the forest, slogging away as head porters and hauling the luxury wares of merchants from the coast to the savanna; clearing land, tilling soil, and harvesting maize and millet; catering to sexual appetites and bearing children in the role of concubines and wives; joining the ranks of low-level functionaries who attended the royals: caretakers, umbrella holders, fan wavers, hammock carriers, gun and sword bearers, personal attendants, sweepers, cleaners, and executioners; suffering the knife and living as a eunuch; passing between the hands of slave traders in a string of interior markets from Elmina to Jenné; heading for a life in the cane fields of São Tomé after being rejected by all the buyers at Mina; laboring as domestic servants and silver miners in Mexico; and toiling away in Lisbon alongside thousands of other black slaves.

Gold dust; copper basins; brass bracelets, bars, and pots; colored textiles; linen and Indian cloth; barrel-shaped coral beads; strings of glass beads; red beads fashioned from bones; enamel beads; felt caps; and horsetails—all these determined the worth of slaves and provided the measure of their existence. The Portuguese referred to them as *braços*, arms or units. The Spanish called them *pieza de India*, which roughly translated into an "Indian piece." A *pieza* was a "mercantile unit of human flesh," which often comprised more than one human being. A male slave in the prime of his life was the standard against which other slaves were measured. Slaves possessing limited physical abilities or who were elderly constituted a fraction of a *pieza*. Two boys or a mother and her child might equal one *pieza*. The Dutch called them *leverbaar*, that is, a healthy or deliverable male or female slave.

The exchanges between persons and things, or property rights exercised in people, were common modes of acquiring wealth in Africa. Unique to the Atlantic slave trade was the immense scale of accumulating persons and the great violence and death required to produce wealth; and this predatory accumulation was often described by the enslaved in the language of "being eaten" or as sorcery. And to their eyes, the Europeans were sorcerers of the worst kind. Who could deny that white men gained their strength from black flesh? It was clear for everyone to see: they possessed the power to transform the bones of slaves into gunpowder, to convert blood into wine, and to dine on their organs.

I COULD NOT DETECT any blood or bones or gunpowder. I had tried, desperately, to wrench tragedy from the landscape and had failed. It had produced the opposite effect. I was blind to everything but the insignificance of the past and the unremarkable routine of the present. Little that I saw seemed noteworthy. Perhaps I had even been mistaken about the ghosts. In the sprawl of the market, I was the creature out of step with time. I was the sole revenant. Even the castle looked spanking new and resplendent in its fresh coat of white paint, as if it were untarnished by the filth and blood of its history.

The African-American residents of Elmina had complained that the refurbishment of the castle offended the dead and "whitewashed the black man's history" by camouflaging the foul character of the place. But the paint was like perfume on a rank body; it exaggerated the stink rather than diminished it. The castle was picturesque in a way that made you cringe, unless, of course, you forgot the cost of its grandeur. And it was easy to forget the slaves crushed under the weight of all that monumentality.

I began to fear that perhaps John was right. Maybe there was no point to being here. I had not wanted to believe this. I was stubborn, so I had convinced myself that I could unearth what others hadn't, but I was wrong. All I could see was a five-hundred-year-old trading fort, a monument to a past that no one wanted to remember.

Monuments, like graves, are intended to preserve the dead and to sus-
pend the past. But everything I could see refuted this. I still thought of the
castle as a tomb, but if it were, then where were the mourners? Didn't a
gravesite require the company of the bereaved?

In Ghana, they took the work of mourning seriously. Professional
mourners were employed at funerals. These expert grievers ensured that
the deceased received the proper amount of crying and keening to guide
them into the spirit world. The failure to properly mourn the dead was
considered a transgression. If not sufficiently honored, the deceased
would punish the living by wreaking havoc among them or sending trouble and misfortune their way. Glorifying the dead was imperative, because it determined the esteem with which the deceased would be
received in the afterlife. Funerals were costly and extravagant, and people
often complained the dead received better treatment than the living and
too often at their expense. *Abusua dò funu*: The family loves the corpse.

But there were no corpses that I could tend in Elmina. There were no
bodies draped in fine cloth, or rum poured down the throat of the dead, or
dirges sung around the laid out figure. No one had sent a message announcing the death of slaves with a pot of palm wine, or fired shots to no-
tify their neighbors, or tied their wrists with amulets and packets of gold
dust for the journey to the next world. No one did these things for them,
or fasted, or held a wake for two nights with drumming and dancing. No
one placed burial gifts alongside the corpse or whispered messages that
were to be delivered to dead relatives in the land of ghosts.

"Africa was a land of graves without bodies." It was a line I recalled
from a poem by the Ghanaian poet Kwadwo Opoku-Agyeman. The poem
was about the millions of people who disappeared from Africa during the
slave trade and the empty homes, deserted villages, and open graves left
behind in their wake. But it made no mention of mourners. Were there no
mourners because the graves were empty?

IF YOU ASKED the peddlers selling drinks and peanuts outside the castle
or the children playing at the foot of the hill about what happened inside

its walls, few could tell you. Most of Elmina's residents, with the recent exception of schoolchildren, had never set foot inside the castle, despite its status as a World Heritage Monument, or in any of the other forts scattered along Ghana's coast. I had colleagues at the university who had grown up in this area, literally in the shadows of the castle, who had never entered it or even inquired about its purpose. No one I spoke with could recall asking a parent about the edifices that lorded over the coast, or shared with me an adolescent adventure about scaling the walls of the castle, sneaking across the bridge, peering into the moat, or dashing through the courtyard. No one volunteered any stories about the slaves sold across the water.

They were baffled that what had happened more than a century ago could still hurt me, although the same individuals recited proudly their family genealogies back ten and eleven generations. I couldn't do the same. I could go back only three or four generations. If Ghanaians wondered why so many from the Americas crossed the water to cry about slave ancestors, it was not because Ghanaians honored their ancestors any less but because of the shame associated with slave origins. To revere your forbears was one thing; to speak openly of slave descent was a different matter altogether. Silence was the only reasonable position to be assumed by a descendant of slaves. Yet each year ten thousand African-American tourists traveled to Ghana and none of them failed to visit the slave dungeons. Ghanaians wondered what kind of people boasted of slave ancestry. Or made such a big show of emotions.

With a shrug of resignation, a taxi driver or clerk or seamstress would tell me that Ghanaians had too many pressing concerns in everyday life to ruminate about the past. The average daily wage was less than a dollar a day and per capita income was two hundred seventy dollars a year. Each year the cedi plunged in value. The unemployment rate was 30 percent. Most laborers didn't make enough in a day to buy a loaf of bread on their way home. "We don't have time to ponder and worry about slavery," they explained with exasperation to another rich American. And all Americans were rich in their eyes.

When I thought of slavery, the images that came most readily to mind were of scorched villages, the corpses abandoned en route to the coast, the filthy hold of slave ships, the bones heaped on the floor of the Atlantic, the breasts and genitalia bared on the auction block, the steel bit in a woman's mouth, the iron mask clamped on a man's face, the white master with a whip in his hand, and ripped apart black flesh. What I discovered was that when Ghanaians, at least those of the elite classes in the south, thought about slavery, they envisioned a "distant cousin from the north" washing clothes and preparing meals in a well-appointed home, the pretty slave wife of their grandfather, or the foreigners in their village. They exulted in the wealth of slave-trading ancestors, if only because it was less humiliating to have been a merchant than to have been a slave. "People pride themselves that their great-grandfathers rather kept slaves, and were not among the numerous slaves that abounded," as one man explained. "To be called a slave is an insignia of shame." The dishonor of the slave had persisted, as had the dignity and self-respect of the affluent and the powerful. The regret was that the wealth had not lasted. In Elmina, they lamented, "In those days we were rich, but now we're poor. The Dutch boat has left Elmina."

Few dared to mention the slaves chained in holding cells or taken off the coast, and if they did, they explained that African traders didn't know how badly the whites treated the slaves across the water. Others called the Atlantic slave trade the European trade, insisting that the West alone was to blame. It sanitized the whole ugly business and permitted them to believe that they were without scars.

Kofi, an assistant curator at the castle's museum, confided that it was difficult for him to think of slavery as a terrible fate. "There were slaves in my family," he told me. "My grandfather owned slaves. I never thought much of it. They were treated no differently than anyone else." I doubted that Kofi believed this, but he supposed that I was gullible enough to accept it as the truth. The terror of slavery, he tried to convince me, had been confined to the Americas.

Terror was what I took for granted. My own understanding of slavery and Kofi's could not have been more contrary. Which wasn't surprising since he was the son of a slave owner and I was the daughter of slaves. In

Ghana, kinship was the idiom of slavery, and in the United States, race was. The language of kinship absorbed the slave and concealed her identity within the family fold (at least that was the official line), whereas the language of race set the slave apart from man and citizen and sentenced her to an interminable servitude. But, as I found out, the line between masters and slaves was no less indelible, even when it wasn't a color line.

Talking with Kofi, I wondered if the problem was mine. I had presumed that the black world shared a thread of connection or a common chord of memory based upon this, our tragic past. In this assumption, I was proved wrong. I didn't experience what Ralph Ellison described as the "identity of passions," which connected the black world through our common suffering and history of struggle. I soon found out that most people didn't have a clue as to the scope of the transatlantic slave trade and didn't imagine that it had any lingering effects, which made them no different from the average American. And if they knew otherwise, they were disinclined to discuss it.

Months later when I met Kwadwo, I asked him, "Where are the mourners?" The poet proceeded to explain, "We, as Africans, are ashamed for our participation in the slave trade, and for this reason are unwilling to talk about the very issue that brings most of you here. And on both sides there is ignorance and a failure to understand one another's lives." It was his way of telling me there weren't any mourners.

I DON'T WANT to paint too simple a picture of things. Slavery was a bitter pill for black folks everywhere. My brother and I argued vigorously about its lasting impact. Were our lives still disfigured by slavery, or were we just haunted by stories of the past that no longer served us? Peter accused me of exaggerating the link between the past and the present and downplaying black people's responsibility in doing badly. My brother was one of those "working two jobs" black men, trying to do better than make ends meet, pay the mortgage, juggle the debts, and have just enough to take care of his family. But he was barely keeping his head above water and he could not forgive himself for this, so he was hard on himself and even harder on black folks. He made no excuses for his failures, so he made none for those of the race.

Whenever Peter and I quarreled, he tried to win the argument simply by speaking louder, which wasn't easy since I could get pretty thunderous myself. During the pitch of battle, my father would weigh in with a measured judgment uttered at an even louder volume. A house full of Hartmans yelling at the top of our lungs about slavery in my parents' modest lower-middle-class dwelling populated by more televisions than persons and outfitted with Ethan Allen furniture set off by muddy abstract paintings, which had been purchased in shopping malls, and cluttered with treadmills and exercise bikes and obsolete encyclopedias and dusty copies of the *Negro Almanac* and *The Miseducation of the Negro*, and dog-eared issues of *Jet*, *Ebony*, *Time*, and *Newsweek* would have made most Ghanaians laugh at the absurdity of it all or suck their teeth in resentment. The fury and the abundance, no doubt, would have made their heads spin.

Whenever we had our "what's wrong with the race" conversation, my brother would punctuate his argument with, "Slavery was a long time ago." I would answer back about the uneven playing field, the disparity between white and black wealth, racial profiling, the war being waged against the poor, and the prison system. He didn't deny these facts; to the contrary, our description of the present wasn't all that different. We simply drew dissimilar conclusions about who was to blame and where to go from here.

"Black people have always been in crisis," he remarked. "We've never been wanted in America, at least not since the Emancipation Proclamation. It's still no excuse for not doing better." No matter how vehemently he and I disagreed, what we both accepted was that the experience of slavery had made *us* an *us*, that is, it had created the conditions under which we had fashioned an identity. Dispossession was our history. That we could agree on.

The solidarity I felt with other black people depended largely on this history, whereas in Ghana their identity as Ghanaians and as Africans depended on silencing a past in which elites sold commoners and southerners viewed northerners as disposable people and alienable goods. The lines of division between kin and stranger, neighbor and alien, became hard and fast during the era of the Atlantic slave trade. It decided who lived and died, who was sold and who was protected. In Ghana, slavery wasn't a rallying cry against the crimes of the West or the evils of white men; to the contrary, it shattered any illusions of a unanimity of sentiment in the black world and exposed the fragility and precariousness of the grand collective *we* that had yet to be actualized.

THREE

The Family Romance

THE WHITE MEN WHO OWNED and sired the family line were phantasmal, as if we had conjured them up and they threatened to vanish under the pressure of scrutiny. We uttered their names reluctantly, never forgetting that their names were also our names, but as if still fearing the punishment of thirty-nine lashes or the auction block for disclosing the identity of the father.

Every now and then my aunt Laura would share a story about "a German from Bonaire" or one of our other shadowy progenitors. Unlike my aunt Beatrice, who believed it was best to leave the past in the past and who was tight-lipped, especially when it concerned matters like indifferent fathers, troublesome origins, or other revelations that could only leave you shamefaced, my aunt Laura was willing to tell all. She relished the perverse details, liberating the skeletons from the closet and dutifully recounting the scandals that comprised our family history. Nothing fazed her, so whenever I wanted to find out some piece of information about the family that others considered taboo, she was the one to whom I turned.

Aunt Laura never shared any anecdotes about the ones who crossed the Atlantic from Africa. There were no anecdotes. "Genealogical trees don't flourish among slaves," as Frederick Douglass remarked. In my

family, too, the past was a mystery. The story boiled down to remote white men, missing black fathers, lies and secrets about paternity, and wayward lines of descent. From time to time, my aunt Laura shared a name, Wilhelm Hartman or Rainer Hermann, or an attribute, "Hermann was a stingy SOB. That was all Mama ever said about him."

Our genealogy added up to little more than a random assortment of details about alcoholics, prosperous merchants, and dispassionate benefactors. Given this paucity of information, all talk of our forebears was sketchy. No matter how much we embellished and dressed things up, the truth couldn't be avoided: slaves did not possess lineages. The "rope of captivity" tethered you to an owner rather than a father and made you offspring rather than an heir.

The classic story of slavery: A gray-haired gentleman succumbs to the evil of the peculiar institution and a wretched dark woman "lays herself low to his lust." Who fails to recognize the figures, the planter and the concubine, the other tragic couple of the New World romance, a romance not of exalted fathers but of defiling ones? Who hasn't heard it all before?

The story of murky adulterated bloodlines, rapacious masters, derelict fathers, and violated mothers.

Bastaard was what the Dutch called their mixed-race brood; the term implied an illegitimate child as well as a mongrel. If these dead white fathers could speak, no doubt they would be hard-pressed to allow "son" or "daughter" to pass through their lips. Yet these ghostly patriarchs commanded more attention than anyone else in our battered line, if only because they could be named.

I HAD READ numerous books and articles about the Dutch slave trade. I knew that the Dutch were the fourth largest slave-trading nation, falling in behind England, Portugal (in combination with Brazil), and France, and that from 1700 until the official end of the slave trade, the Gold Coast was a primary source of slaves for the Dutch. I knew that the Dutch called the female slave hold the *hoeregat*, or whore hold. I knew that Dutch ships were regular freight ships that had been refitted for slaves. I knew that slaves were forced to dance on deck to the accompaniment of African drums, flutes, and whips. I knew that of the 477,782 captives exported by the Dutch from 1630 to 1794, 89,000 were from the Gold Coast. I knew that this number might be an underestimation, but even if I multiplied it by ten or one hundred, all the missing and the dead still would not be of enough significance for the world to care or to acknowledge the crime. I knew that textiles, most of which were manufactured in Haarlem and Leiden, made up 57 percent of the goods the Dutch exchanged with African brokers for captives, and that guns, gunpowder, alcohol, and trinkets made up the rest of the merchandise traded. I knew that anywhere from 3 percent to 15 percent of the slaves held in the storerooms of Elmina Castle died there. I knew that slaves sometimes languished for as long as four months on board a slaver until a "complete cargo" had been purchased and that the journey across the Atlantic could take anywhere from 23 to 284 days. I knew that the slaves were called *kop*, or head, as in head of cattle, and not *hoof'd*, as in human head. I knew a consignment of slaves was called *armaʒoen*, which meant living cargo, as distinct from other kinds of goods, and that the Dutch used the term "Negro" as an equivalent to "slave," so they called the slave ship a *neger schip*. I knew that the death rates of the slave trade, according to one Dutch historian, "reached 70% before the survivors were adjusted to life in the Western Hemisphere."

But what did all this information add up to? None of it would ever compensate for all the other things that I would never know. None of it had brought me any closer to replacing a lacuna with a name or an X-ed space with an ancestral village.

FOR TRACKING PURPOSES, the officials of the Dutch West India Company branded slaves twice. When captives arrived at Elmina Castle, Arabic numerals and/or the letters of the alphabet were seared onto their breasts. When they arrived in Curaçao, which was the way station for the slaves sold by the Dutch West India Company to the Spanish Americas, they were again branded with a red-hot iron. The scars identified the slaves at sales, at criminal proceedings, and in death affidavits, without which company officials were unable to able say little more than, "It is the honest truth that on the first of March this year *a certain purchased woman* slave died, giving as the evidence of our knowledge that we saw the body after she died."

The numbers identified each person as the cargo of a particular ship, or designated the company that purchased him, or simply itemized her as one unit, a *pieza de India*, or *leverbaar*. Slave ship officers traveled with instructions for branding: "Note the following when you do the branding: (1) the area of marking must first be rubbed with candle wax or oil; (2) The marker should only be as hot as when applied to paper, the paper gets red. When these [precautions] are observed, the slaves will not suffer bad effects from the branding."

A vivid picture of the purchase and branding of property was drawn by William Bosman, one of the chief factors at Elmina Castle. The scene he described was repeated at every port of embarkation along the West African coast. When a parcel of slaves arrived, the traders, accompanied by a surgeon, inspected them "without the least distinction or modesty."

The surgeon examined their eyes, prodded their teeth and genitals, and separated the healthy from the infirm. The ones deemed suitable, re-ported Bosman, "are numbered, and it is entered who delivered them. In the meanwhile, a burning Iron, with the arms or names of the companies, lyes in the Fire; with which ours are marked on the breast. This is done that we may distinguish them from the slaves of the English, French or others; (which are also marked with their mark) and to prevent the Negroes ex-changing them for worse. I doubt not but this Trade seems very barbarous to you, but since it is followed by mere necessity it must go on; but we take all possible care that they are not burned too hard, especially the women, who are more tender than the men."

WICS25 or *T99*—no one wants to identify her kin by the cipher of slave-trading companies, or by the brand, which supplanted identity and left only a scar in its place. I'm reminded of the scene in *Beloved* in which Sethe's mother points to her mark, the circle and cross burned on her rib, and says to her daughter, "This is your ma'am . . . If something hap-pens to me and you can't tell me by my face, you can know me by this mark." The mark of property provides the emblem of kinship in the wake of defacement. It acquires the character of a personal trait, as though it were a birthmark.

PARTUS SEQUITUR VENTREM—the child follows in the condition of the mother. The bill of sale includes "future increase," so that even the un-born were fettered. "Mothers could only weep and mourn over their chil-dren," according to the ex-slave Mary Prince, "they could not save them." The stamp of the commodity haunts the maternal line and is transferred from one generation to the next. The daughter, Sethe, will carry the bur-den of her mother's dispossession and inherit her dishonored condition, and she will have her own mark soon enough, as will her daughter Beloved.

The mother's mark, not the father's name, determined your fate. No amount of talk about fathers could suture the wound of kinship or skirt the brute facts. The patronymic was an empty category, "a blank parody," a fiction that masters could be fathers and wayward lovers more than the "begetters of children"; it was as well the placeholder of banished black fathers.

My grandmother had been a Van Eiker, as had her mother and her mother before her. I was a descendant of a long line of fearless and strongwilled women—Leonora Van Eiker, Maria Julia Van Eiker, Elisabeth Juliana Van Eiker—who were denied marriage or eschewed

it. Four generations were born with a blank space where a father's name should be. In its place was the stroke of a bureaucrat's pen, which had left a line less dramatic than an X and which suggested nothing as harsh as erasure but simply "not applicable." My aunts Laura and Beatrice were proud to be Van Eikers; the other path, the dishonor that was the bastard's inheritance as well as the slave's, was too dangerous. The lessons they imparted tried to affirm this maternal inheritance and to make of it something other than monstrosity. The stories my aunts shared were offered as an antidote to shame and they esteemed a web of intimacy and filiation outside the law of paternal sanction.

I WAS A HARTMAN TOO. The predecessors of my grandfather Frederick Leopoldo were spectral figures. All I knew about my great-grandfather was that he had been a prosperous Jewish merchant. My aunts called him "Daddy's father," tacitly acknowledging that this blood relation

WILSON CHINN, a Branded Slave from Louisiana.
Also exhibiting Instruments of Torture
used to punish Slaves.
Photographed by Kimball, 477 Broadway, N.Y.
Entered according to Act of Congress, in the year 1863, by
Geo. H. Hanks, in the Clerk's Office of the United States for
the Southern District of New-York.

did not extend beyond father and son and did not include them within its embrace.

The Hartman name, according to my father, was our anchor in the world. It was our sole inheritance; we possessed no wealth but it. So when my grandfather's white cousins tried to buy back the family name from the brown ones in an attempt to erase a history of owners and property they feared would be mistaken for kinship, our clan doggedly held on to it. It had been passed from Wilhelm to Frederick to three generations of sons who were all named Virgilio.

Tracing the family genealogy at the archives in Willemstad, the capital of Curaçao, I was surprised to discover that my grandfather wasn't a Hartman at all.

On his birth certificate was the name Maduro, the surname of his mother, Clarita. I don't know if his father had acknowledged him belatedly or if he had ever given his son permission to use his name as my aunt Laura insisted, or if Hartman was something my grandfather had pilfered as a man-child when at seventeen he set out into the world. Hartman was the name on his passport and his green card, and no doubt it would have been the name on my grandparents' marriage certificate, if I had ever been able to locate it.

Growing up, I had envied my brother, who as son was the rightful heir to the Hartman name and who in turn would pass it on to his children. My father and mother had placed so much stock in the family name that even after getting married, I held on to it. But, as it turned out, there was no long lineage to which the name had been anchored or to which we had any entitlement. Who, after all, was the Hartman to whom we were staking claim?

Come, Go Back, Child

THE SIGN POSTED on the hurricane fence warned: "No one is allowed inside this area except tourists." As I climbed the muddy incline leading to the entrance of Elmina Castle, a group of adolescent boys approached me yelling, "Sister!" "One Africa!" "Slavery separated us." Kwesi, the leader of the pack, handed me a letter scribbled on the crumpled pages of a school notebook and the other boys followed suit, stuffing my hands with missives that felt like suede because they had been carried in back pockets and sweaty palms too long. When I opened the letters, they threatened to dissolve in my hands, as with old dollar bills that have circulated for ages. Perforations appeared along the folded edges and the penciled script, barely legible, swirled like smoke against the grayed pages.

Kwesi's letter began:

Beloved Sister, please write me. We are one Africa which means we are the same people and I know it's because of the slave trade that's why you left here to U.S.A. and I want you to know that you are my sister and I am your brother according to the history of our ancestors and Africa is both of us motherland so you are welcome back home (Akwaaba) please let keep in touch by letters so that we could learn from each other and know ourselves well as brother and sister. Share my greetings with my other brothers and sisters in America. Thank you. Peace and love to you senior sister.

Francis's letter was a replica of Kwesi's. It opened with me losing my mother and closed imploring me to write. The only difference was that Francis addressed the dead too and wondered when those taken across the Atlantic would return home.

Isaac's letter was short. In three lines he stated the basics: his grade in school, his need of pencils and paper, and my status as a foundling. His letter concluded with the admonishment that I learn my history or risk not knowing who I really was: "Because of the slave trade you lose your mother, if you know your history, you know where you come from." To lose your mother was to be denied your kin, country, and identity. To lose your mother was to forget your past. The letters distilled the history of the transatlantic slave trade to this: I was an orphan.

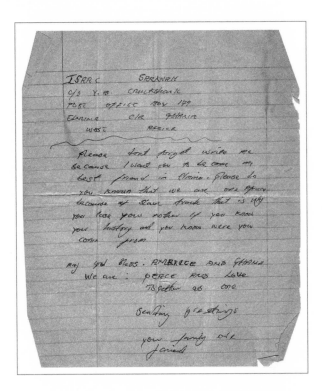

The boys addressed me as if I were the child sold across the Atlantic, as if pledges of love could mend the breach of slavery, as if errant spirits were destined to return home. They mistook me for the *kosanba*—the spirit child—who dies only to return again and again in a succession of rebirths. Because of this cycle of departure and return, exile and home-coming, demise and resurrection, the spirit child is also called the "come, go back, child." The spirit child shuttles back and forth between the worlds of the living and the dead because of the stories not passed on, the ances-tors not remembered, the things lost, and the debts not yet paid. The "come, go back, child" braves the wreckage of history and bears the bur-dens that others refuse.

The comings and goings of the spirit child aggrieve its mother. The first eight days after a child is born are filled with anxiety, because the mother hasn't yet discovered if her infant is a wandering ghost rather than a human child. To prevent the child from dying again and returning to the spirit world, she attempts to trick the forces that would claim its life. So the mother marks the infant to make it ugly or she names the child *odonkor*—slave—fettering the child to keep her in the world. Or she scars the child with the tribal markings of the slave class. This sleight-of-hand convinces the spirits that the child's life is not valuable and thus not worth taking. Mothers, disavowing their love, have called their children *donkor* (slave) in order to save them, while slaveholders have called their prop-erty "beloved child" in order to protect their wealth. Mothers plead with the *kosanba* to remain in the mortal world and not to return to its spirit mother, and masters command the slave to stay put and to forget all thoughts of the mother country, the natal land. Come and stay, child, they both implore.

THE WORD FOR "slave" in Akan that comes closest to what we mean by the term in the West is *odonkor*. It refers to someone who is bought and sold in the market, a commodity. Of all the terms that describe involun-tary servitude—*akoa*, which means "subject," "assistant," or "slave"; *awowa*, which is a pawn ransomed for the debt of a relative; *akyere*, some-one enslaved as punishment for a crime; *domum*, a captive of war—

odonkor is the only derogatory and stigmatized term. It is the one that car-
ries dishonor and shame. Yet the etymology of *odonkor* is not to be found
in words like "idiot," "clod," "oaf," "lout," "dolt," or "barbarian." The
origins of the word *odonkor* are in the words "love" (*odo*) and "don't go"
(*nti nka*). *Odo nti nka*: because of my love for you, don't go.

Love encourages forgetting, which is intended to wash away the
slave's past. Love makes a place for the stranger; it domesticates persons
from "outside of the house" and not "of the blood"; it assuages the slave's
loss of family; it remakes slaveholders as mothers and fathers. Owning
persons and claiming kin are one and the same; so love cannot be separated from dispossession or property in persons. Affection perhaps soft-
ens the sting of dishonor but does not erase it. The slave does not enjoy
the rights and entitlements of "royals" and "nobles," those who are the le-
gitimate heirs of the lineage. Love extends the cover of belonging and
shrouds the slave's origins, which lie in acts of violence and exchange, but
it doesn't remedy the isolation of being severed from your kin and denied
ancestors.

"Don't go." "Stay put." These are the words of the master. The slave
must stay put or stay in her place. *If you have no master, a beast will catch
you. A proud slave is buried with the corpse of his master.* But staying is at
odds with the very definition of a slave; the bought-and-sold person comes
and goes by way of the transactions of the market. The slave is always the
stranger who resides in one place and belongs to another. The slave is always the one missing from home. Being an outsider permits the slave's up-
rooting and her "reduction from a person to a thing that can be owned."

The slave and the master understand differently what staying implies.
The transience of the slave's existence still leaves its traces in how black
people imagine home as well as how we speak of it. We may have forgotten our country, but we haven't forgotten our dispossession. It's why we
never tire of dreaming of a place that we can call home, a place better than
here, wherever here might be. It's why one hundred square blocks of Los
Angeles can be destroyed in an evening. We stay there, but we don't live
there. Ghettos aren't designed for living. The debris awash in the streets,
the broken windows, and the stench of urine in the project elevators and
stairwells are the signs of bare life. "The insistent, maddening, claustro-

phobic pounding in the skull that comes from trying to breathe in a very small room with all the windows shut," writes James Baldwin, daily assaults the residents of the ghetto, the quarters, the 'hood. It produces the need to "destroy tirelessly" or "to smash something," which appears the most obvious path of salvation. As C.L.R. James observes about the San Domingo masses, they destroyed "what they knew was the cause of their sufferings; and if they destroyed much it was because they had suffered much."

Two people meeting on the avenue will ask, "Is this where you stay?" Not, "Is this your house?" "I stayed here all my life" is the reply. Staying is living in a country without exercising any claims on its resources. It is the perilous condition of existing in a world in which you have no investments. It is having never resided in a place that you can say is yours. It is being "of the house" but not having a stake in it. Staying implies transient quarters, a makeshift domicile, a temporary shelter, but no attachment or affiliation.

This sense of not belonging and of being an extraneous element is at the heart of slavery. Love has nothing to do with it; love has everything to do with it.

PEDDLERS, SWINDLERS, and ingenious adolescents were the only ones in Elmina brazen enough to espouse the love of slaves. It was a hustle, and we were all aware of this; nonetheless, we assumed our respective roles. In New York, the game would be three-card monte or a shell game, and two lanky teenagers at a cardboard gaming table would solicit you with "miss" or "sister" initiating the ritual, while the third one keeps an eye out for the police. You'd approach the table knowing that you shouldn't, but something about these boys acting mannish, and the mix of guile and innocence, and the sharp edge of desperation would break down the protective barrier and convince you that you had a chance after all and that you were not predator and prey but somehow all in it together. You'd participate in the game knowing that the odds were stacked against you and that in all likelihood you'd walk away having lost what you staked. But you risk it anyway, and just as you expected, but contrary to what you had hoped, the right card keeps evading you and you never find the elusive object.

In Elmina, the traffic was in redemption. The past was at stake and the odds were not any better. I could not recuperate my losses, nor could *beloved sister* right the balance between things lost and things gained. What I could salvage amounted to flattering words, make-believe brothers, and vows of love. Go, come back, I love you. The tug and pull, the advance and the recoil, the longing and the disappointment: Wasn't this the dance of love? Wasn't this the family romance, a fantasy of exalted strangers, a fantasy of reunited kin? It was an indiscriminate and promiscuous love that did not differentiate between persons; it never required a name or retreated from the wretched and the loathed; it thrived in lowly places. In this game, winning or losing mattered less than the willingness to close your eyes and take the first step.

But how could these scruffy adolescents love me or anyone else like me? You could never love the foreigner whose wealth required you to inveigle a handful of coins. It was not the kind of relationship that cultivated tender feeling. I had fled to their world and the boys yearned to escape to mine. They wanted to break out of this dusty four-cornered town and never see the castle again or the sign barring their entrance; they wanted never to plead for small change from an *obruni* or repeat the words "slave trade" and "one Africa." In their eyes, I must have appeared a foolish woman who acted as if slaves existed only in the past and who conducted herself as if dispossession were her inheritance alone. Looking at me, the boys imagined the wealth and riches they would possess if they lived in the States. After all, who else but a rich American could afford to travel so far to cry about her past? Looking at me, the boys wished their ancestors had been slaves. If so, they would be big men.

"RETURN" WAS THE WORD that reverberated throughout Elmina Castle, as though the only life possible was the one that existed in the past. Travel guides, docents, and wistful Americans tossed it off without an afterthought: *Return to the motherland. Welcome back. It's good to be home.*

Peering through the hatch at the back of the holding cell, I remembered an image from the film *Sankofa*. A file of actors costumed as slaves and weighted with chains exited through this door and onto a slaver. You couldn't see the ship waiting for them because of the mist that hung over the door. So it looked as though the slaves were stepping into the gray haze of oblivion. And as I stood in the cell recalling this, what transpired was almost exactly like what happened in the movie—the assimilated race-traitor heroine, who has now recovered her authentic African identity after being transported back in time to slavery days and beaten and raped on a Louisiana plantation, emerges from the dungeon, stumbles into the courtyard, and embraces her true home—the docent says to me, "It is no longer the door of no return, because now you are back."

We both smiled at the absurdity of it. How could a slave fort be a welcome house? He confirmed what I already knew. The trail back ended at the bars of the holding cell. I later read an article in *The New York Times* about African Americans attempting to fill in the blank spaces of their history with DNA tests. By matching Y chromosomes and mitochondrial DNA with that of contemporary Africans, they had hoped to get closer to an African home than a slave dungeon. History had failed to solve the mystery of an unknown past, so they had put their faith in science, despite the ambiguous and inconclusive results of the test. One man's words stayed with me. Having discovered that his ancestors were from Cameroon, he remarked that he felt more lost than before. Now he was estranged from an ancestral tribe as well as the country of his birth. "It's like being lost and found at the same time," he said. Being in Elmina Castle was like that too.

Wandering through the castle, neither the iron balustrades adorned with the initials of the Dutch West India Company nor the storerooms solicited me. Perhaps it was because nothing was as it had been. The male dungeon was now a gift shop. At the entrance stood life-size cardboard cutouts of an African-American couple, recognizable by the glimmer and shine of the oily waves of their S-curl. Yards of kente were draped around their two-dimensional forms. The trade hall was now a museum and the secret entrance from the female dungeon to the governor's private chamber was the scandal of an otherwise dull tour. The holding cells were empty and the slaves long dead. Nothing was left but the ball and chain outside the women's dungeon, awaiting the prisoners who would never arrive.

◇ ◇ ◇

I shall return to my own land. For at least a century and a half, the slave revolts of the Americas were fueled by this longing. It was not until July 14, 1789, when the Bastille fell, that the word "revolution," according to Hannah Arendt, was first used "without any connotation of a backward revolving motion." Until then, revolution and restoration of an earlier order had been synonymous. No event made this point more directly than the rebellion of Mina slaves that shook St. John. From the outset of the insurrection, the rebels had intended to restore the old world of Akwamu. To do so, they needed first to destroy the prevailing order. For the insurrectionists, return was the language of triumph and political ascendancy. It was also the language of defeat.

While the revolt that erupted on St. John in 1733 was a mere footnote in the annals of the Age of Revolution, this "minor event" registered the reverberations of the Old World in the Americas. It painted in blazing detail the paths opened and impeded when your sights were fixed on the past.

In the spring of 1733, a drought destroyed the majority of St. John's sugarcane crops. In the summer, a hurricane descended upon the island and ruined the few crops that survived. Then a plague of insects afflicted the island, swarming bedchambers, houses, ovens, and pantries, and causing famine. And just when everyone imagined no worse fate was possible, a winter storm beat the already battered island, destroyed the maize crop, and reduced the slaves to starvation. The disasters were of biblical proportions, but what was to follow in the wake of these events was not a story of providential deliverance from slavery but one of bloody rebellion and a short-lived freedom won by the musket and the sword.

In the predawn hours, the rebels struck. An apocryphal account written by a French planter describes in lurid detail the inaugural gesture of the revolt, which mirrored the retribution feared and anticipated by the planters: "That unhappy day was the 23rd of November, 1733, at three in the morning. Mr Soetman's Negroes, assisted by others, broke down their master's door, while he was sleeping, ordered him to get up, and, after having stripped him naked, forced him to sing and dance. Then, after having run a sword through his body, they cut his head off, cut open his body, and washed themselves in his blood. To this execution, they added that of his daughter Hissing, thirteen years old, by slaughtering her on top of her stepfather's body."

The tragic events began, according to a missionary's report, when "a number of Negroes from the warlike Amina nation took control of the fort while fulfilling their accustomed job of supplying the place with firewood." At four in the morning, the rebels commandeered the island's fort. Masquerading as hewers of wood, they entered the garrison with their firearms hidden in bundles of twigs and branches. When the sentry called out, "Who goes there?" they answered, *"Kompni nega mi' hoot,"* company's slaves with wood, and were permitted to enter. They killed the five soldiers on watch and fired the cannons to alert the other slaves of the insurrection. At least one hundred of the island's one thousand slaves heeded the call and joined the rebels. Some say as many as three hundred slaves revolted.

Amina or Elmina slaves, as they were called because they had been shipped from the area surrounding Elmina Castle, comprised the majority of the rebel troops. Amina slaves enjoyed a reputation for being a rebellious and troublesome property. They battled their masters, refused to labor, absconded from plantations, created maroon communities, and committed suicide rather than countenance slavery. Traders and planters complained that Amina slaves were mutinous, treacherous, self-important, and not afraid to die, but no one had ever described them as inclined to forget.

The lines of royals and slaves crossed in the rebel band. The deposed members of the ancien régime of Akwamu led the front ranks of the rebellion. Akwamu was one of the principal states exporting slaves from the Gold Coast between 1680 and 1730. When the king of Akwamu began enslaving and selling his subjects on the pretext of debt, a civil war erupted that destroyed the state. Those allied with the defeated king were sold into slavery by the conquering army. The Amina rebels were part of this defeated elite. The head of the rebels, King June, had been the king's representative in trade relations with Europeans. After the fall of Akwamu, he entered Fort Christiansborg not as a diplomat and trade partner, but as a slave, a *pieza de India.* Five princes, a princess, the king's brother-in law, and other members of the royal court also found themselves aboard a slaver and destined for the fields of St. John.

The royals didn't easily adapt to slavery. They resisted, not because of any commitment to the ideas of the equality of man or opposition to slavery in principle or objection to the idea that some men lived off the labor of others, but because their aristocratic heritage made slavery untenable. Staggered by their arrogance, a missionary stationed on the island observed that the obstinacy of the Amina nation "goes so far that nothing—not even death itself—is capable of dissuading them of their intended course of action." They would break before yielding.

Clashes between masters and slaves were routine. But don't imagine the raised fist of disgruntled and exploited workers, or the righteous indignation of the wretched, or the commoner's bawdy songs of protest and derision, or the collective rage of the downtrodden; be prepared for the complaints of the entitled and the boasts of the superior. When ordered by masters and overseers to complete a task, pick up the pace, carry manure, or haul water, they were likely to refuse what they called "*donkor* work." One young man, explaining the reason for disobedience, told his master, "I am a prince. For the time being, I happen to be in your power; but nothing will ever persuade me to serve you. I would rather die of my own free will and thus end my life as a free man." The prince refused to eat and died as a result of starvation. A young woman, "filled with ideas of her former greatness," shrugged off the command of her mistress: "I was much greater in Guinea than you are here. I had many more slaves in my service than you have. Now you expect me to be your slave? I would rather die of starvation." Others jumped from hills, hanged themselves, and drowned in the ocean.

The rebels decided first to take up arms. They found themselves on the stage of history as actors in a carnival masque, these former traders and raiders now costumed as slaves. But the revelers were eager to cast off the garments of the defeated. They opposed slavery, but the only shackles they were intent on removing were their own. King June, as his title might indicate, was no Toussaint L'Ouverture or Dessalines determined to win complete liberty for all. King June was a man of his time and no charters or declarations yet existed that declared the rights of man and citizen. And even had the Bill of Rights or the Declaration of the Rights of Man and Citizen been written, the black rebels would have fallen outside the embrace of the stated universal principles.

Princes without kingdoms and generals without armies and big men without dependents headed the St. John rebellion. The rebels longed to exercise power again and so planned to reassert their sovereignty by overthrowing the white planter class and assuming their place. An Akan-style polity would replace the plantocracy. When they first gained control of the island, the rebels didn't burn the plantations or factories, because they intended to run them and with slave laborers. They were accustomed to a world ruled by royals and nobles and serviced by slaves, bonded commoners, and peasants. The world they remembered and tried to re-create on the island was not a world in which slavery was abolished but one in which they ruled as a sovereign political class.

During the early months of the revolt, when faced with a shortage of ammunition, they traded ten non-Amina slaves for a barrel of gunpowder (replicating in miniature the gun-slave cycle that helped to fuel the slave trade in Africa). This attitude might explain why the majority of the island's slaves did not join the rebellion. There is the distinct possibility that some of the slaves envisioned the rebels not as their liberators but as the ones responsible for their exile. No doubt, in the eyes of the rebels, the reluctance of the majority of the island's slaves to take up arms consigned them to servitude. It was said that "the Aminas looked at all those who were not on their side as enemies."

It is difficult to narrate the course of events because no single mode can fully describe what happened on St. John. The rebellion was a romance because the enslaved overtook their masters and discarded their chains. It was a farce with deposed royals outfitted as slave rebels seeking to be the new masters. It was a tragedy because the Amina rebels imagined they could preserve their identities and carry on in the New World as they had in the Old. And this failure to establish a language of solidarity with the other slaves of the island doomed the rebellion. Had they been willing to refashion their identities, would the other slaves have joined them? (There would have been few if any Creoles since the island had been colonized for only fifteen years and the enslaved did not reproduce but were replaced.) Would the commoners have envisioned a new social order in which there were no slaves? Would the imperial ambitions of the royals have interdicted the freedom dreams of the lowly? The revolutionary fervor of the Amina rebels could not be separated from their vision of re-creating the Old World, which, ironically, was a social order as dependent on slavery as was the plantation society of St. John.

The St. John revolt toppled, albeit temporarily, the white planter establishment. King June established a new court and controlled the island for six months before being routed by a company of two hundred French troops from Martinique. As the French troops, who were equipped with adequate arms and composed of vigorous men not exhausted by six months of battle, gained on the rebels, they discovered a trail of bodies. On May 4, in a wooded retreat, eleven rebels ended their lives. On May 15, twenty-five rebels, including six women, took their lives in a mass suicide. Some insist that as many as three hundred were assembled on the hill near Brimsbay, when the rebels "sat down in a circle and were mortally shot one after another by the two leaders whom they had selected in the course of the rebellion. When those two completed the task, they then shot themselves." Before they fired their rifles, they avowed, "When I die, I shall return to my own land."

IF DEAR TO THE HEARTS and minds of the rebels was the idea of revolving back to former times, then on the hill at Brimsbay they faced the hard truth that only death would make return possible. Revenants would achieve what rebels could not. On the precipice, return was no longer the language of self-making or reconstruction but of resignation and exhaustion. What the rebels acknowledged by their collective act of suicide was that the past was the only country left, the only horizon visible, the only world inhabitable. Having lost the battle and facing defeat, they hoped they would find their way back home to Akwamu.

The rebels knew that return was bound inextricably with loss. The invocation of who they had been, which earlier had provided the ground of insurgency, now signaled an imminent defeat. Suicide represented not the collapse of their political will but the recognition that their weapons were inadequate to those of their enemies. The lesson offered by their example is vexed and contradictory, because return and remaking, or restoration and transformation, can't be separated into tidy opposing categories. Sometimes *going back to* and *moving toward* coincide.

Remembering the Old World prodded deposed royals to insurrection. But what vision of change stirred those who possessed no home to which they could look back and who failed to see any signposts in the Atlantic? What of the commoners who blamed their abject plight on avaricious kings and imperial states? Their decision to flee and fight would have had little to do with the past and everything to do with hopes for the future. No doubt, the country for which they longed promised first and foremost a radical break with the present. Perhaps what they understood was that restoration was neither the enabling condition nor the end of rebellion and that it was not necessary to look back in order to move forward. And even if they had conjured up the vision of a glorious fanciful past, all that really mattered was the end to which this imagined past—the time before slavery—was mobilized.

The futures anticipated and eclipsed in the course of the rebellion employed the language of return, which lent itself indiscriminately to dreams of a free territory and to recollections of predatory kingdoms. When King June imagined returning home, did he envision himself once again at the side of his deposed king and in the silk robes of the statesman? Did he picture his retinue of dependents dutifully attending to him or foresee reuniting with his lost friends and kin? Could he have remembered the dank holding cell of the fort and still desired to return home?

I shall return home was what he told himself and the others; it gave him the courage needed to point a rifle at his chest and pull the trigger.

I shall return to my native land. The children and grandchildren of the rebels might have reiterated the same vow. Inevitably, time did erase the Old World or, at least, blunted its features and silenced its image. No doubt there were also those who chose to "murder the memory" because it was easier that way. Forgetting might have made it less painful to bear the hardships of slavery and easier to accept a new life in a world of strangers. Perhaps it wasn't a choice at all, and the past slowly disappeared over the course of years, or the shock of enslavement destroyed it in one fell swoop. How long did it take for the mother tongue to be eradicated by a new language? Was the ephemera of everyday life—the pat and scratch of women's feet in the compound at dawn, the low rustle of reeds in the lagoon, the rhythm and nonsense of childhood games, the murmur of trees at nightfall, the mutter of wakeful spirits, the charcoal skies of harmattan, the aroma of boiled cassava, the spire of anthills, or the amber color of grasslands in midafternoon—the first thing to disappear or the only thing that lasted? Was it time or the lash of *watapana* rods or the cat-o'-nine-tails that shattered a mother's image or erased her impression? Did men curse the gods of their country for their captivity? Did women appeal to the gods of their country because of their captivity?

Of course, the children born in the Americas had no other world to forget. They might have tired of stories of life across the water, let the past fall away, and set their eyes on a future different from the present. Unlike the love of the *bozales*, the ones born in Africa or the "saltwater" blacks, for the country they had lost, the love of Creole children for an imagined country across the ocean would not have been weighted by experience but borne by loss and fueled by fantasy. Yet for those bound to a hostile land by shackles, owners, and the threat of death, an imagined place might be better than no home at all, an imagined place might afford you a vision of freedom, an imagined place might provide an alternative to your defeat, an imagined place might save your life.

This inchoate, fugitive *elsewhere* was espoused in their dreams, elaborated in their songs, and envisaged as their future; it was expressed in an idiom, which, like themselves, was born of the new country, a blend of African, Native, and European elements. "Possessing nothing," according to Wilson Harris, "but breath and the calamitous air of broken ties in the New World," enslaved Africans sustained, amended, and abandoned the customs, manners, and proclivities of the Old World. They created a new language out of the languages they had known and the languages foisted upon them. They danced the old dances for new purposes. They built dwellings like the ones in which they had lived with new materials. They remembered and renamed old gods and invented and adopted new ones. Cleavage—the separation from and clinging to the Old World—gave rise not only to dispossession but as well to a new set of possibilities.

For the first and second generations born in captivity, the Americas were the only home they knew. Yet this didn't stop them from dreaming of a province free of masters, plantations, whips, and the four degrees of torture. Even if Creoles could not share the ardor of their parents for the country lost, did they fancy it anyway? Or were imagined countries always doomed to be evanescent? Or did the opposite hold true: Were the only countries able to entice us and to grab hold of our hearts the ones that we imagined?

It is only when you are stranded in a hostile country that you need a romance of origins; it is only when you *lose your mother* that she becomes a myth; it is only when you fear the dislocation of the new that the old ways become precious, imperiled, and what your great-great-grandchildren will one day wistfully describe as African.

BY THE TIME SLAVERY was abolished in 1863, in all likelihood my family in Curaçao had turned their back to the Old World. When my grandfather regaled me with tales of Africa, which he had visited several times as a merchant seaman, he never mentioned any ancestral connection or bond between that place and us. The stories he told me of people who elongated their lips with plates, because this was what they found beautiful, or who prayed five times a day, or of lovely women who adorned the length of their necks with beaded rings, which if removed would cause their death, filled me with wonder. But they were tales of a faraway place that had nothing to do with me.

My grandfather never said Africa was our home because he didn't need it to be. As a polyglot and a sailor, he thought of the world as his home. It was hard to mention a spot on the globe for which he didn't have a story. To him, I imagine, one place was as good as the next. Maybe it was that he had no desire to put down roots or to reclaim them. He had embraced errantry or taking to the sea as the closest thing to freedom he would experience.

He was a fugitive, not from justice but from the confines of a four-cornered world. Even in his later years, when Manhattan was as far away from Brooklyn as he'd ever get, he traveled the world each night listening to foreign news broadcast from Europe and Latin America on his short-wave radio. My grandfather had discovered years back that the only home he would ever know was the imagined country, the promised land of the heart, the territory of dreams. He accepted the peril and promise of being without a country. It explained why, as much as he spoke of Africa, he never imagined it as his natal land. The route he charted back and forth across the Atlantic, as a young sea-

man aboard a merchant ship, was an adventure, a detour, not a *return*. Though I can't believe that as he listened to the rumble of the ocean he was unmindful of that other crossing.

STANDING IN the dark recesses of the holding cell for female slaves, I felt both the pull and the impossibility of regaining the country lost. It has never been more clear than it was then: return is what you hold on to after you have been taken from your country, or when you realize that there is no future in the New World, or that death is the only future. Return is the hunger for all the things you once enjoyed or the yearning for all the things you never enjoyed. It bears the impress of everything that has been taken from you. It is the last resort of the defeated. It is the diversion of suicides and dreamers. It is the elsewhere of insurrectionists. It is the yearning of those who can "summon filial love for persons and places they have never known." Like the myth of the mother, the promise of return is all that remains in the wake of slavery. If you close your eyes, you can imagine yourself once again safe in her arms. With a rifle pointed at your chest, you can travel home.

Every generation confronts the task of choosing its past. Inheritances are chosen as much as they are passed on. The past depends less on "what happened then" than on the desires and discontents of the present. Strivings and failures shape the stories we tell. What we recall has as much to do with the terrible things we hope to avoid as with the good life for which we yearn. But when does one decide to stop looking to the past and instead conceive of a new order? When is it time to dream of another country or to embrace other strangers as allies or to make an opening, an overture, where there is none? When is it clear that the old life is over, a new one has begun, and there is no looking back? From the holding cell, was it possible to see beyond the end of the world and to imagine living and breathing again?

The rebels, the come, go back, child, and I are all returnees, circling back to times past, revisiting the routes that might have led to alternative presents, salvaging the dreams unrealized and defeated, crossing over to parallel lives. The hope is that *return* could resolve the old dilemmas, make a victory out of defeat, and engender a new order. And the disappointment is that there is no going back to a former condition. Loss remakes you. Return is as much about the world to which you no longer belong as it is about the one in which you have yet to make a home.

I shall return to my native land. Those disbelieving in the promise and refusing to make the pledge have no choice but to avow the loss that inaugurates one's existence. It is to be bound to other promises. It is to lose your mother, always.

FIVE

The Tribe of the Middle Passage

The rich ones have come too late. A glance at the luxurious homes towering on the seacoast, which were dwarfed only by Elmina Castle, provided all the proof needed. The stately white residences of the descendants of slaves fueled envy as well as the suspicion that slavery might not have been so bad given the wealth African Americans clearly possessed. Everyone in town agreed they had come too late to change anything and relished seeing the longings of the affluent defeated. Some wondered if the *buronya* had come to Ghana earlier, what might have been possible. Others mocked them, saying the nouveaux riches paraded every stitch of their wealth because they were desperate to show they were big men.

The *ones who had come too late* couldn't rid themselves of the label, so they accepted it grudgingly. Kohain and the others didn't flaunt their wealth, nor were they rich, but the disparity between the way they lived and the way most of the residents of Elmina lived was impossible to miss. The thatch and mud dwellings of the surrounding villages and the shanties, one-room cinder-block houses, and dilapidated colonial buildings of town made the spacious homes occupying the coast appear like mansions.

But the villas, cottages, and bungalows had little to do with wealth.

Debt was what they represented—a history of things owed, stolen, and destroyed. The elegant dwellings lined up along the seacoast reminded me of the mansions built in Liberia by ex-slaves from North and South Carolina and Mississippi, which replicated the world from which they had migrated, except now they were the new masters.

The homes of the rich ones were also the bittersweet reminder of the freedom they would never enjoy in America. The homes announced to the rest of Elmina that the rich ones had disembarked and that they were black *white men*. Every brick and pillar testified to the impossibility of returning and to the imprudence of believing in origins and trying to recover them. Built in the shadow of the castle, as if issuing a provocation—we will now thrive where we once were branded and sold—the homesteads were the product of the struggle still being waged between creditor and debtor races, predators and prey, merchants and slaves. What else could be the point of staking a future in the shadow of a slave fort? It was plain to see: prosperity was the face of dispossession.

The tribe of the Middle Passage was how Kohain and his neighbors, Imakhus and Nana Robinson, identified themselves. As Imakhus often re-

peated, "We are the descendants of Middle Passage survivors." It was the tribe created by the rapacity of African elites, the territorial expansion of strong states, and the greed, cruelty, and arrogance of white men possessing the world. It was the tribe of those stolen from their natal land, stripped of their "country marks," and severed from their kin.

Slavery made your mother into a myth, banished your father's name, and exiled your siblings to the far corners of the earth. The slave was as an orphan, according to Frederick Douglass, even when he knew his kin. "We were brothers and sisters, but what of that? Why should they be attached to me, or I to them? Brothers and sisters we were by blood; but *slavery* had made us strangers. I heard the words brother and sisters, and knew they must mean something; but slavery had robbed these terms of their true meaning." The only sure inheritance passed from one generation to the next was this loss, and it defined the tribe. A philosopher had once described it as an identity produced by negation.

The Middle Passage was the birth canal that spawned the tribe. The Middle Passage was the death canal in which "the African died to what was and to what could have been." Revisiting "what could have been" ex-

plained the presence of this tiny community of African Americans sand-
wiched between two slave forts. Had they come earlier, who knows what
they might have done.

The tribe of the Middle Passage had returned to Africa, but they possessed no kin, clan, or a village home, all of the essential elements that
defined belonging in the eyes of Ghanaians. The arrival of African Americans in Elmina could hardly be called a homecoming. Rather it was a
continuation of a long local tradition of renting land to foreigners, which
had started as early as the fifteenth century when the Portuguese first arrived. No one envisioned Kohain, a black rabbi and activist from Mount
Vernon, New York, or Nana Robinson, a retired fireman, and his wife,
Imahkus, from the Bronx, as errant children who had returned or as chickens come home to roost. No one rejoiced that they were back. They had
been allowed to lease the beachfront property for ninety-nine years, since
no foreigner could own land in Ghana. African Americans were tenants
rather than sons and daughters. No one knew this better than the returnees.

One Africa Productions, which Kohain had founded along with Nana
and Imakhus, organized The Door of No Return Ceremony, a reenact-
ment of the slave trade intended to mend the psychic wounds of the descendants of slaves. At present they were embroiled in a trademark
dispute with a Ghanaian tour operator about who owned the ritual. One
Africa Productions also assisted African Americans who wanted to settle
in Ghana and lobbied for a measure to grant them dual citizenship.
Ghanaians opposed the measure, fearing that waves of African American
riffraff would flood the country and dominate with their U.S. dollars.

It was ironic that the kind of African Americans who would fit best in
Ghana were the ones least attracted to Africa. The straightened-hair,
prim, Bible thumping, flag-waving black Christian conservatives would
be much more at home in Ghana than the frayed band of dreadlocked and
nappy-headed radicals who inundated the place. Evangelicals were welcome; protesters need not apply. Most Ghanaians were Christian, re-
spectful of hierarchy and authority to a fault, straitlaced, and wary of
foreigners in need of love. The country that most of us had come running
from was the one of which they dreamed. They would have traded places
with us in the blink of an eye.

◇ ◇ ◇

I PREFERRED Kohain's house to the hotels in town. Renting a room from him was cheaper than lodging at Oyster Bay or Coconut Grove Hotel. Besides, after a day of wandering around in a slave fort, the last thing I wanted to do was explain myself to an inquisitive desk clerk or own up to the fact that I could not. The sprawling six-bedroom home, which was nestled along the ten-mile stretch of coast between Elmina and Cape Coast castles, provided a reprieve from curious glances and unanswerable questions. All the rooms in the villa had private baths, running water as circumstances permitted, electricity when there wasn't a power cut, and clean sheets and towels always.

Kohain was a pensive man with a broad, handsome smile and *payess*, which he tucked behind his ears. I liked him because he never pontificated about the problems with Africa, which distinguished him from the majority of expatriates. Exhaustion had driven him to Ghana. Thirty years of participating in the struggle for black equality in the United States with seemingly little to show for it had worn him out, so he decided to jump ship. "It doesn't really matter where you live," he said. "Everywhere in the world African people are in struggle. This place is as good as any other."

From the back porch of his house, I could see Elmina Castle jutting into the ocean. I had always intended but never asked him or the Robinsons why they had chosen to build their homes within clear sight of the slave fort. Did the sight of the castle make them rejoice because they had been able to find their way back? Or was their proximity evidence of the fact that this was as near to home as they could get?

A passage from Ayi Kwei Armah's *Two Thousand Seasons* described the folly of ex-slaves, who, blinded by filial duty, tried to return home. Although their villages had been destroyed by the slave trade, they continued to long for the world in which they once had lived. "The sickness of nostalgia," writes Armah, fixed the gaze of the wistful solely on the past. They were like children "hankering after situations forever lost" and "craving the love of blood relatives" who were better in memory "than they could have ever been in their own flesh."

Did *the rich ones* suffer from the sickness of nostalgia? Did I? Was longing or melancholy what defined the tribe of the Middle Passage? I had never thought of my life as being driven by filial duty. I had been a bad daughter, not a good one. My offenses were many: I became an atheist in the eighth grade and never failed to remind Father Cavanaugh of this during confession. I joined the Young Socialist Party at fourteen, primarily because my best friend at the time was high school organizer. I hung out with privileged, disaffected white kids. My mother feared they would lead me astray, and they did. I refused to accept a college scholarship for minority students partly funded by J. P. Stevens. At the time, I was participating in a national boycott campaign because of the company's treatment of its textile workers. I called my mother a handkerchief-head Negro when she tried to force me to attend the scholarship dinner, and she, in retaliation, called me an Oreo. I refused to wear my cap and gown for my high school and college graduations. There had been pressing political reasons for not doing so and the dissenter's armband was red for both occasions. I changed my name and shamed my parents. I lived with a college boyfriend in Lincoln Houses, a Harlem project in which he had been raised. I don't know which my mother was more embarrassed by, the fact that I was cohabiting out of wedlock or that I was living in public housing. Not much besides self-identification divided the lower middle class from the working poor, so my perilous spiral down the class ladder terrified my parents. I went to graduate school to study literature and not to medical school as my mother had hoped. My mother had wanted to become a doctor, following in the footsteps of her uncle, grandaunt, and great-grandmother. I replicated her failure.

I had spent most of my adulthood bucking parental designs, so it was hard to believe that I was now on the path of sacrificial daughters and dutiful sons. Yet I found myself, like the other members of *the tribe*, expecting to discover my legacy in a pile of stones that had been carted across the Atlantic in the fifteenth century. Looking at the castle from Kohain's back porch, I wondered what besides dispossession had been transmitted from one generation to the next? In his *Address to the Slaves of the United States of America*, Henry Highland Garnet had warned that not even death brought an end to the wretchedness of slavery, because the children of the enslaved assumed the condition of their predecessors. Was this as true now as it had been in 1843? Could a negative inheritance be passed from one century to the next, as if, as George Jackson wrote, "time had faded nothing"?

I knew I wasn't in Ghana solely to reckon with slavery; if so, I could have traveled just as easily to Portugal or the Vatican, the localities that had inaugurated the Atlantic slave trade. The unrealized dreams of Nkrumah and King and the unfinished struggle of commoners, slaves, fugitives, and socialists had as much to do with it. I shared Mary Ellen's pessimism about the future, but I wanted to be proved wrong. I wanted to imagine a present not tethered to a long history of defeat, but this was difficult to do with Elmina Castle dominating the shoreline. It entailed a great effort to remind myself that the destruction of the holding cell hadn't been absolute and that I was part of what had lived on. Ghana was as good a place as any other to think about the afterlife of slavery and the future of the ex-slave. Secretly I hoped that it wasn't too late to believe in freedom dreams.

WITH MY EYES SHUT, the ocean sounded louder and even more threatening. It hushed the voices of Kohain and his wife, Chessy, talking at the dining room table and isolated the veranda from the rest of the house as though it were a separate world of its own. The roar and clap of the Atlantic reverberated in my head. I was determined to listen until I couldn't bear it any longer.

The back door screeched across the porch floor and I opened my eyes. A handsome twenty-something-year-old man joined me on the porch. He took the seat next to me.

"It's so beautiful, isn't it?" he said.

"The castle?" I asked.

"No. The ocean."

"Yes. Somehow the Atlantic seems larger here than on the other side."

"Maybe it's just that it feels more tragic," he replied.

"At night it's so loud I can hardly sleep," I said, instantly regretting it. It seemed suggestive.

"Here you can't forget," he said.

I wished that were true, but I didn't contradict him.

Khalid was an aspiring filmmaker from Atlanta. It was his first visit to Ghana. He explained that he had come to Elmina because he felt an ancestral call. "All the folks taken across the waters are returning home through me," he said with absolute earnestness.

"Really," I murmured.

"It's like when I visit my grandmother's grave," he continued. "It feels like the entire family is out there with me. My father, my cousins, I mean everyone."

"I have never felt so alone in my life," I told him, revealing more than I had intended.

He was surprised. "Why?"

"I'm not sure if I can explain it." I heard my voice wavering like it does when I'm about to cry.

"It's okay," he said.

"I'm sorry."

"No reason to be."

"It feels like the crash to me, not the grave," I went on in an unsteady voice. "It's the place where the car hit the tree and your mother and brother died. And your father survived but he becomes an alcoholic, so it's like he's dead too or worse. But it's just a regular street for everyone else." I bit my lower lip but the tears streamed down my face, anyway. Khalid didn't say anything, which I appreciated. The silence allowed me to pull myself together. I laughed nervously and apologized again.

He squeezed my hand. "Sis. It's all right. Don't forget we're survivors."

I wondered if a gesture of tenderness defined a tribe. Or if it was a fantasy of who you once were or who you never were. Was a tribe as fleeting and as treacherous as a promise of love? How was it that a stranger uttered "sis" in exactly the same tone as your brother or that one syllable could make you realize how very far away from home you had come? "I'm okay," I said, too quickly to be convincing.

"How long have you been here?" he asked.

"Five months."

"Tell me what you like about Ghana."

"That's hard. There are lots of things," I replied.

"Just tell me the first thing that comes to mind."

"Okay. I like to watch the boys in my neighborhood play soccer. Some of them own sneakers and some don't. So the boys who have sneakers lend a shoe to the ones who don't. During the game, there are all these boys racing down the field with one sneaker and hoping that foot is going to be the lucky one."

"In Atlanta, kids are killing one another over shoes," he said. We both fell silent.

"They're poor here but less defeated," I said. "Maybe I'm just being romantic." Ghana wasn't Liberia or Sierra Leone or Congo. All reasons for hope hadn't disappeared.

"They didn't lose everything. We did," he responded.

"And all for so little," I said. "The worse thing is that it doesn't hurt any less now. It should, but it doesn't."

"Have you ever thought about staying for the long term?" he asked.

"In Ghana? No, I'm nonreturnable goods," I answered. "What about you?"

"No. I mean it's great here. I totally respect Kohain and the rest of them, but to me it would be like trying to live in a cemetery. I like visiting my grandmother, but I don't plan on taking up residence there."

We laughed and listened to the ocean long after our words had faded away.

SIX

So Many Dungeons

EVERY TALE OF creation I had ever read began in a place like this—in the underworld, in the bowels of the earth, in the gloom of man's prehistory. The cradle of life bore an uncanny resemblance to the grave, making plain the fact that the living eventually would assume their station among the ranks of the dead. Human life sprang from a black abyss, and from dust and muck we traced our beginning. Base elements were the substrate of life. Blood and shit ushered us into the world. Gods vomited human beings into existence or populated the world by raping the earth or coupling with their daughters, or, in their benignity, led us from the darkness into the light.

Adam and Eve were created in this filthy pit. So the British called the first man and woman plucked from the dungeon and bound aboard the slave ship, replaying the drama of birth and expulsion in the Africa trade.

THE SLAVE HOLD WAS BURROWED deep in the earth. Unlike the Portuguese who originally built Elmina Castle to store nonhuman goods, the British designed Cape Coast Castle to warehouse slaves. In the sixteenth century, the British had begun raiding the Gold Coast for slaves and by the end of the seventeenth century they were the foremost slavers in Africa. They alone were responsible for deporting nearly five hundred thousand slaves from the Gold Coast. Half of these captives were shipped from Cape Coast Castle, which provided the headquarters of the Royal Africa Company and its successor, the company of Merchants Trading to Africa. When the company built the fort in 1674, transforming a mud fortification into the largest castle on the coast next to Elmina Castle, which stood only ten miles to the west, they designed the slave pens to deter rebellion and for this reason placed the vaults beneath the earth. "The castle looks very fine from the sea," wrote the French trader Jean Barbot in 1681, but "the most noteworthy item is the slave-house, which lies below ground. It consists of large vaulted cellars, divided into several apartments, which can easily hold a thousand slaves . . . The keeping of the slaves thus under ground is a good security to the garrison."

The lesson imparted to the captives by this grand design was that slavery was a state of death. Who else but the dead resided in a tomb? But the Royal Africa Company and the Company of Merchants didn't imagine their human cargo as a pile of corpses, nor did they consider these dank rooms a grave. As they saw it, the dungeon was a womb in which the slave was born. The harvest of raw material and the manufacture of goods defined the prison's function. The British didn't call it a womb; they called it a factory, which has its first usage in the trading forts of West Africa. (The very word "factory" documents the indissoluble link between England's industrial revolution and the birth of human commodities.)

In the company's view, the dungeon was a way station for human refuse and a cocoon for laborers. The miracle of the slave trade was that it resuscitated useless lives and transformed waste into capital. Africa benefited from this commerce, avowed the merchants, because "her wants were satisfied at a very trifling expense" and paid for with "the refuse and offscourings of her population." What Aimé Césaire later described as "walking compost hideously promising tender cane and silky cotton."

◇ ◇ ◇

THE INTERIOR OF THE DUNGEON exposed an open wound of earth, and the roughly hewn walls perspired, making the chamber dank. The cells were hollowed out of the rocky deposit of a hillside, which had been a sacred shrine devoted to the local pantheon of gods. Nana Taabiri watched over all the creatures on earth and in the sea. When the fort was built, the shrine was displaced and the gods exiled. Two decades ago, the shrine returned to the castle and the gods to the rocks they had once inhabited. The shrine now occupied a wall at the far end of the dungeon. The candles placed on the altar gave off a faint light that was swallowed by the blackness of the hold. Whether the gods were indifferent or attentive to the captives imprisoned in the garrison was of little consequence as far as I could tell. The old man who attended the shrine disagreed with me. He insisted that the gods tended to the slaves and guided them from the places across the water back home. Life is more than matter, he said, there is spirit too. When he convinced African Americans and others from the diaspora of this (the priest did not offer these services to Ghanaian visitors, most of whom, being Christians, eschewed traditional religion and associated it with evil), he received a small donation and then poured libations for the dead.

The arched ceiling of the vault and the tubular shape of the connecting cells resembled a large intestine. Walking from one end of the dungeon to the other, I did feel as though the castle were ingesting me, as though I were inching my way along the entrails of power. The belly of the beast no longer seemed a figure of speech but rather a precise description of this place. What was it about eating that so aptly captured the dynamics of power? The gluttony of the ruling classes was proverbial. As they said in Ghana, *Only the big man has a full belly*. The rich are sated, but the commoner wants. *Seeing is not eating*. The poor man lives in the world but does not own it. *When the slave eats mutton, it irritates his stomach*. The fine things in life are reserved for the powerful. *If one refuses to eat, another's stomach will be filled*. One man takes advantage of another's misfortunes. Ingestion provides a vivid picture of the relation between the haves and the have-nots, the rulers and the ruled, the parasite and the host.

"Everything which is eaten is the food of power," according to Elias Canetti. None knew this better than the slaves. They consistently described their captors as cannibals. Flesh eaters and roasters of men personified the dynamics of plunder and dispossession, unlike the euphemism of *trade*, which made the rout appear bloodless and consensual. None of the enslaved had ever agreed to any bargain that landed them here. Anthropophagy, the practice of eating the flesh of other human beings, aptly described the devouring of life by the machinery of the slave trade.

The mouth was an organ of power. African nations at war vowed to "eat the other," that is, they would seize all their enemies, "sell them as slaves, and enjoy themselves with the goods received in exchange." But white men were the cannibals most feared. Stories of blood orgies and men cooked in boiling cauldrons circulated from the coast to the interior. Upon seeing the slave ship and its European crew, Olaudah Equiano believed he had entered a world of bad spirits: "I no longer doubted of my fate, and, quite overpowered with horror and anguish, I fell motionless on the deck and fainted. When I recovered a little, I found some black people about me . . . I asked them if we were not to be eaten by those white men with horrible looks, red faces, and long hair?" The first time Ottobah Cugoano encountered the white men of the coast, he too was convinced they intended to devour him. "I saw several white people, which made me very afraid they would eat me." Back in the city of Agimaque, he had listened to tales about the *bounsam*, the devil, who resided near the sea and feasted on human flesh.

Slaves were "often under great apprehension at the sight of the sea," according to the slave captain John Newton, because "they imagine they are brought to be eat [*sic*]." An officer in the Africa Corps, testifying before the English Board of Trade, described the great anxiety of the captives upon being delivered to the European traders of the coast. "The [African] masters or Europeans hold out as a general doctrine to their slaves, that Europeans will kill and eat them . . . by which means the slaves are kept in order, and in great fear of being sold to Europeans. This doctrine . . . has a very political effect on the minds of these people."

The fear of white ogres incited mutiny and self-destruction. On the slaving voyage of the *Albion Frigate*, the captain recorded in his journal: "some slaves fancy they are being carried away to be eaten, which makes them desperate, and others are so on account of their captivity, so that if care not be taken, they will mutiny and destroy the ship's crew in hopes to get away." Sengbe Pieh, the leader of the slave revolt aboard the *Amistad*, said he and forty-eight other slaves rebelled after being told by a slave of the ship's captain that they were going to be dismembered and eaten. On other occasions, slaves jumped overboard to escape this gruesome fate or asphyxiated themselves by swallowing their tongues.

A terrible end awaited them, of that they were certain. Paul Isert, a surgeon stationed at a Danish slave fort neighboring Cape Coast, remarked that the slaves don't believe the future could possibly "hold anything good in store for them, when the Europeans use such violent measures to secure them." Reports of the savagery of white men had spread to the most remote corners of the hinterland: "In their own country they have themselves heard such dreadful tales of how the slaves are treated in Columbia [America] that one is appalled when one hears them. I was once asked by a slave, in complete earnest, if the shoes I was wearing had been made of Black skin, since he had observed that they were the same colour as his skin."

Cannibalism provided an allegory for usurping and consuming life. If the wage laborer, according to Marx, was "someone who has brought his own hide to market and now has nothing to expect but a tanning," then the slave was the prey hunted and the flesh eaten by the vampire of merchant capital. The slaves did not doubt it.

IF INGESTION EXEMPLIFIED the merchant's accumulation of capital and the slave's dispossession, then waste was the proof that the powerful had eaten. Excrement was the material residue of this politics of the belly. As Canetti writes of the voracious and bestial character of power:

> Anyone who wants to rule men first tries to humiliate them, to trick them out of their rights and their capacity for resistance, until they are as powerless before him as animals . . . [The] ultimate aim is to incorporate them into himself and to suck the substance out of them. What remains of them afterwards does not matter to him. The worse he has treated them, the more he despises them. When they are no more use at all, he disposes of

them as he does of his excrement . . . The excrement, which is what remains of all this, is loaded with our whole blood guilt. By it we know what we have murdered. It is the compressed sum of all the evidence against us.

Human waste covered the floor of the dungeon. To the naked eye it looked like soot. After the last group of captives had been deported, the holding cells were closed but never cleaned out. For a century and a half after the abolition of the slave trade, the waste remained. To control the stench and the pestilence, the floor had been covered with sand and lime. In 1972, a team of archaeologists excavated the dungeon and cleared away eighteen inches of dirt and waste. They identified the topmost layer of the floor as the compressed remains of captives—feces, blood, and exfoliated skin.

I refused this knowledge. I blocked it out and proceeded across the dungeon as if the floor was just that and not the remnants of slaves pressed further into oblivion by the soles of my shoes. I came to this fort searching for ancestors, but in truth only base matter awaited me.

Waste is the interface of life and death. It incarnates all that has been rendered invisible, peripheral, or expendable to history writ large, that is, history as the tale of great men, empire, and nation. It "evokes the dull ordinary horror of what is vile, worthless and contemptible—a pile of shit." Waste is the remnant of all the lives that are outside of history and "dissolved in utter amnesia."

The only part of my past that I could put my hands on was the filth from which I recoiled, layers of organic material pressed hard against a stone floor.

I HAD ENTERED the dungeon intending to do all the fine things stated in the marble plaque posted at the entrance: commemorate the dead, remember the anguish of the ancestors, and prevent such crimes against humanity from ever happening again. They were the kind of words one encountered at sites of atrocity throughout the world, and, in all likelihood, men would continue to produce the occasions for such words. They were confident words, which promised justice and espoused faith in humanity and quarantined the past with a flurry of boasts. But five minutes in the underground dashed these grand aspirations. The stark facts won out—it was a hold for human cargo, and knowing what happened here couldn't remedy oblivion or betoken a brighter future or lessen the suffering of the dead.

Like most people willing to cross the threshold of a slave dungeon, I wanted to give the dead their due. But I was unsure how to accomplish this. The crush of empty space defeated any surety in the power of memory to deter future crimes. Words like "oblivion" and "catastrophe" crossed my mind. In the dungeon, there were remains but no stories that could resurrect the dead except the stories I invented.

Upstairs in the museum, a glass display case contained the items for which the slaves had been exchanged: checkered cotton cloth, brass and iron bracelets, china, glass beads, red stones, umbrellas, guns, whiskey, mirrors, and chamber pots. There you were educated about the benefits of the trade—new agricultural crops and animals, literacy, and Christianity—as well as the drawbacks of the slave trade—the suffering of millions of enslaved people. You learned that despite the terrible ordeal, the descendants of the slaves triumphed in the end. Large portraits of Bob Marley, Muhammad Ali, Martin Luther King, Jr., James Baldwin, and Angela Davis concluded the story on an upbeat note. But how do you weigh literacy and Jesus and luxury goods against four centuries of rout and the millions gone?

Even in the museum, the slaves were missing. None of their belongings were arranged nicely in well-lit glass cases. None of the waste found in the dungeon was placed neatly on trays with small flags. None of their sayings were quoted on placards throughout the hall. Nor was their family life and social organization described. How they farmed or fished or appealed to their gods or buried their dead goes unmentioned. The museum was as bereft as the underground.

I CLOSED MY EYES and strained to hear the groans and cries that once echoed in the dungeon, but the space was mute. Muffled sounds from other parts of the castle didn't find their way here. I didn't hear a peep, not even the bland reggae covers of Negro spirituals played in the café adjoining the castle, which was owned by a white guy from the United States. Years ago, there had been a café inside the fort. Strains of Ghanaian highlife and R & B blasting from the café drifted into the underground. But visitors complained it was inappropriate to drink beer and hum along with Harold Melvin and the Blue Notes or Marvin Gaye in a slave prison, so the café was shut down.

The first time I entered the underground I was accompanied by a chirpy teenager named Phyllis. I had been waiting for a tro-tro on a road a few miles outside of town when she attached herself to me and decided to become my guide for the day and accompany me to the castle. Had I arrived a few years later, no doubt she would have taken me to Assin Manso to see the Slave River and the graves, but these places were not yet packaged for tourism. Phyllis was a student at the Wesley Girls' School, an elite private school in Cape Coast attended by the best students in Ghana. She chattered nonstop about her plans to study fashion design in the States. She did have an eye for style and sported a retro-mod look. Her shimmering pink lipstick, headband, and cascading hairpiece made her look like one of the Supremes. As we moved through the rooms of the fort, she told me that she loved American movies and ran through the list of the films she had seen most recently. Phyllis was delighted to hear that I lived in California and asked me if I'd ever been to Hollywood. When I said no, I could sense her disappointment in me. Her favorite film was *Waiting to Exhale* because the women were beautiful, independent, and had lots of money. She said I reminded her of those women. I knew she intended it as a compliment so I tried to take it as one. When I asked her if she had been in the castle before, she replied she had. She had visited the castle on a class trip and again on her own. Well, what do you think about what happened here? I asked. "It's a sad story what happened to the slaves," she replied. "We should go to the canteen for lunch."

My first visit had been deflating. With Phyllis trailing at my side, I was certain I had missed something vital. I racked my brain to figure out exactly why the experience had been disappointing. I had entered with the wrong attitude and sailed through the chambers carelessly rather than with the necessary sobriety. I hadn't prepared myself for the encounter. I hadn't been properly attentive. The last thing I expected, of course, was to be talking about Terry McMillan, *Titanic*, and a teenager's favorite stars as I crossed the threshold. I didn't believe this slave fort was sacred ground because terrible things had transpired here. Brutality doesn't make a place worthy of veneration. But I did believe that the gravity of what had happened required a degree of solemnity. I blamed Phyllis for what didn't happen. Only later did I realize there was nothing to see. I hadn't missed a thing.

Since then, I had come to the dungeon more then a dozen times. I had been with tour groups and I had wandered through alone. It had always felt as painfully incomplete as it did on my first visit. That is, when it was not absurd. Once an intoxicated docent led my friends and me through the castle, all the while complaining bitterly about Americans, ignoring our questions and bawling that he was an educated man who deserved better than this. On another occasion, I got into a squabble with a visitor from Sierra Leone when she remarked to her friend, "Why make such a big deal over one slave dungeon. There are so many dungeons in Africa."

Alone, I was the absurd figure. By myself, there was no one else to blame for my discomfort. There was no running away from it. I had come too late for it to make any difference at all, but I kept coming back. I was waiting. For whom or what I couldn't say or perhaps I was just embarrassed to admit. I couldn't explain it because it didn't make sense. I knew only how it felt, which was akin to choking. My chest grew congested and my palms started sweating and I got light-headed. My skin became tight and prickly, as if there was too little of it and too much of everything else. The hollow inside my chest expanded. I could feel my torso bulge and distend like a corpse swelling with gasses. And the emptiness was a huge balloon expanding inside me and pressing against my organs, until I could no longer breathe and was about to explode. Five minutes back in the sunlight and I was breathing easily again. No one could discern it was just the husk and not really me.

Each time it was the same. I failed to discover anything. No revenants lurked in the dungeon. The hold was stark. No hand embraced mine. No voices rang in my ears. Not one living creature dwelled here. Not even a fly darted about. In the silence, my own breath was loud and raucous.

I trudged from one side of the dungeon to the other; each step I took was tottering and indecisive. I moved back and forth with the slumped shoulders of defeat. I traced the perimeter of the cell disappointed. I stepped over the gutters traversing the floor. My hands glided over the walls, as though the rough surfaces were a script that I could read through my dull fingers. But the brush of my hands against stone offered no hint or clue. What I wanted was to feel something other than bricks and lime. What I wanted was to reach through time and touch the prisoners.

NOTHING HAD ENDURED except blood, shit, and dirt. So it was hard to imagine a thousand or more men and boys imprisoned in the male dungeon or to grasp that of this company at least 150 were likely to die here. Among the dead might be ten men offered as tribute to a suzerain, two brothers stolen from a garden, four young men captured while playing within arm's reach of home, five debtors, forty whose village was razed, three adulterers, twenty-five defeated soldiers not sacrificed by the enemy, two teenagers entrapped by neighbors, thirty farmers seized by mercenaries, a nephew pawned by an uncle but never redeemed, a father and son accused of witchcraft, a thief who had stolen a pig, a debt-ridden weaver, three gamblers, and a castle slave deemed incorrigible.

Most had arrived at the castle in small lots conveyed by African brokers and less often by private individuals. Northerners comprised the majority of slaves crammed into the dungeon and shipped from the castle to the Americas. The coffles traveled hundreds of miles before arriving on the coast, and the bodies of the enslaved charted the arduous journey. Traders easily identified them by their bloated stomachs, contusions, and ulcers. Bruises covered their arms and legs, which had been cut and pricked on branches and thorns in narrow forest paths that admitted only one person at a time. Sunken cheeks and distended bellies were the clear signs of scant food and little water. Necks, wrists, and ankles were abraded by the fetters that connected one *donker* to the other, although women and children usually were not chained. Slaves disappeared along the route to the coast; the lucky few escaped, some were sold at interior markets, others died along the way.

Once inside the gates of the fort, the women and men were separated and marched to their respective prisons. Upon being delivered to the dungeon, irons were attached to their feet and necks, replacing the shackles and ropes and heavy logs used by African traders. The double irons used to secure them were so burdensome that even the company officials described them as "too painful" to be endured. Depending on the arrival and departure of ships, captives were confined in this chamber for a few weeks or as long as three or four months. The number of prisoners fluctuated with the trade. Sometimes the rooms were packed with as many as fifteen hundred men and boys, and when trade lagged, a hundred or fewer occupied the dungeon. Each slave was confined to his own place and prevented from moving about in the dungeon.

The slaves slept on bare floors. They ingested and eliminated in the same quarters. Excrement and food debris accumulated on the floor and soiled their limbs. Even when the captives were washed in the sea twice a day, the stench of the dungeon was unbearable. The feculent condition of the hold made dysentery commonplace; it was the leading cause of death in confinement. The disease attacked the stomach and bowels, leading to pains in the abdomen, infected intestines, inflamed mucous membranes, and ulcerated tissues. Overcrowding, poor sanitary conditions, and ingestion of food or water contaminated by feces facilitated the spread of the disease. Traders and surgeons called it the bloody flux because of the profuse discharge of blood, mucus, and pus that were its symptoms. The pools of fluid on the brick floor would have glistened when light trickled through the small openings in the roof.

THE DUNGEON PROVED no less fatal than the Middle Passage. The corpses dragged from the dungeon each week alarmed the surgeon stationed at the castle. To reduce the rate of death the surgeon recommended constructing a platform eighteen inches high in the dungeon for the slaves to rest on during the night, lining the bottoms and sides of the dungeon with boards half an inch thick to protect the slaves from the damp walls, reducing the stench by smoking and cleaning the quarters with citrus and green herbs, and placing sanitary or necessary tubs in the dungeon so that the captives might "ease themselves at night," rather than steep in their waste. None of these recommendations were ever implemented.

A century would pass before an improved prison was built. In 1768, "an enormous vaulted slave prison of seven bays" was built beneath a huge new battery intended to increase the fort's security by adding space for thirteen cannons. These additional cells beneath the battery were considered "more wholesome" than the underground prison because of the large openings in the ceilings. The portholes were designed to permit supervision by guards, but they also enabled greater circulation of air. Indifferent to the spirit of reform, slaves continued to die. And a pile of corpses was not the kind of refuse that was of any use to the Company of Merchants Trading to Africa. A corpse was unresponsive to the logic of conversion that transformed dead men into commodities.

NO ONE IMPRISONED in the dungeon of Cape Coast Castle had ever described it. There was no record left behind by the captives who entered and exited the underground. Not a single account. All the journals, reports, letters, and trade documents belonged to merchants and company men. The rare instances of slave testimony described neighboring forts or slave holds elsewhere on the West African coast, but these recollections didn't amount to more than a few lines, none of which provided the merest hint of their experience in the holding cell. Was the scene too horrible to describe or too painful or both? Or was forgetting the price exacted by survival? All that Venture Smith was willing to say was, "All of us were then put into the castle and kept for market. On a certain time, I and other prisoners were put on board a canoe." Perhaps he no longer remembered the six-and-a-half-year-old boy who had been confined inside the cell with its rocky floor and towering dark walls, or he preferred not to conjure up an image of what he had spent his adult life trying to erase.

The nine lines written by Ottobah Cugoano in his 1787 antislavery tract, *Thoughts and Sentiments on the Evil of Slavery*, provided the most detailed account of the slave hold. (Cugoano, in all likelihood, had been imprisoned at Anomabu or Cormantin, which were the neighboring trade posts of the British. He had forgotten the name of the fort.) But even he

conceded it was impossible to convey the horror of the prison or to describe "the miserable situation of the poor exiled Africans." In 1787, he
said it was already too late for such testimony to change hearts and minds;
the world had become habituated to black suffering. According to Cugoano, it was "needless to give a description of all the horrible scenes
which we saw, and the base treatment which we met in this dreadful captive situation, as the similar cases of thousands, which suffer by this infer-
nal traffic, are well known." Given this, he was reluctant to share the
details of his captivity. What he remembered most vividly about the dungeon were the groans and cries of his fellow inmates.

I had read *Thoughts and Sentiments on the Evil of Slavery* at least a
dozen times, so it was impossible for me not to think of Cugoano as I
roamed through the empty chambers. I tried to picture him here, but I
couldn't. The only image I had ever seen of him was in the etching *Mr and
Mrs Cosway with a Black Slave*. He was the anonymous manservant standing to the left of Mrs. Cosway, with his head bowed, his eyes cast down-
ward, and donning the fashionable black wig of his times. Only the hand

of Mrs. Cosway hanging awkwardly in midair as she blindly grabbed for a handful of grapes acknowledged his presence.

But the image of the dutiful convert and the faithful black retainer was already after the fall. I preferred not to think about him tucked away in the servants' quarters of a stately house in London. I was most interested in the story he had been disinclined to share. I wanted to imagine the boy entering the gates of the fort on the day he lost his name.

HIS NAME WAS Kwabena. But once he was shoved inside the fort it no longer mattered. No one would ever call him by that name again. Trudging across the threshold, the boy asked, "Why am I here?" The keeper replied, "To learn the ways of the *browfow*: the white-faced people." Then he jerked the boy's hand and pulled him into the trade hall. For a gun, a bolt of cloth, and three bars of lead, he was handed over to the soldiers. The boy begged, please don't abandon me, but the man only quickened his pace as he headed out the gate. Please, don't leave me with the *browfow*. The white-faced men twisted his arms and trussed his limbs like he was a shoat and they intended to flay and roast him.

He didn't cry and he didn't shout until he saw the men in the courtyard chained two and two with their hands bound behind their backs. He cried because he had never seen terrible things like this before and he shouted because he was happy to see his countrymen.

Inside the cell, it was so dark he could barely discern the other bodies chained to the wall. The odor made his insides spill out. The filth from the floor clung to his legs and buttocks and he made an even worse mess of things. After the first day, his eyes adjusted to the gloom and he saw more clearly the men and boys imprisoned in the room. Ashamed, he pretended not to see. The odor of rotting things no longer made his stomach heave. He no longer recoiled when vermin scuttled across his body. He learned to take shallow gulps of the fetid air.

Chained in the holding cell, he never stopped thinking about that afternoon in Assine. It was too late, but he imagined all the ways his captivity might have been avoided. He should have stayed inside his uncle's house. He had said no when his friends asked him to come out and play, but they had teased and tormented him. "He feared the devil would capture him," they taunted. To prove he wasn't afraid of the devil he set out with the band of children. The bad feeling he had he kept inside; he didn't say anything when they stepped into the woods and his heart quickened.

They had gathered white plums, star apples, tamarind, and mangoes and then feasted on the fruit. The juice left sticky white streaks that ran from their palms to their elbows. Before they could trap a lovebird or a fire-crowned bishop, men with pistols and cutlasses surrounded them. The children pleaded, "What have we done wrong?" "You have committed offenses against our lord," one of the men replied, without providing details of their crime. Kwabena and a few of the others tried to run away, but they were caught and threatened with death if they stirred.

The gunmen divided the twenty children into small groups and herded them to the town of the *ohene* (great man). The journey took many hours, and by the time they arrived it was too late to appear before the *lord* and make amends. The next day the *ohene* left town before they could offer their apologies. With the *great man* gone for the day, one of the kidnappers invited the children to a feast a day's journey away.

When they arrived at the town after a full day's trek, multitudes of people filled the square playing drums and horns and flutes, others sang and clapped their hands, a circle of dancers swirled and gyrated as onlookers encouraged them with ululations and praise. The children watched the festivities entranced and afraid. That night they slept in the homes of the very nice singing and dancing townspeople. When Kwabena awoke the next morning, all of his companions had disappeared. The kind man with whom he lodged assured him that his companions had gone to the seaside to fetch provisions and would return in the afternoon. But none of them returned that day or the days that followed.

When Kwabena stopped eating and drinking, his host promised to return him to his mother and father. Days later he set out for Ajumako with a stranger who introduced himself as a friend of his father's. Kwabena was relieved to hear this. They traveled for two days before arriving at the seaside. Is this where my friends are? Kwabena asked. Before his keeper could reply, he saw the white-faced men and then the fort.

Three days locked in the dungeon made him feel as though he had always been missing from his uncle's house. Time was at a standstill. In the underground, there was no measure of the days, just walls of stone and mortar. The sky was barely visible from the small holes cut in the ceiling. So he could not tell when the sun transformed the sky from slate to gold, or if it was the time of the day when the sun washed away his shadow, or when it fell behind his shoulders making him twice as tall, or when the sun slipped below the horizon and colored the millet fields ocher.

Now his only bearings in the world were the groans and cries that echoed through the chamber, the ring and clank of the chains, the smack and hiss of the whip. When the *browfow* began leading the men from the cell to the ship, a number of them clung to the ground already anticipating a worse place and refusing the next leg of the journey. Then the *browfow* with the whip started beating them, but they still would not move, more rushed into the cell whipping and kicking until they dragged the limp bodies from the ground.

The boy hung back. He didn't affix his body to the floor, but he allowed his legs to slacken and his feet to inch along. He didn't know what the future held, but by this point he knew enough to dread what awaited him aboard the slaver. From the holding cell, he didn't see the two years laboring in a slave gang in Grenada, he didn't feel the sting of the lash on his back, he didn't ache from a belly distended with hunger, he didn't know the delight of a piece of stolen sugarcane or if caught that the price of the feast was having your teeth knocked out with a cudgel or your mouth stuffed with excrement. He didn't wish he was dead yet, but he was wise enough to fear the future.

As the men filed out of the dungeon, he rightly suspected there was no way back to his parents' house in Ajumako. But he told himself otherwise. Like every other person who crossed the threshold before him, he promised he would find a way back. But the sight of the ocean made even the stalwart crumble. When Kwabena boarded the slaver he knew why the men had clenched the muck of the floor as though it were the soil of their country.

IF THE GREAT NOISE of the dungeon drifted into the chaplain's residence, Philip Quaque never mentioned it in the fifty-four letters he wrote from his quarters above the holding cells to the Society for the Propagation of the Gospel in Foreign Parts (SPG). If the priest caught sight of the boy Kwabena as he was being shipped from the fort, it was unlikely that Quaque would have ever suspected that their paths would cross again as black writers in the Age of Enlightenment, as representative men of the era of the slave trade. If they encountered one another in the courtyard, it is unlikely that they would have exchanged words, or that the boy, the captive, would have guessed that residing in this fort the priest was as cut off from his past as any slave. How could the boy have known that the priest no longer spoke his mother tongue and that his country too had withered away?

Before I stumbled over his grave in the courtyard of Cape Coast Castle I had never heard of the black priest. Only later did I read his letters in a dusty folio box at the Bodleian Library at Oxford University. Buried alongside Governor Maclean and his wife, an English poet rumored to have been poisoned by the governor's African mistress, and a soldier killed during the war with Asante, Quaque commanded the respect and attention that eluded him during his life. As he lay dying, he asked to be buried in the spur of the castle so that he would be remembered. No doubt he feared being forgotten given his lackluster career and frustrated ambitions and agonized that he too might be unceremoniously buried, another corpse hastily dispatched. For half a century he had watched countless slaves disappear without leaving behind any indication that they had ever existed. Seeing such things might have made him feel vulnerable and caused him to question whether his own life was as ephemeral. By his own admission, he had been a failure. A deathbed plea saved him from oblivion.

Quaque was born in the Gold Coast, the son of a wealthy slave trader. At thirteen, he had been sent to England along with two other boys to be educated for service in the slave trade. The other two boys never returned home. They died in England. Thomas Coboro died from tuberculosis and the other, William Cudjo, Quaque's cousin, descended into madness and died in confinement. After twelve years abroad, Quaque returned to the Gold Coast at twenty-five, the first African priest ordained in the Anglican church. The Company of Merchants paid him to serve as chaplain at Cape Coast Castle and the SPG employed him as a missionary, schoolmaster, and catechist to convert the Akan.

On September 28, 1766, in his fourth letter to the SPG after six months of residing at Cape Coast, he described the "wretched creatures who [were] now languishing under despair in the shadow of death," by which he meant not the slaves but his heathen countrymen who refused "the glorious light of the gospel." The African traders and *caboceers* (headmen) were interested in commerce, not conversion. Quaque had been unable to secure a single convert among them. His inability to speak any language other than English must have appeared ridiculous and pretentious to them. He had come back from what he described as "the blessed country of God," with no words of his own except those of the whites. As Phyllis Wheatley remarked about Quaque, "How like a Barbarian shou'd I look to the natives . . . being an utter stranger to the language."

By his own estimation, he was a shepherd attending to the lost souls of the fort, that is, the European officers and personnel. After a year of indifference, hostility, and insult, he considered himself the lamb and the men he had come to shepherd as wolves. The company personnel had refused to listen to the Gospel delivered from "sooty lips."

From the perch of his quarters, he was able to watch one of the largest migrations, albeit forced, that had yet occurred in history. He observed the coffles of slaves arriving on the coast, "bulked" in the underground by the governor, transported by canoes to the slavers waiting offshore, but he mentioned none of this in his letters. He had viewed it all but decided not to write a word about the slaves imprisoned two floors below him. Why had he refused to be a witness? Was the sight of his "poor abject countrymen . . . in cruel bondage" too awful to describe? Rumors and secondhand reports detailing the violence, which he failed to disclose in his reports to the SPG, circulated in Britain. A paycheck and a chaplaincy made him a servant of the company. Silence was the proof of his loyalty.

Quaque was writing into a void and he knew it. After seven years in residence on the coast, he had not received "so much as a line from [his] worthy benefactors" since he arrived. His missives were self-pitying, obsequious, and percolating with rage. Page after page recited a litany of complaints about the dissolute ways of Europeans on the coast, the poverty of his quarters, not being paid by the company, the vicious rumors spread about him, the silence of the SPG, his lack of prayer books, the governor's refusal to support his work, the lack of robes for service, and the poor example of Christian principles offered by slave traders. As long as there were slaves to be purchased at cheap rates, he commented, the fort personnel would have no more to do with prayers. Most of Quaque's time was spent instructing the mixed-race offspring of company personnel in reading, writing, and the catechism.

The SPG blamed the failure of Quaque's mission on his taste for commodities. "Paying more attention to the purposes of trade than of religion" was, according to them, the primary reason Quaque had never been able to win any converts. The Company of Merchants promoted "private trading" by the officers because it encouraged African brokers to deliver their slaves and commodities even in the absence of ships. Eking out an existence on small wages or, at times, no wages at all might have encouraged Quaque to buy and sell slaves.

Quaque resided in the castle for two decades before he dared mention the slaves in a letter to the SPG. Even then, he focused not on the ones languishing below him but on the captives of a Dutch slaver. This single paragraph in a lifetime of correspondence made him a better man than his counterpart, the black chaplain at Elmina, Jacobus Capitein, who wrote a thesis at the University of Leiden defending the slave trade on the basis of Christian principles. That Capitein had been a slave himself had made no difference.

The nine sentences of Quaque's letter described a "most melancholy and unhappy circumstance" aboard a Dutch slaver. The captives had revolted and overtaken the ship's crew, but the victory was short-lived. "They consisted in number about 150. But the most dreadful circumstance of all is that after having laid their scheme with subtlety and art, and decoying as many of their countrymen who came far and near to plunder on board and near the ship, and also some white sailors of the English in hopes of relieving them, were all indiscriminately blown up to upwards of three to four hundred souls." Quaque blamed the captain's "brutish" behavior for the tragedy. The captain had denied the slaves sufficient provisions of food and water.

If even before the slaves arrived at markets in the Americas they could be treated with such cruelty, Quaque wondered, then what fate awaited them in the West Indies? "Can we help but figuring to ourselves the true picture of the inhumanity those unhappy creatures suffer in their miserable state of bondage, under the different degrees if austere masters they unfortunately fall in with in the West Indies?" When a month later the castle slaves ran away, he wrote, "It is easy to conceive that the evils which they seem to complain of, to bear an affinity to the excess of burden the Children of Israel suffered in the reign of Pharaoh, King of Egypt, under their task masters."

After twenty years spent on the coast whining about the respect he had been denied and the invitations he hadn't received and the important men who had snubbed him, he had finally turned his glance elsewhere, at least for one long paragraph. He had seen the traders and the slaves in a new light. The hierarchy was turned upside down. The traders were now the benighted and the slaves the chosen. The English had disappointed him, so he turned to the slaves. Looking at them, he awaited a confirmation of the workings of Providence, some proof that the venture had been worth it, some assurance that he hadn't risked everything but had nothing to show for it.

I, TOO, WAS a failed witness. Reckoning with my inheritance had driven me to the dungeon, but now it all seemed elusive. I struggled to connect the dots between then and now and to chart the trajectory between the Gold Coast and Curaçao and Montgomery and Brooklyn. But I kept fumbling.

I could rattle off all the arguments about the devastating effects of having been property, denied the protection of citizenship, and stripped of rights of equality. The simple fact was that we still lived in a world in which racism sorts the haves and have-nots and decides who lives and who dies. Racism, according to Michel Foucault, is the social distribution of death; like an actuarial chart, it predicts who would thrive and who would not. Blacks are twice more likely to die than whites at every stage of life and have shorter life spans. In my city, black men have life spans twenty years shorter than white men's, and the infant mortality rate among black women rivals that of a third-world country. Blacks are five times more likely to die of homicide and ten times more likely to be HIV positive. Half of black children grow up in poverty and one-third of all African Americans live in poverty. Nearly half of black men between the ages of eighteen and twenty-five are in jail, on probation, or on parole, and are four times more likely to be sentenced to death than whites; and black women are eight times more likely to be imprisoned than white women.

The distribution of wealth is no less dire. Forty years after the passage of the Civil Rights Act, black households possess one-tenth of the wealth of white families; blacks own seven cents for every dollar owned by whites.

This in part explained why I was in the dungeon. But it was personal too. Hovering in an empty room was my attempt to figure out how this underground had created and marked me. Could I trace my despair back to the first generation stolen from their country? Was it why I sometimes felt as weary of America as if I too had landed in what was now South Carolina in 1526 or in Jamestown in 1619? Was it the tug of all the lost mothers and orphaned children? Or was it that each generation felt anew the yoke of a damaged life and the distress of being a native stranger, an eternal alien?

I was loitering in a slave dungeon less because I hoped to discover what really happened here than because of what lived on from this history. Why else begin an autobiography in a graveyard?

THERE WAS a whole set of proscriptions about what I should and should not do based upon my mother's childhood in Montgomery, Alabama. When she came to New York after graduating from college, her understanding of the color line changed little, if at all. As she saw it, New York was even more dangerous than Alabama because Northerners said one thing but believed another; at least with Southerners you knew where you stood. She taught my brother and me that an array of expected and unforeseen dangers lay in wait for us because we were black. For my brother, things were really dire. The smallest mishap could result in his imminent death. I think Peter was nine when he received his first lecture about white police officers. That our father was a police officer at the time didn't make my brother's prospects any less terrifying, but only made the dangers more vivid. The rule was simple: policemen were to be avoided whenever possible. It was the exact opposite of the lesson white children were taught.

But it was I, not my brother, who stepped out of line and flouted all of my mother's rules. She was on her way to pick me up from the dentist's office late on a freezing February afternoon when her car skidded across an ice patch and she ran a red light. She didn't see the police officer but he saw her. He followed her the block to the dentist's office where I was waiting. My mother retrieved me from the office, and when we returned to the parking lot the officer was waiting for us. He said she ran the light at the corner and told her to hand over her license. My mother didn't have her license because in the rush to pick me up she had left her purse on the dining room table. I feared that everything my mother had warned me of was about to happen.

"Hand over your license, miss," the officer repeated in a gruff voice. When I looked over at my mother, tears were running down her face. I didn't know if the tears were due to the cold or if they were the signs of her distress, but seeing my mother cry made me reckless. I called the officer every foul name a good twelve-year-old girl who attended Catholic school and who was prohibited from cursing could utter, the first being a racist and the second being a bully; had I known the word "fascist" then, I would have called him that too. I asked the officer if he was going to lock us up or shoot us because my mother's brakes failed and she left her license at home. He closed his ticket book with my mother's half-written ticket inside and said, "Young lady, I'm sorry you believe all that," and walked back to his patrol car.

I'm certain the police officer could not have imagined his daughter saying the awful things I had said to him. A black girl with two ponytails and ashy knees and a plaid school jumper had shared her view of the world and it frightened him or it shamed him. He recoiled from the ugliness of it. To put on that uniform each day, he needed to believe it wasn't true. As he drove away, I'm sure he was thankful no child of his lived in the same country I did.

My mother and I drove home in silence. To speak about it would have been to invite bad luck. Nor did we breathe a sigh of relief, because we didn't feel any safer. That evening we had been fortunate, but we might not be so again.

Looking back, I wonder if my mother worried that the rules she had drilled into my brother and me to protect us in fact might endanger us, or worse, that there was nothing she could do to protect her children. Even as a child I knew that a wrong turn off the highway, a whistle, or a walk on the wrong side of town could cost you your life if you were black.

Like many black children, my brother and I were taught a set of contradictory lessons about our country and our place within it. The picture of the world my mother drew was one of infinite possibilities and absolute limitations. Her vision of America was an amalgam of dream and nightmare: spacious skies, amber waves, and niggers hanging from trees.

I inherited this vision. My understanding of being black was defined by some rudimentary notion of *us* and *them* that was clarified whenever my mother spoke of Governor Wallace, White Citizen's Councils, and her life in Alabama, or when I witnessed the anxiety that filled her body as she watched the evening news waiting for word of some new terrible thing that had happened to black people or of some crime of which we had been accused.

My mother had grown up in a context in which white violence was something you took for granted and tried your best to avoid. She taught us the lesson her mother had taught her: "Be careful. All the white world sees is black skin." My mother's stories had become mine. Soon enough I would have my own stories with my own names.

None of the lessons imparted by my mother had anything to do with radical politics, at least not officially. She was an integrationist and a striver; she, along with my grandmother, had participated in the bus boycott in Montgomery. Yet the map of racial power in America she handed me might as well have been taken from a Black Power handbook. It was perhaps the one way I saw the world as my mother did. I too saw it as being ruled by the color line. It was a world in which blackness too often translated into "no human involved."

◇ ◇ ◇

I, TOO, LIVE in the time of slavery, by which I mean I am living in the future created by it. It is the ongoing crisis of citizenship. Questions first posed in 1773 about the disparity between "the sublime ideal of freedom" and the "facts of blackness" are uncannily relevant today. The echoes could be heard in a plea, still waiting for an answer, chalked onto a rooftop in the Ninth Ward of New Orleans: "Help. The water is rising. Pleas." Six people are trapped on the roof and two of them are waving American flags, hoping against the odds that the Stars and Stripes might make their plight visible, keep them afloat, and demonstrate unequivocally, "We are citizens too." But the anxiety and the doubt fueling the assertion was made plain by the photograph's caption: "Cast Away."

History doesn't unfold with one era bound to and determining the next in an unbroken chain of causality. It is "without providence or final cause," writes Foucault. "There is only 'the iron hand of necessity shaking the dice-box of chance.'" So the point isn't the impossibility of escaping the stranglehold of the past, or that history is a succession of uninterrupted defeats, or that the virulence and tenacity of racism is inexorable. But rather that the perilous conditions of the present establish the link between our age and a previous one in which freedom too was yet to be realized.

The past is neither inert nor given. The stories we tell about *what happened then*, the correspondences we discern between today and times past, and the ethical and political stakes of these stories redound in the present. If slavery feels proximate rather than remote and freedom seems increasingly elusive, this has everything to do with our own dark times. If the ghost of slavery still haunts our present, it is because we are still looking for an exit from the prison.

IN THE PHOTOGRAPH of the dungeon in the tourist guide for Cape Coast Castle, the space is crammed with boys and girls from the local school costumed as slaves. Eight adolescent boys are chained to the walls with their arms spread in giant Ys. Their scrawny bare chests jut out as they pull against the iron fetters. Rows of boys and girls are packed in front of them. The girls in the first row are wearing plain cotton wrappers, which make them appear like village girls rather than like slaves. They are sitting primly in front of the boys as if posed for the annual classroom picture. The girls seem uncomfortable and a bit shy. Most of them have averted their gazes from the camera and are looking toward the far left corner of the room, where I imagine a teacher is standing. One girl stares head-on at the camera with a furtive smile. The boys, squatting in rows behind the girls and filling the entirety of the room, have affected a more stolid and downcast look. Their arms are folded across the tops of their knees with the elbows sticking out at sharp angles. The photo is underexposed so I could barely make out their brown faces in the dark room.

I wondered how the children made sense of pretending to be slaves. Did being crammed into the dungeon and forced to sit on the cold grimy stones help them to understand the past? Did it frighten them, or did they daydream as the photographer counted to three? It was not the kind of make-believe they would have dreamed up on their own. Explaining that the slaves had been forced to stay in this room for as long as three months wouldn't have made the children any less uncomfortable. It might have made them feel sad for the people locked inside or they might have giggled nervously because they didn't really understand it or they might have shifted restlessly because they wanted to be outside playing. Their teacher would have told them that in the eighteenth century one-fourth of the slaves transported were children and in the nineteenth century children made up nearly 40 percent of the Atlantic slave trade. But history was one thing, and having to pretend something bad was happening to you was another.

The photograph tried to create an endearing image of the captives. How could you look at children in chains and not be moved? But the effort to invoke the dead and to lodge experience in tangible persons failed. By providing the anonymous with faces, the image succeeded only in killing the dead a second time by replacing them with stand-ins. The loss that the photo struggled to articulate was at cross-purposes with the gaggle of children huddled in the dungeon. Through a sleight of hand, by substituting one set of bodies with another, the photo tried to remedy the slave's oblivion. It didn't bring them any nearer but hid the one true thing—they were gone. The photo could only express the loss, not repair it.

No one looking at the photograph could forget for a moment that the picture did not reproduce or document the past. "The hell holes of the most horrific conditions imaginable" read the text in the brochure. But what did a picture of hell look like? All the photograph really expressed was yearning. But proxies and surrogates couldn't mend the wound or bridge the distance between the living and the dead.

The picture was a fiction of love. It permitted us to believe that we could coexist with the captives, witness their suffering, and remedy their defacement. The photo intended to bind our love to persons rather than totems. But the crowd packed in this room would remain without names and faces. That was the nature of the crime that had transformed persons into cargo. It was now impossible to fill in the blank spaces.

Love longed for an object, but the slaves were gone. In the dungeon, missing the dead was as close to them as I would come. And all that stood between artifice and oblivion was the muck on the floor.

SEVEN

The Dead Book

IT IS SAID that if you look at the sea long enough, scenes from the past come back to life. It is said that "the sea is history." And "the sea has nothing to give but a well excavated grave." Looking at the Atlantic, I thought of the girl. There were countless others buried at the bottom of the ocean, but she was the one I had my eyes set on. If I concentrated hard enough I could see it all happening again.

The billow of the ship's sail shuddered in the rush of air. The canvas awning occluded the sky. It could have been dawn or noon or dusk. Time had stopped. The *Recovery* was a world all its own. Three sailors, the captain, and the girl were the only ones visible on the ship. What happened next, no one could agree on, except, of course, that the girl ended up dead.

Everything else depends upon how you look at things or where you were standing when her body was suspended from the slaver's mast. No one saw the same girl; she was outfitted in a different guise for each who dared look. She appeared as a tortured virgin, a pregnant woman, a syphilitic tart, and a budding saint. And the explanation of how she came to hang in the air, flailing like a tattered banner, was no less fanciful: The girl declined to dance naked with the captain on the deck. The girl

snubbed the captain and refused his bed. The girl had the pox and the captain flogged her as a cure for the venereal disease.

The captain, the surgeon, and the abolitionist all disagreed about what happened on the deck of the *Recovery*, yet they all insisted they were trying to save the girl's life. In this respect, I am as guilty as the rest. I too am trying to save the girl, not from death or sickness or a tyrant but from oblivion. Yet I am unsure if it is possible to salvage an existence from a handful of words: *the supposed murder of a Negro girl*. Hers is a life impossible to reconstruct, not even her name survived. I suppose I could have called her Phibba or Theresa or Sally or Belinda. With a name she might have been more difficult to forget. A name would have afforded the illusion of knowing her and made less painful the fact that the girl "never will have any existence outside the precarious domicile of words" that allowed her to be murdered.

A few lines from a musty trial transcript are the entire story of a girl's life. Barring this, she would have been extinguished without a trace. These words are the only defense of her existence, the only barrier against her disappearance; and these words killed her a second time and consigned her to the bottom of the Atlantic.

Of the twenty-one slaves who died aboard the *Recovery*, and the million and more tossed into the Atlantic, one girl comes into view. Exceptional circumstances prevented her from simply vanishing into the heap of obscure lives scattered along the ocean's floor: a captain was tried for her murder.

The Committee for the Abolition of the Slave Trade first brought the case to the attention of the public. On April 2, 1792, William Wilberforce immortalized the girl in a speech delivered before the House of Commons and the world lent its attention, at least for a few days. When the trial ended, so did any interest in the girl. No one has thought of her for at least two centuries, but her life still casts a shadow.

THE CAPTAIN TIED a gun tackle around her wrist, fastened it to the mizzen stay, and suspended the naked girl above the deck. Her skin was covered with pustules, the ribs jutted out of her slight torso, and one of her legs was misshapen. The captain held the tackle while one of the cabin boys pulled and jerked her limbs as her body hung in the air. She swung for five minutes before the captain released the tackle and the girl fell to the deck. Then the captain suspended her by the other wrist. He watched the body writhe and then let her drop to the deck. He strung her up by her right leg, then he repeated the ritual with the left leg. Gravity emptied her upper half of blood. Her appendages turned gray, then blue from the lack of oxygen. The pressure of the rope made bloody cuffs around her wrists and ankles and caused her limbs to swell. The color in her face drained. Her insides gave way. Her wrist and elbow were dislocated from bearing the weight of her body.

The captain then tied the tackle around both wrists and pulled her into the air. He reached for his whip and he beat the girl on her back, buttocks, behind her knees, then slashed her with his whip across her arms, her ribs, the sides of her abdomen, her hips, and then across her breasts, torso, and the front of her legs. Her body twisted and turned as the rawhide struck her. The whip tore and blistered her flesh, covering her with welts.

The captain let go the rope and the girl crashed onto the deck. She didn't budge. She was still breathing, but she didn't move. She collapsed on the deck, with her head drooping toward her knees. The captain lifted her head, slapped her face, and said, "The bitch is sulky."

Watching the girl crawl on hands and knees back to the ship's hold, the third mate asked the captain if he should help the girl down. The captain cursed her again and said, "She may find her own way."

The girl crept to the hatchway and tumbled down the steps of the ladder. The ship's surgeon retrieved the girl from the hold the next day. She had fouled herself, so he washed her and attempted to revive her by rubbing alcohol on her temples, her nose, and her back. He spooned water into her mouth but she would not swallow. For three days she refused all sustenance. As the girl lay on the deck, she racked with convulsions. Fluids escaped her body and formed a puddle beneath her. The open wounds and the smell of decay attracted vermin. When a sailor discovered that she was dead, he notified the captain and then threw her overboard.

THE THIRD MATE ARRANGED the dancers. The women moved with grudging and perfunctory steps and kept their arms locked close to their sides and clasped around their waists. The rows of faces were dull and impassive. The figures swayed and jiggled and bounced, and he danced alongside them. The sun crept overhead as the women shifted back and forth and reeled from side to side. The girl sat alone at the outskirts of the group, drowsy and lethargic. She hung back like she always did and ignored the third mate when he motioned for her to join the others. Not even the threat of the whip could stir her, so he let her be. When the captain saw she was idle, he called to the boy Evans, "Get the tackle." Since they had left Old Calabar three weeks earlier, the captain had singled this girl out and beaten her for not eating or not dancing or some other thing.

When the third mate looked up again, the girl was hoisted into the air.

From where he was standing, just to the side of the barricado, the slave quarters on deck, he saw her clearly. The surgeon was on the awning deck next to him. The rest of the men were scattered about the ship doing their chores and didn't much notice the girl hanging from the rigging. They didn't observe the girl because you couldn't see that well around the barricado; it was about seven feet high and partly concealed the captain and the girl, and the men didn't give much attention to such things, anyway. Many of them had been in irons and on the receiving end of the captain's blows. It was best to stay away from what didn't concern you.

He was watching the women and laughing with the surgeon when they caught sight of the girl. The women continued to dance but they had turned to look at the girl thrashing at the end of the rope. They paid more attention to the girl than to their jig and shuffle. All you could hear was their feet pounding on the deck and the dull thump of the whip on the girl.

She didn't cry out. The captain beat the girl himself, and he tugged at her leg as she hung in the air. The captain sputtered something at the girl, but the third mate couldn't hear what was said. The whole thing took about half an hour, but it seemed longer. When the captain untied her and she fell to the deck, the girl was still alive. She was sitting all rolled up like a ball with her head touching her knees. Then she started to crawl back to the hatchway, but the third mate could see she would never make it on her own. Wanting to assist the girl, he asked the captain, "Sir, should I put her down?" But the captain forbade anyone to help the girl.

The third mate couldn't say for sure if the captain was trying to heal the girl or to harm her. It might have been for either purpose. Mostly the captain was a fair man.

THE GIRL WAS SICK from the time she set foot on the *Recovery*. It was gonorrhea, the surgeon was sure of it. The pox was what they called it. A few days after she had come on board, he perceived it. Pus-filled sores covered her skin, a discharge ran down her legs, and she was falling away in the flesh. It was definitely not the bloody flux, which when bad so covered the deck with blood and mucus that it resembled a slaughterhouse. The venereal distemper was common among the blacks, which was no surprise. The other dead one, Venus, which was what the crew called her, had it too. No, the girl didn't die because of it. It was a simple discharge, which was why he hadn't given her any mercury. Bleeding, purging, injections, and medicine of niter (potassium nitrate) and gum arabic—he had used all the precautions in his power. It was his first voyage as a surgeon on a slaver and he didn't intend to set foot on another.

The disease had been stable, although the girl could not eat as the other slaves did, or join in any of their amusements. Had the surgeon not been much interrupted in his treatment by the captain—that is, by the captain beating her—the girl would have recovered. The pox didn't kill the girl, the captain did. She died in consequence of the flogging. If it had not been so, she would have gone to market.

None of the other sailors besides the surgeon himself and the third mate and the two boys who assisted the captain ever talked about what happened with the girl. Such things were customary aboard a slaver. Everyone knew murder was part of "work at sea." "Outrages of that nature were so common on board the slave ships that they were looked upon with as much indifference as any trifling occurrence; their frequency had rendered them familiar."

The surgeon meant the flogging, but taking the women was customary too. It was common knowledge. Any seamen would tell you, "Sailors were allowed to have intercourse with such of the black women whose consent they can procure. The officers were permitted to indulge their passions among them at pleasure, and sometimes were guilty of such brutal excesses, as disgraced human nature." When the girls came on board, the sailors decided which ones they'd take for themselves. "The prey was divided, upon the spot, and only reserved until opportunity offered. Where resistance or refusal would be utterly in vain."

He had not mentioned the girl or any of the others in the journal he handed over to the customhouse in Grenada because he was afraid. It was a record of the white people only. He would not swear to the *dead book*, the journal of the black people who died on board. There happened so many deaths among the slaves and so many cruelties committed by the captain that the surgeon couldn't swear to the dead book. He pretended to kiss the Bible and muttered the oath, but he kissed his thumb and not the book.

A true account would have been very disagreeable to the captain and dangerous for himself.

The captain had locked him in irons, cheated him of half his pay, and deceived him of two slaves, but this had nothing to do with his testimony. He never told anyone he would ruin Captain Kimber. It was as false as God was true. "Revenge" wasn't a word that had crossed his lips. He was promised two slaves and it was only fair that he should get them.

WILLIAM WILBERFORCE ONLY HALF LISTENED to what the surgeon told him about the girl. The details weren't the truth of it, anyway. He had heard them before, the accounts of slaves trussed, burned, mutilated, ravaged, and dumped into the sea, and had learned by heart the facts about person-to-tonnage ratios, the most efficient arrangements of slaves tightly packed in the hold, the seasonal fluctuations of mortality rates, and the portion of each cargo likely to suffer from dehydration, malnutrition, and dysentery. But the captain and the girl—it was allegory. Wilberforce didn't see the wreck the surgeon described or the unsightly creature shunned by the other women, but a bashful girl costumed as an English maiden, a *Venus pudica* whose modesty dictated that she hide herself, a virgin persecuted by a monster.

It sickened him to think about her pudenda exposed and her wrists tied and her long legs and buttocks covered with stripes, so frighteningly vulnerable to the whims of the captain. She was no Bridgetown prostitute or Kingston whore, but a chaste girl who died trying to shield herself from the tyrant's eyes. She had fallen into the hands of a brute, when she needed a protector.

The girl touched something in Wilberforce. It was his shame. He wanted others to feel it too.

On April 2, 1792, when the fiery young moderate stood before the House of Commons arguing yet again for the abolition of the slave trade, he was desperate. In 1789 he had presented his first motion; it had been postponed for nearly two years and then defeated. This time he had chosen his words carefully, so as not to offend his adversaries. He wanted the men assembled before him aroused by the urgency of the task. He wanted them to smell the stench of slavery and to feel the great misery condensed into the small space of the slave ship. He wanted them to envision the girl and to know what he knew: *we are all guilty.* What he wanted them to see was not the girl's disgrace but their own. *It is we ourselves that degraded them to that wretched brutishness. It is we ourselves that have been degraded so much more than them.* He wanted the members of Parliament to squirm in their seats, to flinch before her battered body, to recoil with every lash that cut the girl's flesh. He wanted them to bear the burden of shame, so he paraded her before them:

> A young girl of fifteen, of extreme modesty, who finding herself in a situation incident to her sex, was extremely anxious to conceal it. The captain of the vessel, instead of encouraging so laudable a disposition, tied her to the waist, and placed her in a position so as to make her a spectacle to the whole crew. In this situation he beat her; but not thinking the exhibition he had made sufficiently conspicuous, he tied her up by the legs, and then also beat her. But his cruel ingenuity was not yet exhausted, for he next tied her up by one leg, after which she lost all sensation, and in the course of three days expired. This was an indisputable fact. If anything could in the annals of human depravity, go beyond this, he owned he did not know where to look for it.

He chose not to speak of Venus, the other dead girl. The pet name licensed debauchery and made it sound agreeable. Nor did he mention the nineteen men who died. Too many dead slaves would have had the opposite effect and diminished the significance of the tragedy. From the *Zong* case he had learned that 132 live slaves dumped into the sea were just cargo. It was easier to feel fully the loss of one life and to hang your hopes on one girl. Too many deaths were unmanageable.

THE CAPTAIN HAD CALCULATED wrong. It was too late by the time he realized it. She was a rack of skin and bones and he had tried everything, but she wouldn't eat horse beans or yams or manioc with slabber sauce. He had used the *speculum orbis* (to pry her teeth apart and shovel in some food), thumbscrews (to make her submit), coals pressed near the lips (to scare her), and four days of the whip (to break her stubbornness), all to no avail. Melted lead poured on the head sometimes worked, but none of the surgeon's remedies improved her lethargy or sulkiness. Nor would she dance, which likely would have lifted the black cloud of melancholy. The girl's low spirits and refusal to eat were the telltale signs. He had once heard a surgeon say, "No one who had the melancholy was ever cured."

When he observed her to be wasting away, she had been aboard only a few days. He knew enough to be suspicious. Slaves from Old Calabar had a reputation for destroying themselves. The first mate confirmed it. The girl had not taken her food and refused to take any. Mild means were used to divert her from her resolution but she still refused to eat. He believed he could save her, but then the girl forced his hand.

When they first left the Guinea coast he had been hopeful for a good journey. But with two boys and seven men dead, he began to fear all his labor was in vain. *To be frustrated by their mortality after all his efforts* was too much to bear. What had to be suffered to load and transport a slave cargo was beyond the capability of most men. The natives would steal you blind if you let them. A fixed price was a game to them and the terms of trade changed on a whim: one season it would be striped cloth, then the next season only red was acceptable, but you had none and a ship to load. Sometimes the gun was the only way to strike a bargain. But the slaves were the true affliction. *The slaves were filthier than swine.* To endure that reek for months, to have the violent smell of waste and sickness and death cling to your clothes and your skin and inside your lungs (the camphor and citrus and the smoke didn't make a damned difference), and to watch it all, everything you had hoped for, disappear with each morning's count. Well, it was hard to maintain your wits about you.

On the awning deck, he saw it all slip away and they still had a month to go before they reached Grenada. When the girl refused to dance with the others . . . well, what could he do? The girl would never be corrected. That much was apparent. Such a waste. His attempts at instruction had failed with her, but by God the others would learn. Otherwise, he'd have to stave off an insurrection. It took only one bad seed to plant the idea of rebellion, so you had to destroy it quickly, before it took root and spread.

The others would take their lead from how he handled the girl. It was essential to teach them that their will was no match for his. He'd see them all dead first.

Each time the whip hit her, her head jerked around as if she was trying to find him to stare him down with those cold, flat eyes. The slattern was trying to show him she still had some fight left. One way or the other, she'd be dead in a few days. It was a defeat and a small comfort. "Let her down," he shouted to the boy.

EIGHT DAYS AFTER Wilberforce's speech, London gawked at the girl being beaten. A satirical print depicting the flogging was plastered in taverns and coffeehouses and print shops. All that bruised flesh on display attracted pornographers, flagellants, and abolitionists alike. There was no hiding from English vice. In order to fight depravity, it had to be exposed. Gazing at the girl's buttocks and shapely legs caused a riot of warring passions in gentleman viewers who would have been familiar with the lubricity that attended whipping bottoms. Parlor room reading of Abbé Boileau's *Historia Flagellantium* would have explained the relation between the loins and the buttocks. When the buttocks are stricken, "the animal spirits are forced back violently towards the *os pubis* and they excite lascivious movements on account of the proximity of the genitals." And *The Memoirs of a Woman of Pleasure* schooled them in the rejuvenating effects of flogging on "sluggish juices and flagging, shrivelly parts, that rise to life only by virtue of those titillating ardors created by the discipline of their opposites."

The public was flummoxed. Clearly the illustration, titled *The Abolition of the Slave Trade* in homage to Wilberforce's motion, was intended to arouse, but *how* was the question? Was it protest or a send-up? Was the print ridiculing Wilberforce's moral conceits or mocking the captain? Was the girl a tart or a suffering innocent? The nubile maiden persecuted by the leering captain provoked indignation and stirred those flagging shriveled parts too. The white cloth draped over the girl's dark sprawled limbs made her appear indecent and exposed, more so than if she were simply naked. The cloth was an indulgence of the artist. It created a peekaboo or striptease effect and called attention to the parts of her body—the long legs, round bottom, and pert breasts—that it should be covering but failed to. The girl's nudity was exaggerated by the contrast with the fully outfitted captain and the similarly attired sailors, and the threat made plain by the vertical pole behind her.

No doubt the gentlemen tried to avert their gazes, but everywhere they looked, they could see her. They assured themselves that what held their attention was a loathing of depravity, rather than depravity itself. The exposed body of the *negresse* exercised a certain gravitational pull, which they fought to subdue, at least in public. Luckily there was the captain to blame for having to behold the girl's battered body. He was the brute responsible. An enlightened man could not enjoy looking at a picture like this, but morally they were required to.

Unlike a man of decency, the captain enjoyed what he saw. It was clear from the way he leered at the girl. The line of his mouth was squiggled up in a smile. His hands fondled his chest in the way a man might after eating a delicious meal of mutton and sweetbreads and fancy iced cakes and tea

thick with spoonfuls of sugar, then pushing away from the table, drowsy and sated. Contented was how he looked.

It was plain to see there was no delight in the boy's face. He wanted to look away, although he didn't, fearing how the captain might take it. The girl writhing like that made him tremble too. Torn between hauling the girl as the captain demanded and letting her down, which was what he wanted, he decided to protect his hide. What could a boy do? He himself had been badly used but could do nothing to stop it. It was between him and the girl, well what could he do?

The two sailors made a joke of it. The first sailor remarked, "Our girlies at Wapping are never flogged for protecting their modesty." And the other responded, "By God that's too bad if he had taken her to bed with him it would have been well enough. I'm sick of this black business." The girlies at Wapping (a parish on the Thames notorious for its ale-houses filled with pirates, mutineers, and sailors) were prostitutes, loose women, and disorderly persons, the female complements of the picaresque proletarian.

The joke derailed the terror of the scene and relieved the gentlemen viewers' anxiety. "No difference, no-none at night" when all beauteous dames, whether slaves or whores, were alike. Then the gentlemen could imagine themselves as either the spanker or the spanked and relish the pleasures and dangers of slavery. After a few chuckles and the exchange of a bawdy wisecrack, it was easy to turn your back and walk away.

HAD JOHN WESKETT SEEN the girl slumped on the deck, no doubt he would have decided that her death was the result of melancholy, in which case it was an uninsurable loss. The standard cargo policy covered slaves against all accidents except "death from natural causes." The London Assurance Company Policy on slaves provided "that it was free from the death of slaves either natural, violent or voluntary." No, the insurers were not liable for natural or self-inflicted death; such deaths were the result of "an inherent vice in the slaves themselves."

In his eighteenth-century tome on English insurance law, *A Complete Digest of the Theory, Laws, and Practice of Insurance*, John Weskett defined the parameters of damages needing to be taken into account by insurers. Under the entry "slaves," he wrote: "The insurer takes upon him the risk of loss, capture and death of slaves, or any other unavoidable accident to them; but natural death is always understood to be expected: by natural death is meant, not only when it happens by disease or sickness, but also when the captive destroys himself through despair, which often happens: but when slaves were killed or thrown into the sea in order to quell an insurrection on their part, then the insurers must answer."

Weskett arranged *things* in classes according to degrees of perishability. A slave cargo was no different from other commodities. Slaves, like china, limes, or silk, were susceptible to risks of many different kinds and were in the median range of peril. The hazards presented by the transport of slave commodities at sea were divided into two classes—accidental destruction and natural death. Yet natural death was not in itself sufficient to distinguish slaves from other commodities that withered and decayed. Death was just a variant of spoilage. A dead girl was not really all that different from rotten fruit.

WHEN CAPTAIN KIMBER WAS DELIVERED to Newgate prison seven days after Wilberforce delivered his speech at the House of Commons, he didn't write a word about what had happened on the ship's deck in the note he sent to his lawyer. During the trial, he never took the stand or tried to defend what he had done. Nor did he bring forth a single witness to contradict the charges of the third mate and the surgeon. He counted on his peers to understand what was required of him. Forms of correction, which might on first appearance seem harsh, were sometimes necessary in achieving the desired results. His sole aim had been to keep the girl alive and healthy until they reached the market at Grenada. As master it was his duty to manage the risks and hazards as best he could. A ship was its own government and none could be safe with a fainthearted commander.

The abolitionists had made a big scandal of one dead nigger, two now that they had added the second girl, with all their lies. The whole of the country was pointing the finger and laughing at him. In Cruikshank's illustration, he looked like a degenerate and the wench a tormented sprite.

He had wanted to smash his fist through the pane of the print shop window. Wilberforce would answer for sullying his name.

It was his good fortune that the owners of the *Recovery* hadn't lost faith in him. Mr. Jacks reassured him that nothing would come of the charge. The Duke of Clarence supported him, and he trusted the Admiralty Court to do what was right. Were two dead girls more important than the prosperity and commerce of Great Britain? Were the fools and idiots ranting about abolition blind? The fruits and majesty of the empire would be impossible without slavery. Prosperity had a price. There was no getting around it—death was the cost of the Africa trade. It was as certain as the day was long. An iron hand was the only way to manage it.

The judge said as much during the opening of the trial. He advised the jury, when deciding the matter of the captain's guilt, to take into consideration the particular circumstances of the high seas, "where all life is violence. This consideration makes a very great difference between the actions done upon sea and actions done upon land . . . You have to judge of ferocious men, who have few but strong ideas, peculiar to their own employment, hardened by danger, fearless by habit. The preservation of ships and lives depends often upon some act of severity, to command instant obedience to discipline and supreme command. These scenes of violence present a picture of human nature not very amiable, but are frequently justifiable, and absolutely requisite; as without which no commerce, no navigation, no defence of the kingdom can be maintained or exist." When the jury acquitted him of the murder of the two girls and charged the third mate and the surgeon with perjury, the captain knew they believed it too.

EVEN AFTER Wilberforce's measure for the abolition of the trade had been eviscerated by the addition of the word "gradual," which allowed the trade to flourish for another fifteen years, the great emancipator experienced the bliss of knowing that he had demanded justice for millions who could not ask for it themselves. He did not permit the ugly truth of things to contaminate this joy. The girl's death had changed nothing.

Had she lived, however, everything would have been different. While he would have preferred that the girl never have been stolen and sold to a trader on the Guinea coast and stowed away in the hold of a merchant ship bound for the Americas, had she arrived in Grenada, then he too would have clung to the word "gradual" and used it like a shield or a barricade or a rampart before the word "emancipation." Liberty was a seed that if planted in poor soil failed to vegetate into maturity. It was the child of reason. "Before men can benefit from the wisdom of laws, it was necessary they should have some idea of freedom. Freedom itself was a blessing the most valuable in nature; but it could be enjoyed only by a nation where the faculty of thought had been for some time employed. He hoped the day would arrive when all mankind would enjoy its blessings; but this neither was nor could be the case at present with the unhappy negroes in the West Indies; and from these reflections he was led to believe that no man could in reality be their friend, who proposed anything that could lead them to hope for their emancipation." The course toward freedom need not be precipitous. The thought of slaves set loose in the world without masters seemed reckless and likely to end in atrocity—the cane fields aflame with French ideas.

He regretted deeply the circumstances that destroyed the girl's life, but in truth she was more useful dead than alive. Her sacrifice had not been without purpose; *it afforded a salutary lesson*. In this respect she had been fortunate. He hoped as much for himself. It was this embrace of sacrifice that led others to call him a saint. He held his own life to be no more important than the girl's, and this was tested when the captain threatened to kill him. On the advice of the prime minister, who was a close friend, Wilberforce had quickly dispatched a memorandum refusing the captain's ridiculous demands for a public apology, five thousand pounds in cash, and a comfortable place in government. Unfortunately, the captain persisted. The rascal had followed him in the streets shouting insults, challenged him to a duel, stalked his private residence, and promised revenge. A friend (Lord Rokeby), concerned that his life was in danger, had insisted on sharing his carriage and riding with a pistol in his pocket. Entertaining the idea of a revolver in his own hand made Wilberforce wince. He had allowed himself to be called a coward rather than duel with another enraged slave captain whom he had offended. By his own estima-

tion, the right was with the bleeding lamb and not the raging tiger. Un-
afraid, he reassured his friend that "if the captain were to commit any act
of violence it would be beneficial rather than injurious to the cause."

THE LADLE OF cold horse beans settled in her palms. She pressed her
fingers together and the fibrous mash oozed between them and made a
squishing sound like a foot stuck in mud. The boatswain eyed her as he
passed among the rows of women and watched her lips move. There was
nothing inside her mouth, since she had decided against eating. Her lips
moved slowly as she talked to herself and her head was tilted to one side
as if she were listening to someone at the same time. The other women
couldn't understand her words, but from her eyes they knew she was
gone.

When she landed on the ship, the wish, which had taken root in the
holding pen in Calabar, blossomed. No matter what new torments the
captain inflicted, nothing would pass her lips. Not even the hands attack-
ing her each night could break her resolve. The hands swarmed her body
and pinched her thighs and stabbed her insides and nipped her breasts and
strangled her throat and stuffed their claws in her mouth so that she could
hardly breathe. They plucked her eyes out. They tore off her limbs. A rat
scampered away with her tongue. The others pretended not to notice anything. But she knew they were not sleeping. She could hear the racing
hearts of the women packed around her. The hands were trying to kill
her, and the women didn't budge from the wooden planks, acting as
though they were already dead. In the morning, her missing arms and
legs were replaced, waterlogged and twisted; her tongue no longer fit her
mouth; her eyes sank to the back of her head. Her middle was bloated and
stretched tight like the skin of a drum.

For twenty-eight days, she had climbed through the hatchway and
poured onto the deck with the others and not eaten. Once they had lost
sight of the coast, her hunger had disappeared too. Four weeks without
food left her dreamy and intoxicated. Short-lived bouts of elation made
her feel unoccupied, disburdened, sovereign, as though she had found a
country of her own. When the rapture ebbed, she was just a worldless girl

again; her belly turned into stones and the thing gnawing her intestines took a ferocious bite. The leaden feeling radiated from the pit of her stomach and spread through her body, and she nearly collapsed from its weight. Her feet became unsteady and her legs crumpled, forcing her to recline on the deck.

The women were assembled a few feet away, but it might well have been a thousand. They held back from the girl, steering clear of her bad luck, pestilence, and recklessness. Some said she had lost her mind. What could they do, anyway? The women danced and sang as she lay dying.

One hundred forty-eight women pounded the deck. The sound entered the girl's body in small tremors. She listened to the songs, uncomprehending. The din in her head prevented her from keeping track of what they were saying. The world clamored. In the jumble of sound, she discerned the creaking of the ship as it expanded and contracted, the grumble and complaint of the sailors, the men wrestling with their chains belowdecks, the barked orders of the captain, rats scuttling in the hold, the whirr of ropes, canvas whipping in the air, the ring and tug of the pulleys, the gulls squawking, the whales spurting, flying fish slicing through the water, the low rumble of sharks, the high-pitched hum of the sea, and the cities of the dead laughing and crying out.

She had discovered a way off the ship. It worried her that the ancestors might shun her, or the gods might be angry and punish her by bringing her back as a goat or a dog, or she would roam the earth directionless and never find her way beyond the sea, but she risked it anyway, it was the only path open. When the two boys plummeted into the sea, they had made leaving look so easy.

She curled into a ball in the corner of the deck. Her body hurt and she trembled. The furtive glances of the women made her feel pitiful and weak. Had she been capable of tears, they would have streamed down her face. Had her tongue not made speech impracticable, had it been possible for a corpse to speak, she would have said, "You are wrong. I am going to meet my friends." All they could see was a girl slumped in a dirty puddle and not the one soaring and on her way home.

◊ ◊ ◊

IF THE STORY ENDED there, I could feel a small measure of comfort. I could hold on to this instant of possibility. I could find a salutary lesson in the girl's suffering and pretend a story was enough to save her from oblivion. I could sigh with relief and say, "It all happened so long ago." Then I could wade into the Atlantic and not think of the *dead book*.

EIGHT

Lose Your Mother

AS I TRAVELED through Ghana, no one failed to recognize me as the daughter of slaves, so the few stories people shared were kinder and less severe than they would be otherwise. No one said things like slaves were a bunch of stupid and backward people, or confided they were fit only for manual labor that required strong arms, or called them barbarians or criminals. If you believed that slavery was a relatively benign institution in Africa, then you certainly would not expect to hear such things, but in fact, masters and traders spoke about their slaves in exactly these terms and people continue to do so today. In my company, the polite refrained from such remarks and instead made jokes about how I had found my way back home or teased me about searching for my roots. They were used to Americans with identity problems. None openly expressed surprise or amazement that nearly two centuries after the abolition of the Atlantic slave trade, I was still hoping to find a hint or sign of the captives. If they experienced a twinge of remorse, no one let on. And even if I was indiscreet enough to mention my slave origins, most refused to follow me down this dangerous path and responded with studied indifference to all my talk of slavery. But silence and withholding were not the same as forgetting. Despite the dictates of law and masters, which prohibited the discussion of a person's origins, everyone remembered the stranger in the village, everyone recalled who had been a slave and with a discerning glance just as easily identified their descendants.

As it turned out, the slave was the only one expected to discount her past. It surprised me at first. Why would those who had lost the most be inclined or likely to forget? Clearly even someone like me, who was three generations away from slavery and who had neither a country nor a clan to reclaim, hadn't been deterred from searching. But as I traveled along the slave route, I soon found out about all the elaborate methods that had been employed to make slaves forget their country.

In every slave society, slave owners attempted to eradicate the slave's memory, that is, to erase all the evidence of an existence before slavery. This was as true in Africa as in the Americas. A slave without a past had no life to avenge. No time was wasted yearning for home, no recollections of a distant country slowed her down as she tilled the soil, no image of her mother came to mind when she looked into the face of her child. The pain of all she had lost did not rattle in her chest and make it feel tight. The absentminded posed no menace. Yet more than guns, shackles, and whips were required to obliterate the past. Lordship and bondage required sorcery too.

EVERYONE TOLD ME a different story about how the slaves began to forget their past. Words like "zombie," "sorcerer," "witch," "succubus," and "vampire" were whispered to explain it. In these stories, which circulated throughout West Africa, the particulars varied, but all of them ended the same—the slave loses mother. Never did the captive choose to forget; she was always tricked or bewitched or coerced into forgetting. Amnesia, like an accident or a stroke of bad fortune, was never an act of volition.

When I asked, "What happened to the ones taken across the waters?" people passed on twice-told tales in which herbs, baths, talismans, and incantations transformed slaves into blank and passive automatons. In

Ouidah, a town that had been a significant port on the Slave Coast, a university student told me that slaves were marched through a grove that induced forgetting, or that they encircled a tree of forgetfulness. Women had to circle the tree seven times, and men had to circle it nine times in order to forget their origins and accept their slave status.

The student joked, "The tree didn't work because now you are back." He pointed out the tree of return on the slave route.

"It doesn't make sense," I replied. "Why did they want the ones who had forgotten to return?"

He just smiled.

"Well, how do you say tree of return in the Fon language?" I asked.

"There's no word for it in our language because it's just something we tell foreigners."

Every part of West Africa that trafficked in slaves possessed its own Lethe, rivers and streams whose water made slaves forget their pasts, dense groves that trapped old memories in the web of leaves, rocks that obstructed entrance to the past, amulets that deafened a man to his mother tongue, and shrines that pared and pruned time so that only today was left. Traditional healers devised herbal concoctions that could make the most devoted husband forget his wife in the blink of an eye, marabouts applied potions and dispensed talismans that erased the trail home, priests forced captives to vow oaths of allegiance to their captors, sorcerers tamed recalcitrants with the powers of the left hand. European traders, too, employed occultists to pacify and entrance slaves with medicinal plants.

A famous slave trader on the Rio Pongo subdued his captives with the aid of an enchanted rock. He lined them up and forced each in turn to take a seat on the rock, which drained away all will. After this treatment, the prisoners no longer resisted their bonds, recalled their pasts, or attempted to flee the trader. After being washed with a brew distilled from plant roots, the slave was integrated into a group of the newly pacified.

In Ghana, captives were given ceremonial baths before sale to wash them clean of old identities. Medicine men, fetish priests, and slave traders recited songs and incantations that lulled the captive into embracing servitude and that eradicated all visions of home. In Ewe country, on the eastern coast, people still told stories of a brew or tonic that prevented slaves from retracing the path back to their country.

In the north, they possessed medicine so powerful that it transformed able-bodied men and women into vacuous and tractable slaves. The plant *Crotalaria arenaria*, a leguminous undershrub found in the savanna, was called *manta uwa*, which means "forget mother" in Hausa. Traders boasted that slaves ingesting the plant soon forgot their origins and no longer attempted to run away.

Manta uwa made you forget your kin, lose sight of your country, and cease to think of freedom. It expunged all memories of a natal land, and it robbed the slave of spiritual protection. Ignorant of her lineage, to whom could the slave appeal? No longer able to recall the shrines or sacred groves or water deities or ancestor spirits or fetishes that could exact revenge on her behalf, she was defenseless. No longer anyone's child, the slave had no choice but to bear the visible marks of servitude and accept a new identity in the household of the owner.

It was one thing to be a stranger in a strange land, and an entirely worse state to be a stranger to yourself.

This was the fate from which the boys in Elmina were trying to rescue me. Through their letters, they were trying to call me back from *donkorland*, not the territory raided for slaves but the land of oblivion. But what, if anything, could I remember after hundreds of years of forgetting?

THE PATHS LEADING from the hinterland to the coast, to listen to slave traders tell it, swarmed with amnesiacs, soulless men, and walking corpses. As early as the fifteenth century, European traders had described their black captives as absentminded and innately servile. "In time," one traveler observed, "they soon forgot all about their own country." And by the eighteenth century these accounts had been repeated so often that they were accepted as truth. These people of no country were called "negroes" and "donkors." In the end these names were just another way of identifying them as the living dead. Race, Hannah Arendt observed, "is, politically speaking, not the beginning of humanity but its end . . . not the natural birth of man but his unnatural death."

Like the term "Negro," *donkor* was a badge of servitude, a stamp of those who had been uprooted, an earmark of dead men. It did not refer to any home or country or history but only to a dishonored condition. Like the term "nigger," *donkor* implied that "the human pulse stops at the gate of the barracoon."

Donkor was used as an epithet in Asante, the powerful inland state that controlled the traffic in slaves to the coast. It was "synonymous with the barbarian of the Greeks and Romans," a European factor explained, "which they [the Asante] apply to all people of the interior but themselves, and implies an ignorant fellow." A tome on Asante law and custom held that *donkor* was "applied strictly to any man or woman, other than an Asante, who had been purchased with the express purpose of making him or her a slave."

With the knowledge gained from ten slaving voyages to Africa, in which he traversed the territory from Cape Palmas to the Congo River, Captain John Adams judged "the Dunco" to be the most passive of all the people he encountered north of the equator. He first noted their appearance— "they were middle size and the color of their skin is not of so deep a black as those of the Fantee or Asshantee"—and then provided an assessment of their character: mild, tractable, and inoffensive. "They may be called a simple people, who never exhibit any sullenness of manner, but a uniform willingness to do to the best of their ability whatever they are desired; and the term Dunco, which in the Fante language signifies stupid fellow, or ignorant man, from the back country, is invariably given to them by the Fantees, as a term of derision, in consequence. To the Fantees, as well as to the Asshantees, they have a strong aversion, because they consider these people as the authors of their misfortunes."

In the opinion of Ludewig Roemer, a trader at Fort Christiansborg, a Danish settlement, "One could hardly call them human . . . The farther up in the land the slaves come from, the more stupid they are." But contrary to the prevailing view of northerners as a "well-mannered nation," Roemer insisted they were wilder and more savage than other slaves. To his eyes, they possessed a physiognomy like that of a tiger with comparable teeth in their mouths. Notwithstanding their wild nature and feral appearance, Roemer conceded that the fear of men like him hid behind their truculence. "The slaves who come from far north in the land think we Europeans have bought them to be fattened like swine, and that we eat them when they become fat. I cannot describe to what degree of desperation this fear drives them, so they seek to kill us."

Roemer was not the only trader fearful of slaves set upon destruction and revenge. The occult practices to induce forgetting were attempts to avert rebellion and forestall retribution. It wasn't only the memory of their kin and country that royals and merchants wanted the captives to forget but, as well, those responsible for their wretched circumstances.

AN ELDERLY AKAN MAN RUMINATED about the cost of enrichment while conducting business with Roemer.

"It is you, you Whites," they say, "who have brought all the evil among us. Indeed, would we have sold one another if you, as purchasers, had not come to us? The desire we have for your fascinating goods and your brandy, bring it to pass that one brother cannot trust the other, nor one friend another. Indeed, a father hardly his own son! We know from our forefathers that only those malefactors who had thrice committed murder were stoned or drowned. Otherwise the normal punishment was that anyone who had committed a misdeed had to carry to the injured party a large piece of firewood for his house or hut, and ask on his knees for forgiveness, for one, two, or three days in a row. In our youth, we knew many thousands of families here and at the coast, and now not a hundred individuals can be counted. And what is worse, you have remained among us as a necessary evil, since if you left, the Negroes up-country would not let us live for half a year, but would come and kill us, our wives and our children. That they bear this hatred for us is your fault."

This man was not alone in fearing the punishment to be meted out by slaves. Others shared his apprehension. By the middle of the eighteenth century, African merchants had begun to ponder the consequences of the

Atlantic trade. While many weren't aware of the population decline occurring in West Africa as a result of the slave trade, which has been likened by scholars to the demographic impact of centuries of war, they had started to experience the social disruptions of the trade. The state of emergency caused by predatory greed was becoming slowly apparent and fears of social collapse or personal affliction haunted the ruling class. Royals, big men, and merchants feared the revenge of slave spirits, the envy of their inferiors, and the indictment of their riches. Like ruling men everywhere, they dreaded the hewers of wood, the rabble, the multitudes. They fretted about the course of events that might place the bottom rail on top. They nervously anticipated the retribution of slaves. The lives sacrificed for cloth, guns, rum, and cowries left their traces in the anxieties of the ruling class.

In the Congo, a group of traders formed an association called Lemba, which was a therapeutic cult for those afflicted with the disease of wealth. Lemba, which means "to calm," contained the disruptions caused by the slave trade with ritual and medicine. Like Keynesian economists, Lemba priests tried to cure capitalism by regulating the violence of the market and redistributing wealth to their kin and community. The members of the Lemba cult were the elite: healers, chiefs, judges, and the affluent. They were the ones vulnerable to the envy of the less fortunate and blamed for the social ills associated with the trade. Infirmity, sterility, and witchcraft tainted those allied with merchant capital. Gifts offered to high-ranking priests and riches shared with subordinates provided the remedy.

In Senegambia, the Diola built altars to their captives. Shrines adorned with wooden fetters (*hudjenk*) and consecrated with palm wine and the blood of animal sacrifice protected raiders and their captives and also determined who could and could not be seized as a captive. The priests who tended these shrines were required to have captured at least one slave with their own hands. A shrine was named after the first slave taken so that his or her name would perdure and the songs performed at the altar invoked the name of the man or woman responsible for the family's prosperity. The Diola traders recognized that slaves produced their wealth and for this reason they committed the names of their captives to memory. (In Antwerp or Lisbon, Nantes or Bristol, Charleston or Providence, no one invoked the names of the persons responsible for their riches.)

The spirit shrines of the Diola protected the communities involved in slave raiding from internal disruption. If the rules governing raiding were violated, traders were afflicted with a disease called *hupila*, which "made one feel like all one's limbs were bound in a rope." The disease replicated the bonds and immobility of the captive.

On the Slave Coast, the Ewe incorporated the *donkor* into their pantheon of spirits. In the Gorovodu religious practice, the spirits are *amefeflewo*—bought-and-sold people. This practice of spirit possession by slaves, explains an anthropologist, was a form of sacred debt payment by which the stolen lives of captives were redressed. The Ewe host offered her body as a vessel for *donkor* spirits. Possession, as a form of spiritual expenditure or loss, reversed the theft and accumulation of slave trading. By honoring slave spirits, the Ewe endeavored to amend the past and to make a place for strangers.

Even if the captives had managed to forget the acts of violence that made them slaves, ironically the traders could not. They remembered the riches and debts they had incurred by their participation in the trade. Apprehension regarding what they had done and how it might come back to them motivated these rituals of atonement. Royals and merchants could not afford to forget, at least not without risking all they had gained and being engulfed by the chaos and disorder of the slave trade.

FEW OF THE ENSLAVED forgot the royals, merchants, and thieves responsible for their captivity, even when they had forgotten their country. Each generation passed on tales of men who bled dry the lives of other men, who stank from the smell of corpses, and who gorged themselves on human flesh. The ones made property didn't take pleasure in the great wealth of ruling men, so their stories recounted the gruesome means by which the big men had acquired coffers of gold and cowries. In a volume of folktales titled *Nigger to Nigger*, collected in South Carolina by a white amateur folklorist, E.C.L. Adams, there is a portrait of a slave-trading king. The storytellers called him a "big nigger."

Way back in slavery time and way back in Africa, there had been a chief who betrayed his own tribe by helping white folks catch and entrap slaves. White folks used to give him money and trinkets, and, for this the king sent thousands into bondage. He would trick them onto the boat where the white men trapped and chained them. The last time the white men came to the coast, they "knocked dat nigger down an' put chain on him an' brung him to dis country."

When the king died, he was not desired in heaven and was barred from hell. God, the Greatest Master, condemned the king to roam the earth for all times. As retribution for having killed the spirits of men and women as well as their bodies, he would never be permitted any resting place. He would forever wander with the other marauding spirits of the bush. Banished to the dismal swamp, he was forbidden from ever touching a living thing and allowed to feed only off the dead. As he had sucked away the life of men, so he would spend the rest of his days as a buzzard with carrion as his only food.

Sometimes he would appear before those wandering or lost in the swamp, but his doom had been settled. He wouldn't ever hurt another person again. His evil beak and claw would never poke, scratch, or wound any creature still alive. Known all over the spirit world as the King Buzzard, he would travel forever alone.

IF IN THE ERA of the trade the enslaved had been forced to *forget mother*, now their descendants were being encouraged to do the impossible and reclaim her. In the 1990s, Ghana discovered that remembering the suffering of slaves might not be such a bad thing after all, if for no other reason than it was profitable. So contrary to the legal precedents and prohibitions of three centuries, the state was now trying to create a public memory of slavery. Under the stewardship of Shell Oil, USAID, and a consortium of North American universities, the Ghanaian Ministry of Tourism and the Museum and Monuments Board crafted a story for the ten thousand black tourists who visited the country every year hungering for knowledge of slave ancestors. Tourism provided a ready response with a tale of the At-

lantic slave trade as a distinctly African American story, with no mention
of the expansion and increasing severity of African slavery in response to
the Atlantic trade or of destitute commoners.

Local cottage industries in slave route tourism began sprouting up all
over Ghana. In 1998, the Ministry of Tourism encouraged every district
to form a Tourism Development Committee. Every town or village had
an atrocity to promote—a mass grave, an auction block, a slave river,
a massacre. It was Ghana's equivalent to a fried chicken franchise.
McDonald's had already organized McRoots tours to Senegal and Gambia. No one knew for sure, but Ghana might be next. Few of the tour oper-
ators, docents, and guides put any stock in the potted history of the "white
man's barbarism" and the "crimes against humanity" that they marketed
to black tourists or believed the Atlantic trade had anything to do with
them. They only hoped that slavery would help make them prosperous.

For Ghana, the slave route was a desperate measure to generate
needed revenue and to develop a viable economy. For towns and villages
scattered throughout the countryside, it was the possibility of digging
new wells, building a school, or buying a vehicle to transport the sick to
the small hospital one hundred miles away. For the jobless, it was the opportunity for employment in the tourism industry. For petty traders, it
was an expanded market for their goods. For dreamers, it was the chance
of a ticket to America.

Door of No Return rituals, reenactments of captivity, certificates of
pilgrimage, and African naming ceremonies framed slavery primarily as
an American issue and as one of Africa's relation to her "lost children."
The biennial Panafest Historical Theatre Festival (Panafest), which began in 1992, attracted participants from all over the African diaspora. The
reunification of the African family and the return of its children to the
homeland were the animating themes of the festival. On the ground, this
often translated into a comedy of errors, as in 1994 when the Ghanaian Con-
cert Party Union decided to welcome black Americans to Ghana and pay
homage to their culture with an old-style blackface performance. (A bureaucratic obstacle prevented the show from being performed.) A "take their
heads" crusade was the response of taxi drivers, peddlers, and merchants.

Most recently, the Ministry of Tourism launched an advertising campaign to change the common perception of African Americans from one of rich tourists to one of brothers and sisters. This effort to make Ghana feel more like Jerusalem and less like Disneyland required Ghanaians to strike *obruni* from their vocabulary and welcome their African American kin back home.

"Remembering slavery" became a potent means of silencing the past in the very guise of preserving it, since it effectively curbed all discussion of African slavery and its entailments—class exploitation, gender inequality, ethnic clashes, and regional conflict. The sorcery of the state, like the sorcery of marabouts and herbalists, was also intended to wash away the past (at least those aspects that might create conflict) and to pacify the heirs of slaves, except that now this process was described as memorializing rather than forgetting. The arrival of "the ones who had been taken away" did not encourage a working through of this history but a bittersweet celebration of return, reunion, and progress.

So the descendants of slaves were welcomed with the red carpet treatment. They mourned their ancestors in great public ceremonies where chiefs assembled to atone for the past and to collect alms. And the brothers and sisters gave generous donations and shopped vigorously, perhaps hoping that the breach of the Atlantic would be bridged by their new roles as consumers. It was to everyone's advantage to believe this.

The heirs of slaves wanted a past of which they could be proud, so they conveniently forgot the distinctions between the rulers and the ruled and closed their eyes to slavery in Africa. They pretended that their ancestors had once worn the king's vestments and assumed the grand civilization of Asante as their own. They preferred to overlook the fact that the Asantehene (king of Asante) had helped to shove their ancestors onto slave ships and refused to admit royal power emanated from "the abuse of human beings and things." It was comic and tragic at the same time. The children of slaves were as reluctant to assume their place among toilers, laborers, and peasants as the elites. The irony of this was suggested by Aime Césaire: "We've never been Amazons of the King of Dahomey, nor princes of Ghana with eight hundred camels, nor wise men in Timbucktu under Askia the Great, nor the architects of Djenné, nor Madhis, nor warriors . . . I may as well confess that we were at all times pretty mediocre dishwashers, shoeblacks without ambition, at best conscientious sorcerers and the only unquestionable record that we broke was that of endurance under the chicote [whip]."

And even if African Americans were seduced by tourism's promise of an African home and willing to dance joyfully around trees of return and eager to experience solidarity with their newfound kin through freshly minted memories of slavery, most Ghanaians weren't fooled by the mirage, even when their survival necessitated that they indulge the delusion. The story of slavery fabricated for African Americans had nothing to do with the present struggles of most Ghanaians. What each community made of slavery and how they understood it provided little ground for solidarity. African Americans wanted to regain their African patrimony and to escape racism in the United States. Ghanaians wanted an escape from the impoverishment of the present, and the road to freedom, which they most often imagined, was migration to the United States. African Americans entertained fantasies of return and Ghanaians of departure. From where we each were standing, we did not see the same past, nor did we share a common vision of the Promised Land. The ghost of slavery was being conjured to very different ends.

IN THE UNITED STATES, black people's insistence on reckoning with slavery in the face of national indifference, if not downright hostility, has been an effort to illuminate the crushing effects of racism in our lives. It is less a historical exercise than an ethical and political mandate. Simply put, the "legacy of slavery" is a way of saying that we had been treated badly for a very long time and that the nation owes us. Martin Luther King, Jr., employed the language of creditor and debtor races to underscore the elusive quest for racial justice. In the speech delivered at the March on Washington, he said, "America has given the Negro people a bad check, a check which has come back marked with insufficient funds." The promissory note to which King referred was the Constitution and the Declaration of

Independence. As he saw it, the civil rights movement was an effort to "cash this check, a check that will give us upon demand the riches of freedom and the security of justice."

No one has ever been able to make the case persuasively enough to convince the government that this was true or even to be granted a day in court, despite the recent flurry of lawsuits for reparations. In overturning the use of affirmative action in granting city contracts, Justice Antonin Scalia wrote, "Under our Constitution there can be no such thing as either a creditor or a debtor race . . . We are just one race here. It is American." In the eyes of the court, no enduring harm had been passed across generations. And, even if it had been, we had slumbered on our rights for too long. Too much time had passed between the injury and the claim for redress. But for us the opposite was true. The time passed had only intensified the injury. History was an open wound, as Jamaica Kincaid writes, that "began in 1492 and has come to no end yet."

Who could deny that the United States had been founded on slavery or disregard the wealth created by enslaved laborers? Or brush aside three centuries of legal subjection? Yet I remain agnostic about reparations. I fear that petitions for redress are forms of political appeal that have outlived their usefulness. Did the bid to make a legal or political claim in an officially "post-racist" society require us to make arguments in a moral language that appeals to the abolitionist consciousness of white folks, who accept that slavery was wrong *and* believe that racism has ended? Are reparations a way of cloaking the disasters of the present in the guise of the past because even our opponents can't defend slavery now? Did we want a Federal Bureau of African American Affairs to decide and manage what we were owed? Or did we hope that the civil suits could accomplish what a social movement had failed to do, that is, to eradicate racism and poverty?

I had grown weary of pleading our case and repeating our complaint. It seems to me that there is something innately servile about making an appeal to a deaf ear or praying for relief to an indifferent and hostile court or expecting remedy from a government unwilling even to acknowledge that slavery was a crime against humanity.

In 1817, the black abolitionist Robert Wedderburn had warned of the dangers of appeal. In an address to the slaves of Jamaica, he encouraged them to stage a general strike to win their liberty. "Union among you, will strike tremendous terror to the receivers of stolen persons. But do not petition, for it is degrading to human nature to petition your oppressors." In 1845, Frederick Douglass echoed this sentiment when he described the slave's appeal as "a privilege so dangerous" that anyone exercising it "runs a fearful hazard" of inviting even greater violence.

I couldn't help but think of Josiah Wedgwood's famous antislavery medallion of the chained slave on bended knee, begging in supplication, "Am I not a man and a brother?" The medallion had enjoyed such popularity that it became the favored icon of the abolition movement and was worn as a brooch or hairpin by women of fashion in the 1780s and '90s. But the bid for emancipation reproduced the abject position of the slave. And the pleading and praying for relief before the bar struck me in exactly

the same way—it was as an act of state worship. I didn't want to get down on my knees as a precondition to arriving at freedom. I didn't want to plead my case, "Yes, I have suffered too." I didn't want to display my scars.

When I envisioned the slave I didn't think of this fellow on bended knee, trying to maintain his dignity as he made the case for his humanity. His clasped hands were folded as if he were praying and his head was up-turned slightly as if he were looking for God, but I understood that it wasn't God to whom he was looking and praying but to the people of England or France, who might as well have been God. And anyone looking down upon his naked figure could see that this man was helpless and needed their assistance despite his rippling muscles and broad chest and mighty shoulders. His humiliation moved them and made them feel guilty and excited their sympathy.

Of course, once you have assumed the position of supplicant and find

yourself genuflecting before the court or the bar of public opinion, then, like the strapping man on the medallion, you have conceded the battle. It is hard to demand anything when you are on bended knee or even to keep your head raised. And you can forget trying to counter the violence that had landed you on your knee in the first place. Being so low to the ground, it is difficult not to grovel or to think of freedom as a gift dispensed by a kind benefactor or to imagine that your fate rests in the hands of a higher authority, a great emancipator, the state, or to implore that you are human too. "Am I not a man and a brother?" Having to ask such a question, no doubt, would have made the petitioner's nostrils flare with anger and perspiration bead on his forehead and the bile rise to the back of his throat.

Needing to make the case that we have suffered and that slavery, segregation, and racism have had a devastating effect on black life is the contemporary analogue to the defeated posture of Wedgwood's pet Negro. The apologetic density of the plea for recognition is staggering. It assumes both the ignorance and the innocence of the white world. If only they knew the truth, they would act otherwise. I am reminded of the letter that James Baldwin wrote his nephew on the centennial anniversary of the Emancipation Proclamation. "The crime of which I accuse my country and my countrymen," he wrote, "and for which neither I nor time nor history will ever forgive them, that they have destroyed and are destroying hundreds of thousands of lives and do not know it and do not want to know it . . . It is not permissible that the authors of devastation should also be innocent. It is the innocence which constitutes the crime."

To believe, as I do, that the enslaved are our contemporaries is to understand that we share their aspirations and defeats, which isn't to say that we are owed what they were due but rather to acknowledge that they accompany our every effort to fight against domination, to abolish the color line, and to imagine a free territory, a new commons. It is to take to heart their knowledge of freedom. The enslaved knew that freedom had to be taken; it was not the kind of thing that could ever be given to you. The kind of freedom that could be given to you could just as easily be taken back. Freedom is the kind of thing that required you to leave your bones on the hills at Brimsbay, or to burn the cane fields, or to live in a garret for seven years, or to stage a general strike, or to create a new republic. It is won and lost, again and again. It is a glimpse of possibility, an opening, a solicitation without any guarantee of duration before it flickers and then is extinguished.

The demands of the slave on the present have everything to do with making good the promise of abolition, and this entails much more than the end of property in slaves. It requires the reconstruction of society, which is the only way to honor our debt to the dead. This is the intimacy of our age with theirs—an unfinished struggle. To what end does one conjure the ghost of slavery, if not to incite the hopes of transforming the present? Given this, I refuse to believe that the slave's most capacious political claims or wildest imaginings are for back wages or debt relief. There are too many lives at peril to recycle the forms of appeal that, at best, have delivered the limited emancipation against which we now struggle.

IN GHANA, they joked that if a slave ship bound for America docked off the coast today so many Ghanaians would volunteer for the passage that they would stampede one another trying to get on board.

But who would ever envy slaves or view a cargo hold as an opportunity or risk death to arrive in the Americas? Every year Ghanaians stowed away in packing crates, cargo holds, and ship containers trying to make their way to the United States or Europe. Twenty-three men arrived in New York in 2003 hidden in a cargo ship. The year before, two Ghanaian boys were found dead in the baggage compartment of a plane at Heathrow Airport. The subzero temperatures and lack of oxygen killed them. Each year young men and boys risked deadly voyages to escape poverty and joblessness, while girls fled to Abidjan and other cities and were trafficked internationally as prostitutes. It was the dire circumstances of the present that caused Ghanaians to make wisecracks about volunteering for the Middle Passage and to view black tourists as the fortunate heirs of Kunta Kinte.

What they didn't discern were the two decades of political setbacks and economic decline that had inspired these trips to the dungeon; what they didn't understand was that many of us also lived in poverty. (It didn't look the same, but the assault of poverty was life threatening in the United States too.) A growing sense of despair and an exhausted political imagination incapable of dreaming of radical change had everything to do with the busloads of black strangers looking to shed tears in a slave fort. There were no obvious signs of this diminished hope for the future. The grief of African Americans was opaque here. We were encouraged to mourn because it generated revenue, but our grief struck no common chord of memory, no bedrock of shared sentiment.

To most Ghanaians the government's efforts to commemorate the Atlantic slave trade were irrelevant. Besides, what had Jamaicans and Americans to do with their lives? When President Rawlings declared that on August 1, 1998, Ghana would celebrate Emancipation Day to commemorate the abolition of slavery in the British Caribbean, Ghanaians retorted, "Has slavery ended in Africa?" The British had also abolished slavery in Ghana, but President Rawlings had not planned any public celebrations of the colonial ordinances that ended slavery in the Gold Coast in 1874 and in the Northern Territories in 1897. Had Rawlings asked, "Are we yet free?" most Ghanaians would have answered with a resounding, "No."

This "no" resonated on both sides of the Atlantic. It was the reminder of what abolition and decolonization had failed to deliver. This "no" was the language we shared, and within it resided a promise of affiliation better than that of brothers and sisters.

The Dark Days

"OPEN YOUR EYES," John had been scolding me for months. Now, through no fault of my own, I spent most of my time in the dark. In the mornings, I was bleary-eyed as I labored to make out the world concealed beneath the blustery gray sky of harmattan. In the evenings, the city slowly disappeared as the light shifted from the color of ash to a charcoal black, as if Accra had been buried under a mound of soot. From my terrace, I watched the city vanish at nightfall, straining my eyes to make out the human forms hidden in the shadows, training myself to discern the subtle intimations of life in the sea of blackness.

I had scoffed at the December headlines in the *Daily Graphic* and the *Ghanaian Times*, "Power Cut in Half," and dismissed the articles warning of the severity of the energy crisis. I didn't imagine that it would be possible to go without electricity for three and a half days of the week. I didn't worry about living in darkness, because I was convinced the headlines had to be mistaken or that the news reports were a scheme intended to increase readership by alarming the public about an event that would never come to pass. I hadn't stopped to think that at least 60 percent of Ghanaians regularly lived without electricity. So I was unprepared when the middle classes were also plunged into darkness.

The rationing of electricity began at the end of January. A shortage of rainfall had lowered by half the water level of the Volta Lake and drastically reduced the hydroelectric power provided by the Akosombo Dam. Power was available only on a rotating schedule: twelve hours on and then twelve hours off. This soon increased to power on for twenty-four hours and off for twenty-four hours, but there were periods as long as thirty-six and forty-eight hours when there was no electricity. Since the water system employed an electric pump, no electricity meant there wasn't any running water. Nor could you predict when it would come back on. So at whatever hour the power was restored, whether it was eight p.m. or two a.m., you had to get moving. When the electricity returned I would often stay up all night writing on my computer or watching videos with my friend Anna and her daughters.

Osu was divided into zones of darkness and light. The clubs, restaurants, and elite residences owned private generators, but most of the neighborhood was dependent on the whims and calculations of the Volta River Authority. The glare of the brilliant main drag cast the rest of us into an even greater obscurity. Once you left Osu Road, the neighborhood was immersed in shadow and the streets were pitch-black. It was the kind of velvety black that was rare ever to see in cities, because artificial light robbed the sky of this jetty density.

Walking through the streets after eight p.m., I navigated with a flashlight. I wasn't afraid that I would be robbed or assaulted, as I would have been in New York or Oakland. Instead, I feared twisting my ankle in a pothole or stumbling into a sewage-filled ditch or being attacked by field rats. I was self-conscious about my flashlight and feared it was the equivalent of the pith helmet worn by colonial administrators. Illuminating the world seemed like an act of violence, when everyone else was willing to fare in darkness.

I lived in darkness, not the darkness of African inscrutability or the gloomy cast of a benighted landscape but rather in a blind alley of my own making, in the deep hole of my ignorance. And what is truth if not insight? In Western philosophy, knowledge has been conceived of primarily as an ocular function. To know is to see and to see is the inception of thought. The mind has been described as an inner eye and knowledge as a series of visual perceptions or pictures. Sight is the sense elevated above all others in apprehending the world. Not being able to see clearly is tantamount to ignorance, and since early modernity the ignorance of the West had been projected onto Africa—the heart of darkness, the dark continent, the blighted territory.

But I knew better. My flashlight was a defense not against dark, dark Africa but against my own compromised sight, my own thickheadedness. I had been in Ghana nearly half a year and I barely understood the world around me. All I had discovered was a series of empty rooms and abandoned warehouses. I had nothing to show for the time endured. I had collected no artifacts. I had found no stories.

Initially, I tried to beat back the darkness. But over the course of weeks, I began to experience a kind of relief when the lights went out, as if the world were meeting me on my own terms or pardoning me for my flawed perception. The darkness provided a welcome retreat from my failure and, to my surprise, the threshold to a world I had failed to notice.

The world I glimpsed at night was not one that I had encountered previously. It was a tenebrous realm, which, prior to the blackout, usually emerged around eleven p.m. or midnight and disappeared every morning by dawn, but now it flourished under the cover of twilight and crossed paths with my own. Midnight began at eight o'clock in the evening because the world had shut down earlier. Businesses had reduced hours and people retired shortly after dusk, often just to escape the boredom of having nothing to do. But I became a roving nocturnal creature, at first just to get away from the heat of my apartment, which without a fan was unbearable. In a month I had adjusted to a city without lights and I began prowling the neighborhood. As I made my way through streets, familiar and unknown, the people hidden from view and the things I had failed to notice now bumped into me in the night.

My light stabbed through the darkness and haphazardly entered intimate spaces, which were also public spaces since the poor commanded no place that was truly private. I stumbled upon an old man bathing himself in a plastic tub near the gutter of Lokko Road. His gangly limbs were sprawled over a large red container, so that the lower half of his body formed an inverted U. The white lather covering his dark skin was luminous in the small beam of light, but the foam didn't hide his nakedness. The flash of illumination froze him in time, as though he were a photograph of a moment that had already passed, rather than a flesh-and-blood man scrubbing himself before my eyes. I caught a pair of lovers holding hands as they crossed the lot of the soccer field and my wayward stream of light exposed their tryst. I spotted a night soil man surreptitiously carting away a pan of waste that he balanced on his head, and my gaze made him cringe. I saw ordinary flies darting above the sewers and in the artificial ray they appeared incandescent. I discovered that the seamstress, Sarah, who during the day was always busily at work on her foot-powered sewing machine, slept in her kiosk at night with her daughter. Others, never more than two or three, slumbered in the alley right outside the Kwatchie compound. In the dark, they crept up the lane and huddled against the compound's high walls, which were crowned with broken glass bottles to deter trespassers, and they slept on makeshift cardboard beds, no longer fearing being discovered or chased away. I watched little orbs of pulsating light from charcoal fires fade away against the black backdrop, as if they were dead stars emitting their last light. The women tending the flames were invisible.

In the deep hole of night lived all the people whom I passed by during the day but failed to see. They had not been tucked away in some remote corner of the city; they lived within arm's reach of me but at the periphery of my world and beyond my notice. The beggars, the poor, the ragtag street children, the whores down on their luck, the slum dwellers, the discharged small boys and small girls with no place to go, the refugees who had escaped camp, the soldiers for hire between assignments, the derelict and the drunk, the sleepwalkers, the toilers who tidied and swept the world for those who owned it, and the roaming and lost spirits who would never become anyone's ancestors—all resided in this nocturnal world.

Shortly after I had first arrived in Osu, Mary Ellen had encouraged me to walk through the neighborhood just before dawn to see how people really lived. "You don't have any idea," she said. "The First World and the Third World are reproduced in a one-mile square. Guess which world is bigger? The zone of privilege doesn't extend very far. Get out and see."

I promised her I would, but I had never gotten around to it. The blackout introduced me to the multitude outside the circle of light. They were the ones Nkrumah had wanted to lead to the New Jerusalem and catapult into a new era. But the dark days hadn't ended with the demise of colonialism. Nkrumah had hoped one generation was enough to jump-start development, eradicate backwardness, and deliver the masses from poverty. "What other countries have taken three hundred years or more to achieve," he said, "a once dependent territory must try to accomplish in a generation if it is to survive. Unless it is, as it were, 'jet-propelled,' it will lag behind and then risk everything for which it has fought." For Nkrumah, dispelling the shadows was the aim of progress. "Electricity in abundance" would flood the country with light and accelerate the nation into a new era.

In September 1965, when Nkrumah switched on the power at the Akosombo Dam, which had been his brainchild, he believed the nation had taken a giant leap forward on the road to development. A few months after unveiling the facility, he was overthrown by a military coup and his dreams for Ghana were swept away. The future envisioned by Nkrumah, in which each would give according to his ability and receive according to his needs, had been eclipsed.

Four decades after independence, most of Ghana was still in darkness. The "natives" were now citizens of a sovereign nation, with its own flag and national anthem, but they struggled against the same poverty and the same heavy darkness. I didn't know if they were resigned to it or if they longed for new eras as they readied for the night.

But the slumbering city was not placated; it was volatile. Who could predict when it might rouse, bolt, and hurtle us all into the future?

TEN

The Famished Road

THE LAND OF BARBARIANS was what southerners called it. Most of them had never been north of Kumasi, so a full day's journey from Accra to Salaga was unthinkable, but this didn't prevent them from sharing fanciful tales about air so thick with dust you could hardly breathe, or describing bare-breasted women with the kind of revulsion and fascination you would expect from an American provincial opening the pages of *National Geographic* for the first time, or mapping the north-south divide along the lines of brawn versus intelligence, or bemoaning a world without indoor toilets or electricity, or complaining of lazy and untrustworthy servants. Listening to them you would have imagined that northerners had stumbled out of their caves just yesterday and had yet to lose their scraggy feral manner. My landlady in Accra swore you could smell the stench of the untamed at the edge of the forest. Her daughter openly mocked primitives who had never set eyes on the sea, as if this alone were enough to damn them for eternity. The crudeness and poverty of northerners would send me running back to Accra, they warned. It was an inhospitable country. The north was the heartland of slavery.

◇ ◇ ◇

THE ROAD to Salaga was more an idea than an actual path. Craters threatened to swallow our mammoth van as we inched our way along. It was harmattan. Billowy gray clouds of sand from the Sahara extinguished the first light of daybreak and colored the world slate. The pall of dust hid everything more than a foot away: dwellings, people, the whole lot of it. The world receded from our gaze; everything was bleary and indistinct. A boy on a bike emerged from the swirl of dust and disappeared a moment later. Thatched dwellings bobbed in and out of sight, here one moment and gone the next, as if a trickster god alternately cast the world into light and shadow.

On this road, people had always arrived unawares and as swiftly disappeared. Slaves trekked on rutted pathways like this one en route from sacked villages surrounding the upper reaches of the Volta River, or from the barren stretches of land bordering Mossi country, to the string of markets extending from the north all the way to the coast. A woman named Thiamba had stumbled along this route before she arrived in Louisiana in the latter half of the eighteenth century, where she was renamed Ester and sold once again with a parcel of slaves in 1790, but this time with her four-year-old son Raphael and fourteen-month-old daughter Marguerite. All three of them estimated together were valued at 550 piastres. As she marched along, trying to avoid rocks and thorn covered bushes, had she expected the ship's hold or the master? Had she feared an existence as an object in an inventory of belongings? Had she anticipated the children born as slaves in a country she would have preferred never to see? It was unlikely that Thiamba ever forgot the road that led to the hell of St. Charles Parish.

SEVEN ROADS RADIATED from the hub of Salaga. Had you been traveling along this road in the eighteenth or nineteenth century, no doubt you would have seen a band of strangers, whose chains were the clear sign that they would never pass this way again, heading toward the market. A fleeting horseman with a young girl tied across the back of his steed reminded everyone they passed that life was at the mercy of men with guns and horses—*kambonga*. The hefty bags of cowries saddling the pack animals of mercenary soldiers sauntering home at dusk were the only remnant of the hamlet upon which they had descended, the houses they had burned, the men they had slaughtered, and the women and children they had sold at the market.

Caravans from Hausaland (Nigeria) and Mossi (Burkina Faso) approached from the north and the east with as many as four and five hundred slaves in tow. The slaves were exhausted from traveling hundreds of miles and hauling the goods, textiles, hides, copper, jewelry, and pots of shea butter that, like they themselves, were to be traded. They were filthy from trailing alongside cattle, oxen, sheep, and donkeys. When the caravans entered Salaga, the residents rushed toward the procession, greeting them with shouts and rejoicing.

The largest caravans contained between one and two thousand travelers. Armed men mounted on horses accompanied the leaders of the caravan at the head of the procession. A drummer directed the group, announcing rest stops and departures, and guiding the expedition. The livestock followed behind the advance party. Hundreds of donkeys were loaded with textiles, leather, and natron (an alkaline substance used as a medicine for stomach- and headaches, mixed with ash and palm oil to make soap, used in dying and tanning, and fed to livestock). Slaves, pawns, and apprentices guided the donkeys. The rich merchants and their families were mounted on horses and asses behind them. The commander of the caravan brought up the rear. The expedition was well armed to prevent attacks from bandits and hostile states. In the most dangerous stretches of the journey, women were dressed like men to exaggerate the appearance of able-bodied warriors. Those unable to keep up with the arduous trek, as well as the ailing and pregnant, were abandoned along the way.

Jihadists and soldiers of fortune drove throngs of stunned captives through the entrance of the market. Dagomba and Gonja raiders trotted in on horses with every single inhabitant of a newly desolate village in tow. On the road from Kafaba, Ashanti merchants advanced with a caravan of donkeys and head porters saddled with baskets of kola. An "assload" of kola was an official unit of measure, just as large amounts of currency were calibrated in units of slaves. On the road from Daboja, salt dealers ambled toward the bazaar. Petty traders approached from all directions carrying their produce on the backs of donkeys, mules, bullocks, and, sometimes, camels.

On these roads, men, women, and children stolen from their homes became commodities destined for the market. Men were bound with ropes and chains. Little children two years old and upward, and women, young and old, trailed along beside them. Most were prisoners of war or victims of raiding. Reeling along this gutted pathway, they began to anticipate what awaited them. The sinking feeling that they had seen their home for the last time and the fear that at the next town they would lose their son or sister made them drag their feet, search out an escape route through the grasslands, and with their eyes ask one another what they might do. What they knew was that one life had ended and the one they could foresee was terrifying. The first steps propelling them away from home had cut loose the familiar. Once inside the market at Salaga, it was clear: the old life was a pile of ruins.

The Salaga road, like the one immortalized by Ben Okri, was a famished road that devoured those who trod on it. The people walking along the road didn't suspect this; they thought it was a path like any other, until the road revealed its true nature and they discovered that it was the kind of road that didn't lead you anywhere—this was the end of you. It was a road of torment and devastation, a road of insatiable and cruel appetites, a road where you lost everything, and remade yourself from the wreckage.

SALAGA WAS the grand emporium of the kingdom of Gonja and the crossroads of a traffic in slaves, which traversed the Sahara and extended as far south as the Atlantic coast. The trans-Saharan, transatlantic, and African trade all fed upon the northern territories of Ghana. Salaga was perched above the Volta River in a broad belt of grassland that stretched across West Africa. To the north of Salaga was the Sahel and to the south was the forest.

The famed warriors of Gonja began raiding for slaves from the moment the state was founded in the seventeenth century. It was not by chance that the emblem of Gonja was a hand clenching a spear. The cavalrymen of the warrior state swept through the savanna capturing those they deemed prey. The raiding expeditions were bountiful and the captives sold at local markets were many.

At its peak in the nineteenth century, Salaga was a bustling metropolis of forty to fifty thousand people. There were four mosques in the town. At least a thousand dwellings, each one consisting of ten to twenty small conical buildings and enclosed within a circular wall that divided one compound from the next, covered the grassy plain of the valley and spread over one or two miles. Slaves were posted at the entrance of the outermost buildings facing the street. The royal farms, which were on the outskirts of town and extended for miles, were cultivated entirely by slave labor.

Nearly all of the male residents were literate and read and wrote in Arabic. The Salaga people, most of whom were landlords and brokers in the slave trade, were most often described by nineteenth-century travelers as intelligent, diligent, industrious, and cruel. All the rich and important people owned horses, and when riding they were accompanied by footmen and attendants. Horse races took place on Friday afternoons at an open-air track. The town's inhabitants dressed in finery, the women wore silk wrappers and heavily embroidered Hausa gowns and lovely

head ties and bangles of gold and ivory, and the men were outfitted with silk caps and turbans, voluminous trousers, smocks and Arab robes, and finely tooled leather slippers and sandals; even the horses were decorated for the entertainment. After the races, the jockeys would amuse the crowds by making their horses canter to the tune of trumpets. The good life sprang from a thriving market.

The Salaga marketplace was legendary; it was called the Timbuktu of the south. Slaves and kola were the prized commodities in the market. *"Zaa ni gun ja goro"*: I am going to the place of the red kola nuts, said Hausa merchants en route to Salaga. Each year, an estimated 15,000 to 20,000 slaves and 150,000 to 300,000 pounds of kola were sold to merchants from as far away as Timbuktu and the Niger bend. Both the demand for kola and the growing number of slaves sold at the marketplace were a consequence of the Islamic reform movement that swept through the savanna at the beginning of the nineteenth century.

Kola was the only stimulant permitted by Islam and it replaced alcohol among reformed Muslims and new converts. The devout treasured it because kola liberated the spirit from the cravings of the physical body. The nut sustained the body in the absence of food and water, reduced fatigue, cured headaches and sexual impotence, and improved the taste of brackish water.

The spread of Islam also expanded the slaving frontier. "Infidels" and "nonbelievers" who resisted the call to conversion were captured and sold. That the appetites of nobles and merchants for rum, brandy, and tobacco stoked the transatlantic slave trade is, by now, common knowledge. More surprising, perhaps, is the fact that devotion to Allah and the renunciation of appetites also contributed to the development of one of the most famous slave markets in the savanna.

SALAGA HOUSED the largest slave market in Ghana and trafficked in slaves from the beginning of the nineteenth century to its end. Near the entrance of the market, rows of beggars lined up along the street and with extended palms pleaded for assistance. They thanked the generous with the stock phrase: "May Muhammad reward you with much riches, slaves, and many kola nuts." Each day upward of ten thousand people entered the market. A dazzling variety of goods was on display in the stalls: piles of kola nuts, balls of shea butter, lumps of natron the size of duck eggs, stacks of animal hides, small mountains of gold dust, finely crafted bags and saddles and footwear, leathers tanned red, blue, and yellow, pelt rugs, shawls and girdles of silk from Timbuktu, heaps of woolen and silk and cotton textiles, pyramids of blue and green glass containers, neat rows of sweet and pungent spices, tobacco in balls and plaited leaf, bowls of henna, glistening copper pots, earthenware jars filled with perfume and sweet oils, ostrich feathers, ivory tusks, Arabian horses, braying asses, and bleating sheep. The aisles of the bazaar were filled with people speaking nearly all the languages of Africa. All kinds of currency—gold dust, silver, coins from all of Europe from the British shilling to the Prussian thaler, and cowries—changed hands. The music of the drummers and the poems and songs of minstrels entranced buyers. The distracted and weary lingered at the barbers' booths listening to the tales being swapped. The carpenters' workshops and ironsmiths created a din in the market. Small crowds gathered to watch the blind basket and mat weavers. The scent of myrrh and frankincense, the reek of freshly slaughtered oxen, and the stench of offal wafted through the air.

AND THEN THERE WERE the slaves. Small groups of slaves bound to one another with ropes and iron shackles attached to their legs or cords fastening their wrists to their throats could be found scattered throughout the market. Bodies were washed and oiled for display. Medicines were dispensed to shrink the appetite and herbs were utilized to enhance appearance and perk up a sad lot. According to one trader, "Every slave had a cut in the tongue and medicine was put in it so that it healed quickly; then the slave ate little and still stayed of good appearance." The healthiest and the most attractive were grabbed quickly. Others lingered in the market for months because they were in poor condition or a missing ear had raised doubts about their character and steered buyers away, and others, considered defective, the sickly and the disabled, were sold for rock-bottom prices—a few thousand cowries or a secondhand robe—or were left behind when the traders returned home.

Acts of sale all took on the same trappings. Potential buyers appraised the fettered bodies looking for hardy slaves suited for agricultural labor on the farms of Salaga, gold panning and kola production in Asante, and palm oil processing in Krobo and Akuapem; or polite and refined persons suited to attend to the needs of the household; or young pretty women to be taken as concubines and wives; or the average and the unexceptional to be used as head porters or hammock carriers on the return journey. Then the slaves too would play their part. They would step forward or turn or bow or speak as the buyer demanded. Cowries would change hands, or if the buyer was also a trader, he might exchange his goods for the price of the slave. And the man or woman purchased would leave behind the rest of the lot and follow after his or her new master.

In the journal he kept during his three-week stay in Salaga in March 1877, the Reverend Theophil Opoku, an African pastor with the Basel Missionary, described the great number of slaves who passed through the market:

> Among the numerous articles of trade, unfortunately human wares ever and anon play the main part. On 14 March, for example a caravan led by Mossi and Hausa traders arrived with some 400 slaves, as well as horses, asses, oxen, cows and many others. On March 19 I saw another troop of Hausa and Mossi people with many slaves, cattle and shea butter. The slaves, 350 to 400 in number were mostly young people, boys and girls, and people of middle age. They were all sold in a few days . . . These pitiful people are chained together in groups of ten to fifteen, by the neck, and exposed the whole day from morning to evening in the piercing sun, hungry and thirsty, naked and ailing, often sick and deadly weak, standing there till one after another is sold. And how hunger plagues them. A lad of gruel is their entire nourishment, morning and evening. If you stand in front of them and they catch sight of you, they look at you imploringly and make signs of their longing for you to buy them . . . Mothers show their empty breasts and their small hungry chil-

dren. And how fortunate they feel when they are bought together with their children by the same master. For it frequently happens that young children are taken from their mothers and fall in the hand of different buyers.

By the time Opoku left Salaga, he had seen emaciated old slaves sold for a trifle, others scarred from being lashed by the whip or toothless from blows to the face, and sickly slaves abandoned in the market and left to die.

Each year tens of thousands of slaves exchanged hands in Salaga. After the official abolition of the Atlantic slave trade in 1807, the volume of slave trading increased. Extensive smuggling continued well into the 1840s and not until the 1850s did the abolition of the overseas trade become decisive. In 1860, the last group of African captives arrived in the United States aboard the slave ship *Clotilde*. As late as 1881, a slave ship from the port of Bahia, *The Spade*, was reported near the mouth of the Volta River. More than three million slaves were shipped from Africa to the Americas in the nineteenth century. On average, at least a third of a million people were deported each decade.

After the Atlantic outlets disappeared, the pillage of slave trading continued. The prices of slaves decreased, enabling people other than royals and merchants to purchase them. The internal trade persisted until the end of the nineteenth century. As late as 1899, Hausa merchants conducted slaves along hidden paths from Salaga to the coast. The greater demand for slaves increased the numbers of captives hauled to the market and widened the expanse of conquered and depopulated territory in the savanna.

IN THE CENTRAL SQUARE of Salaga, we piled out of the van. Ours was a small group. Yaya, Lawrence, and I lived in the same apartment complex in Osu. Ayanna, Lawrence's fiancée, was visiting from the States. Yaya and Lawrence were junior Fulbrighters who were headed to Columbia University in the fall for graduate degrees in international relations. They were both working on development projects, but, like most African Americans, they were very interested in the history of slavery.

One evening at dinner I had shared with them my plans to travel north to the site of the largest slave market in Ghana. They were shocked to learn that the domestic trade in slaves had continued until the end of the nineteenth century, decades after the transatlantic slave trade had been abolished. Their mouths fell open in disbelief when I explained that there were more slaves in Africa in the nineteenth century than in the Americas and that slaves and the descendants of slaves comprised anywhere from one-half to three-quarters of the total population of West Africa. When I invited them to join me on the trip, they eagerly accepted.

Orbiting the square, all I saw was a sleepy dusty town, not unlike the old mill or mining towns one passes through in West Virginia or California, so on first glance Salaga seemed vaguely familiar, as if I had been there before, but the first visit left no lasting impression. In such places the signs of inevitable decline and diminished prospects are more readily discernible than the former glory. This was true of Salaga. There were no fine dwellings in sprawling compounds, or sumptuously clad residents, or any recognizable features of a once vibrant metropolis. The town consisted of mud-walled dwellings with thatched roofs, and if they were once beautiful it was no longer possible to see. A battered old wooden building, which looked like it was about to tumble, squatted at the far end of the plaza.

Everything was as it had been. Nothing was as it had been. The earmarks of the distinctly contemporary were readily visible in the landscape, the recycled car parts housed in a makeshift shelter, the sputter and clack of a motorbike speeding up the road, and denim-clad youth with faux American university T-shirts. They were the overlay of the present on the past. As were we—the only strangers in the square.

An elderly man approached and introduced himself to what was clearly a group of stray travelers. He was stout and well dressed, wearing the classic indigo and white striped smock typical to the north, khaki trousers, and polished loafers. With the formality that was customary when addressing strangers, he stated his name and profession. Haruna had lived in Salaga all of his life. He was a retired schoolteacher. After welcoming us, he asked why we had come to Salaga. When I uttered the words "slave trade," the schoolteacher interrupted me in midsentence and reeled off the names Gasare and Babatu and Samori. "They were the ones responsible," he said, nodding his head.

Gasare and Babatu entered northern Ghana in the 1870s as mercenaries for hire, and as soon as their stint was completed, they began pillaging towns and villages and selling the conquered in the Salaga marketplace. The anticolonial fighter Samori Touré swept through the upper regions of Ghana kidnapping conscripts to replenish his anticolonial army and selling them cheaply to fund his war, feed the troops, and purchase arms to battle the French. These late-nineteenth-century slave raiders were the ones who came most immediately to mind when you asked anyone in the north about the slave trade.

"What happened to the ones sold here?" I asked. "Where did they go?"

"The white man shipped them across the waters," he said. "The Dutch and the Portuguese came into the hinterland and seduced people with their merchandise. They were the landlords and the slave traders." Together we retraced the history.

"The Europeans started this trade in people," the teacher explained.

"But who sold the ones here?" I asked.

"We were the middlemen, but others introduced us to the trade," he said defensively.

"But it wasn't until 1876 that the first European claimed to have reached Salaga," I replied. "The captives passed through the hands of African traders before they arrived on the coast."

"The white men lied about what happened."

"Didn't Africans control this leg of the trade?"

"Those who sold slaves no longer lived in Salaga," the teacher insisted. "The Salaga people involved in the trade were landlords. They were go-betweens." Not exclusively. The Gonja state was predatory and raided the less powerful and decentralized societies of the savanna.

"The human trade has stopped. Those who sold slaves are dead or have gone away. The people in Salaga, those who remain here, are the descendants of slaves." The teacher separated the innocent from the guilty, but I was curious about the ones gone.

"The Gonjas too were sold," continued the teacher. "Asante raided the Gonjas and captured entire villages." Gonja was also under the thumb of Asante, the powerful empire to the south. Each year the Gonjas were required to hand over one thousand slaves as tribute to Asante. When the British defeated the famed Asante empire, no less with the sons of slaves, the paramount chief of Gonja welcomed the British with songs of praise: "You, the white man, come from a great nation which has freed us from our enemies. Every year we had to send one thousand of our brothers to the Kumasi knife, and to the Kumasi king all our money without complaint."

It was a complex history. Even the small communities ravaged by the trade on occasion captured others rather than hand over their own members as tribute to predatory states and freebooters or sold captives to purchase the guns and powder necessary to battle raiders and mercenaries. The peoples raided had to resort to the tactics of their enemies in order to survive. The slave trade created a state of emergency in which firearms were essential for defense and wars of capture extended over more and more territory.

"We suffered too," the teacher reminded me. "The big market was called *ubancaswah*, which means 'we captured our own people.'" He sounded like Aeschylus: A kingdom *laid upon its house a treacherous destruction*. It was a house divided against itself and eventually it fell.

It was a lovely tale of who "we" never were. No chain of common ancestors supported the Gonja and the peoples they raided. Violence was the sole link between them. The teacher knew this as well as I did.

The Gonjas or *ngbanya* were the ruling class. They conquered the area and subjugated the original inhabitants, who first became their slaves and then their subjects or who fled to other parts of the savanna. The Gonja called these people *nyemase*, which means "he has it but won't give it away unless he is forced to do so." Need anymore be said?

The Gonjas also enslaved *grunshi*, which was a pejorative term equivalent to pagan, primitive, or barbarian. Like *nyemase*, *grunsi*, or *grunshi*, was a ragtag name for the "stateless" people living on both sides of the Ghana and Burkina Faso border and to the north and west of Gonja. *Grunshi* was a name synonymous with defeat. Most of the slaves sold in the marketplace were *grunshi*. They came from small-scale, non-Islamic, agricultural societies without chiefs. Aristocratic warrior states viewed them as inferior, savage, and weak. African royals and elites, like their European counterparts, envisioned the stateless and the sovereignless as suited for slavery. Vassals, subjects, and commodities were what they were made for in the eyes of the Gonja.

"It is hard to speak of these things," the teacher admitted wearily. "Africans prefer to forget slavery. If we tell the story, we weep."

In wrestling with the past, he and I redrew the lines of blame and responsibility. Where I saw a raiding empire fattened by the slave trade, the teacher saw his own people suffering. He was convinced that the slave trade had been responsible for Salaga's decline.

"No one wanted to come here because of the slave trade. Trade in other areas never developed because of it," he complained. His ire was directed at Asante, the coastal middlemen, and European merchants. Mine was floating and amorphous.

What we chose to disclose and what we withheld was determined as much by who we were—strangers meeting in a square—as by who we feigned to be—a singular we. The story that unfolded was less about what happened then than it was a way of navigating our present. Telling it over and over again, we hoped to discover a way of changing our lives. If history attended to the dead as "a way of establishing a place for the living," then what the teacher and I were reaching toward was a world in which we might thrive.

PLUNDERING KINGS AND WARRIOR STATES had not ceased to be victorious, at least not in memory. The history that lived on in Salaga mostly recounted the glories of the slave trading past and, in so doing, defeated the enslaved yet again. The drum histories, founding myths, and Arabic texts about Gonja's past concerned themselves with Ndewura Jakpa, the founder of the state, and with the activities of rulers, the *ngbanya*. Slaves have no place in the myth of empires. There were no drum histories of the captives. When they appeared in the historical record, they were booty—the spoils of war. Even today the perspective of the rulers still governed what could be said about the past.

I had read an oral history of Gonja in which the *ngbanya* recollected their former splendor. I plowed through story after story about warriors plundering their stateless neighbors, tales of a fierce cavalry empire that spared no one, not even children, recitations of the great wealth accumulated through slave raiding, and boasts about the prowess and dominance of Gonja.

The conquerors never failed to broadcast their achievements, and virtually every royal repeated a story of a golden age when cowries were plentiful. I could recite the words of the *ngbanya* with my eyes closed:

We used to raid slaves in the thousands and exchange them with guns and alcoholic drinks.

If a chief needed slaves he mobilized his army and they attacked a village. If they succeeded they came back with the slaves if they failed they themselves might be sold into slavery.

Before the actual raid, they came together, armed themselves and attacked a village, if they defeated the inhabitants they took everybody away leaving the old men and women . . . Some people married the beautiful slave women.

When hard times arrived, we went to war. When poverty caught [us, we] went with war.

Exhilarated by the glories of the past, the royals spared no details, reveling in the fine points of pillage and plunder. The elders spoke wistfully about a time when Gonja was powerful and prosperous. As one man said, "It is today that the Gonjas are working, [then] they were fighting." The cowries realized from the sales of slaves were so great according to one chief, that "they could not be carried back home, the money was therefore used for buying guns and gunpowder, drinks [alcohol] and return home."

The Gonjas considered raiding dishonorable only when the *ngbanya* were its victims. When sharing tales of battling with Samori and Babatu, all insisted that no Gonjas had been taken as slaves. As the paramount chief recalled, "It was only Samori who attempted, but he did not take away a single Gonja soul. All he succeeded in doing was burning villages and slaughtering people." For warriors, death was preferable to the dishonor of slavery, which was a state suitable only to their inferiors.

When the white man came, their prosperity ended. "The white man said nobody should sell a slave again, so the money we made by selling slaves stopped coming and we became poor."

I haven't yet been able to get these voices out of my head. And there is no path from the "sumptuous memories of plundering kings" and elites to the lives of the enslaved. History is a battle royal, a contest between the powerful and the powerless in "what happened" as well as in the stories we tell about what has happened—a fight to the death over the meaning of the past. The narrative of the defeated never triumphs; like them, it ekes out an existence in the shadow of the victors. But must the story of the defeated always be a story of defeat? Is it too late to imagine that their lives might be redeemed or to fashion an antidote to oblivion? Is it too late to believe their struggles cast a shadow into a future in which they might finally win?

THE PALACE OF the Salagawura, the chief of Salaga, was only a few hundred feet away from the central square. "Palace" was too grand a word to describe the modest concrete dwellings that comprised the large compound. Upon entering the anteroom of the Salagawura's dwelling, we were assigned seats on a bench opposite Chief Suleiman. He was seated on a throne of animal skins and surrounded by several men of his inner circle. The Salagawura welcomed us to Salaga and invited us to think of it as our home. "You must come again many times."

The linguist Muhammed Issah translated for the chief, as was dictated by protocol. But it had the odd effect of separating the chief from his words, as if he were a puppet and the linguist the true speaker. It also exaggerated the gulf between the chief and us as it was intended to do.

We nodded in mock agreement on hearing these words of welcome and mumbled thank you, uncertain whether to address our words to the linguist or the chief. Ignorance made us awkward. We had come bearing gifts, but they were the wrong ones. In the south, one offered schnapps to the chief; but this was not the custom in the north. They were polite and didn't say anything, so we didn't find out until later.

I was tongue-tied and smiled blankly, not knowing how to proceed. Should we say something first or wait for them to speak? Luckily, the linguist asked, "What is the purpose of your visit?"

I paused, searching for words and suddenly self-conscious about the reason we were here. Yaya and Lawrence looked toward me, since I was the one who had organized the trip. I was the one working on slavery. My voice wavered as I answered, "We have come to Salaga because of its importance in the slave trade."

"Many, like you, have visited Salaga for this reason." Chief Suleiman's words skirted the awkwardness of the matter as he continued, "Some people, like you, came ten years ago, they asked us about slavery, we told them, and they cried." To him, slavery was not the territory we shared but the story that could make someone like me weep.

"What about the slaves of Salaga? Are there people in town who are the descendants of slaves?"

The chief visibly stiffened upon hearing my question. He spoke with pursed lips and Muhammad translated. "It is still difficult for us to speak of slavery. One cannot point a finger and say he or she is a slave. It is prohibited to do so."

The taboo on revealing someone's origins extended back to the seventeenth century. Ndewura Jakpa forbade people to refer to their own or anyone else's origins. It was said that tracing genealogy destroyed a state. Those who defied the law risked the punishment of death. Everyone who had ever mentioned the law to me had explained that it was intended to protect those of slave origin. In practice it prevented the enslaved from speaking of a life before servitude and it abolished their ancestry. The slave existed in the world, but without either a history or an inheritance. Robbed of their kin and denied their lineage, slaves were a tabula rasa. It was as if they had just appeared in the world without ever having been born, without ever having known a mother or father. Like Topsy, in *Un-*

cle Tom's Cabin, who, when asked about the parents she had never known, replied, "I jes grew."

"Why shame someone and say he or she is a slave?" the chief added. I wondered if the chief was shocked that I had been so tactless. "Those who were slaves have married and become incorporated into Salaga."

The Salagawura says one thing, but I hear another: "We still know who they are."

My friend Gyeman told me that he could tell who was of slave origin in his village because on the whole they were more attractive than everyone else. As a child his understanding of slavery was limited to pretty girls purchased as "wives." Most of those sold in the internal trade were women and children. But neither beauty nor affection mitigated the relations of power and dependence. It was not uncommon, a Gonja elder recalled, for an owner to trade a slave woman simply because he preferred another. "If you had your woman, you could say to someone else, 'Give her to me and I will give you mine,' then you exchanged."

The children born to a slave wife shared the mother's disinheritance and belonged entirely to the genealogy of the father. It was said that only the penis touched the child of a slave woman, since the mother passed no birthright that she could transfer to her child. Slave women extended the owner's lineage without enjoying the privileges or protection entitled to wives supported by their families. Inequality suffused the idiom of kinship. Nor did families ever forget who was "of the house" (the slaves absorbed and remade in the line of the master) and "of the blood" (royals possessing legal rights of inheritance and succession). Slaves were the ghosts in the machine of kinship.

There were no women in the chief's inner circle whom I might ask about the rewards of being pretty or about the trials of being a wife. The men had appointed themselves the official custodians of history. Besides, the women never had an afternoon to waste ruminating about history. They didn't have an hour to spare; they were selling goods in the market or laboring in the fields or carrying pails of water or hauling a load of firewood or washing laundry, the very chores that made the labor of slave women so highly prized. Who could stop to talk when there were children to be tended, food to be cooked, rooms to be swept, and a husband to be maintained? When later I asked the women in town about slavery, they joked, "The wife is the true slave."

"IF EVERYONE KNOWS who is a slave, then why not discuss it?" I badgered the chief. I wondered if in pointing a finger at the slave the trader was exposed too. And what about the raider? Who benefited from avoiding the past? Silence didn't protect and it never had. All that it offered was a tentative belonging in the master's house.

"It is the law," the chief replied. "You cannot point to someone and say he is a slave."

"But doesn't everyone know anyway?"

If the chief found my questions impertinent, he did not let on. We were at cross-purposes. The very thing I wanted to know, he was duty bound not to tell. It was a mistake coming to the palace, but etiquette dictated that when a stranger arrived in a town or village, she must first introduce herself to the chief or headman. It reproduced the very hierarchy I wanted to tumble. I knew the elites couldn't speak for slaves.

We went on talking about it at considerable length, not really confronting the heated issues as much as circling around them. Raging questions stormed in my head, but the ones I shared issued from some reasonable and polite person, not at all like me. I was even-keeled. For each word spoken, there were one hundred others stuck in the back of my throat. My smile was studied; my deference was a lie. I was as slippery as the chief.

All of the indirection and polite back-and-forth, the chief's refusal to show his hand and my attempts to best the chief by sheer doggedness were part of the contest being waged over the past. We were careful to steer clear of open expressions of animosity and outright declarations of war. I realized I should stop hammering the chief with questions, but I couldn't rein myself in. I thought he must be a kind man or a desperate one to indulge me like this. It was a cliché any way you looked at it: the ugly American making demands or the slave baby pleading for recognition. But my awareness of the script in which we were cast didn't make the slightest bit of difference. We played it out until its end.

Was Gonja ashamed of its past? It was the question I didn't dare ask. The Salagawura had spoken only of the dishonor attached to slave status. And what of the traders and raiders? Didn't the victors ever feel ashamed? Or was shame the kind of feeling reserved only for the powerless and the defeated? There was no answer to this kind of question. If the chief had answered, "Yes, we are ashamed of our past," of what use would it have been? And if he had denied it and said, "No, we are proud of our state," I would have been offended. It was the kind of rhetorical question that one raised not to get an answer but to communicate indirectly to the person who is not ashamed that he should be. Broaching it as a question softened the blow.

It was not easy to own the past, especially in a place like Gonja where the victories and conquests of previous eras hadn't amounted to much and the prestige of the *ngbanya* has eroded over time. Unlike the case of Europe and the Americas, where the profits gained from slave trading and slave labor fueled the Industrial Revolution, expanded the shipping and insurance industries, founded banking institutions, increased national treasuries, and provided the foundation for even greater economic development, in Gonja the boons of slave trading were short-lived.

"YOU CANNOT COME to Salaga for a few hours and hope to know the whole story. You must spend time here," the chief said. "After spending time, maybe people will be willing to talk."

I suspected the chief was trying to bring our visit to a close. We had been inside the palace for at least two hours. I imagined he found the conversation tiresome and I wondered how many times he had gone through this ritual. I decided to ask him. "How do you feel about people like me coming here to talk about slavery? Do you welcome it or feel it as an imposition?"

"We welcome it," he said enthusiastically. "We want more people to come. All the tourists go to Cape Coast and Elmina Castle, when they should be coming to Salaga because the trade was centered here." He was candid, even perky, about Salaga's role in the slave trade when considering the prospects of tourism. African-American visitors would mean dollars flowing into the town, which, given the impoverishment of Salaga, was no small thing. In another ten years, tourism would be Ghana's number one industry.

Turning the tables, the chief asked us, "Do you talk about slavery in your country? Over there do people know who the slaves are?" The question took us by surprise and we looked at one another, searching for the words to respond.

"Only the blacks were slaves," Yaya responded. "If you are black and in America, people know that you came to the country as a slave." It was more complex than this, but it was difficult to explain what the arrival of four Africans in Jamestown set in motion, what the Thirteenth Amendment hadn't finished, and what time hadn't healed. How could you explain that four hundred years in a place didn't make it home? All of us tried and failed. We talked about chattel slavery, a century of Jim Crow, the million plus black prisoners, poverty, death row, but it seemed abstract and disjointed. The lives connected with these words were hard to see. They were as elusive as the ones tied in the square. What could they bring to mind for the chief?

He listened intently as we stumbled along trying to describe the world from which we had come. "Things over there were terrible," the chief replied. America was less dangerous territory for him than the marketplace in Salaga. The evils of chattel slavery and Jim Crow and neosegregation had no social repercussions here. What happened in Ghana was terrible too, but the chief refused to discuss the ugly history that had unfolded a few yards away in the square.

In West Africa, the Atlantic slave trade intensified inequality and fueled war. Public roads were unsafe. Commoners became impoverished and endangered. The merchant princes and traders became fat. The wealth accumulated by wars and plunder and theft created aristocratic and merchant societies in which the economy was divided between subsistence and luxury. The predatory state fed upon the communities within its reach, and then the British, French, and Germans took over, carved up the territory, and made themselves the new masters. Being a "native" wasn't all that different from being a Negro. This was the terrible history with which the chief was already familiar. Ours was the mystery.

"What is it you want from Ghana?" he asked us. Again, we were at a loss for words. After six months in Ghana I was no better able to explain it. Whenever I tried, I saw the puzzlement on the face of whomever I was speaking to and I would falter trying to convince them of what I took for granted. I could tell from the way he looked at us that the chief too wanted to know why we acted as if our lives depended on what he had to tell us.

We cobbled together an answer. Not an argument, just sentences piled on top of one another, Yaya's response interrupting mine and me adding something to what Lawrence and Ayanna said. In the States, nearly every day you are reminded of your losses. You keep waiting for it to get better, but then you see another picture of a dead boy in the newspaper or someone else has gone missing for fifteen to life and you get really tired. You're tired of being a problem; you're tired of loving a country that doesn't love you or hating the place you call home. It's the kind of weariness old folks say you can feel in your bones.

We didn't mention the hardest things. No one said what it has done to us or disclosed the terrible things we do to one another. It would be difficult to explain gangbangers, drive-by shootings, homicide tolls, and missing fathers. Nor did we share the best things, like the way a song born in the cotton and cane fields became something wondrous on the lips of a trumpet player in New Orleans, or something able to cut your heart in two even when the words were as silly as what a little moonlight can do, or a rant about a distant lover, or a chant to bring Babylon down in the mouth of a trench town boy; or the raw-edged beauty that grew between the cracks of everything that was wrong in the urban gulag; or the miracle that we were still here.

We didn't really have an answer to the chief's question. Yaya had begun to explain, "It's not like we're looking for a particular place or person when we come here, but it's just the feeling that something is missing back home. So we come here."

"Do you find it here?" the chief asked.

"No" was on our lips, but none of us said it.

Had we possessed the words, we might have said that it was not as if we expected to find something that could make history hurt less or fill the hole inside of us, because it was not the kind of hole that could be filled and then would go away. Coming here was simply a way to acknowledge it. There was no turning back the clock. But it didn't feel like it was moving forward, either.

As we were about to depart, the Salagawura gave each of us a handful of cowries so that we would remember Salaga. "No one ever leaves my home," he said. By which he meant that we must return; we couldn't come, take what we wanted, and then leave. But this was precisely what we would do. "Salaga is your home. Come and build a house here. We welcome it."

I had been waiting a long time to be embraced, so more surprising than the chief's invitation was how little comfort it brought. If secretly I had been hoping that there was some cure to feeling extraneous in the world, then at that moment I knew there wasn't a remedy for my homelessness. I was an orphan and the breach between me and my origins was irreparable. Being a stranger was an inveterate condition that a journey across the Atlantic could not cure. I could never make Salaga my home.

Nor did the irony of the offer escape me. How could I put down roots in a slave market, which was what Salaga would always be in my eyes? I would never be able to think of the place in any other way. I would always be haunted by the lives exchanged in the square. I would always stick out as the kind of person easily identified as having slave origins. So I would be a stranger here too. At last someone was saying, "There is a place for you here," and it sent me running in the opposite direction. But I was not seeking a proxy for a relationship severed centuries ago. Fictive kinship was too close to the heart of slavery's violence for my comfort. Perhaps this was the bastard's view, disloyal to both blood and house.

"We have never shown these sites to anyone," Muhammed said, as we made our way across the central square. I knew it was a lie, because they had shown these exact sites to my friend Mary when she was doing research several years earlier, but it didn't bother me. It was the kind of lie lovers told one another, less to deceive than to create the feeling of something unique and exclusive. Because we all knew that walking through Salaga was neither special nor exclusive and that they had trod this path many times before, the linguist invented something better than the truth. "For your eyes only" was what he promised as he lifted the veil from the past. Besides the linguist, two other men from the chief's inner circle decided to accompany us on a tour of the town's slave sites, which for the most part were hardly noteworthy.

"The tree was over there," said Muhammed, pointing toward an empty spot in the distance. "It occupied the center of the market. The slaves would gather around it waiting for sale. It fell in 1973. A new tree will be planted to replace the old one since so many people visiting Salaga ask for the tree." We looked in the direction indicated by his arm and tried to envision the huge baobab tree, where private traders assembled the slaves for sale and where the paramount chief of Gonja corralled the tribute slaves to be offered to the Asantehene.

"Only the difficult ones were held in chains," Muhammed reassured us. Baba and Idaissu exchanged quick glances and smiled nervously. They seemed uncomfortable with this careless remark about such a sensitive matter. Perhaps they feared we would be offended by talk of recalcitrant slaves.

Jitneys crossed the plaza scurrying passengers to and fro in the business of the day. A few pressed their faces closer to the glass to get a better look at us. I stared back until the bus sped past, making a blur of the tan, brown, and black faces. We walked to the far end of the square to inspect what we were told had been a holding pen for slaves. I went in and took a few pictures. There was nothing to record, but I kept shooting, as if the empty space would become something significant by being pressed onto film. My imagination captured no more than the camera. A year later I would look at these photographs and struggle to make out the contents. And when I showed the muddy images to friends, no one was able to discern what they were looking at. When I explained it was a slave pen, they said, "Oh," and passed on to the next photograph. But I could not bring myself to discard them. I would put one of the images on my desk alongside the cowries from the Salagawura and next to a small blue vial that contained Langston Hughes's ashes, as if that were enough to transform a photo of an empty shack into a memento mori.

Ruins were the only monuments to slavery in Salaga. Mounds of dirt, uprooted trees, brackish sinkholes, and decayed structures. This landscape in ruins seemed an appropriate reminder of the destruction produced by slavery, more so than a gleaming white fortress. And, as well, it was a statement about the impoverishment of the present. Our path zigzagged through small clusters of homes. The signs of affluence— enclosed compounds, corrugated tin roofs, cylinder block or concrete houses, bicycles—were rare. We passed two women pounding cassava and they looked at us shyly, smiled, and then returned to work. The pupils at an open-air school rushed out to greet the strangers. We introduced ourselves to the teacher and the students gawked, whispered, and giggled as the adults talked. The teacher, Bismarck, who was one of the sons of the paramount chief of Pembe, informed us that the students were without pencils and paper and three students were required to share the same slate chalkboard. He instructed a mixed-grade classroom of more than forty students. We promised to send them pencils and pads when we returned to Accra.

Baba, who was also a teacher, shared with us Salaga's hardships as we made our way to the slave wells. There was a dire shortage of teachers and school supplies. Many children were unable to attend school because the fees were greater than their family could afford and their labor was essential to the family's survival. In years past not one student from the north qualified for entry to the University of Ghana at Legon. The town was in desperate need of medical services. The nearest clinic was in Tamale, and irregular hours, costly fees, and the difficulty of transportation severely limited its usefulness. A sole Cuban doctor serviced an area of thousands.

Muhammad gestured toward the eroded holes sunk into the ground. The slave wells looked like blisters that had erupted in the soil. "Water for the slaves was collected here and carried back to the square," he explained. The town's residents still used them. The wells were polluted, but there was no supply of freshwater. People were forced to drink the brackish water from these wells or the water the women hauled in buckets from infested ponds nearby. The government promised to assist them in creating freshwater facilities; however, they had to raise the equivalent of twenty thousand U.S. dollars to begin the project. In a country where the average wage was less than two hundred dollars per year and most people survived by subsistence agriculture and petty trading, this was virtually impossible.

Water had always been a problem in Salaga, even when the town was thriving. European travelers complained that Salaga was "a most miserable town, where even water is very scarce and can only be purchased at an exorbitant price, the merchants always manage to make their stay here as short as possible." The slaves in the market bore the brunt of this scarcity. They often suffered from dehydration. As one visitor to the market observed, "In harmattan time drinking water is brought to Salaga from far away, and sold there, it is understandable that the slaves who are set out without shelter in the burning sun, get little of it." A century later, water was just as valuable and as scarce.

We contributed $225 to the water project. Touring the village, we made a thousand promises, heady from being embraced and overwhelmed with all that was expected of us. Like the other Americans who had visited Salaga before us, we would leave a trail of broken promises in our wake. The few we were able to make good on, the few within our means—pencils and pads and a few hundred dollars—were not capable of changing anything.

On the way to Wankan-Baye, the stream where the slaves were bathed before sale and some say cleansed of their memories of the past, Idaissu whispered to me that his grandfather had been a slave. When Idaissu was a schoolboy, his father told him that his grandfather had been carried away from the Niger bend when he was a child and sold as a slave. As his father began recounting the story, Idaissu shook his head sadly and his eyes filled with tears. When his father noticed the tears, he reprimanded his son, "Is your grandfather's suffering too much for you to hear?"

As a boy, Idaissu had been ashamed that his grandfather was a slave. His father had been right; the tears were as much for himself as for his grandfather. Many of the children and grandchildren of slaves felt this way, especially the children of slave women who were identifiable as foreigners by tattoos and facial markings. If the marks were there, as the grandson of a slave recalled, "there was nothing to clean them. The children they felt ashamed because their mother had slave marks. They did not want her to come out much. And they kept her in the house, in the room when she was an old woman." The offspring of slaves continued to feel this shame, so some changed their names to mask their origins, lied about their families, or moved to cities and towns where their dishonor could remain a secret.

I explained, "Black skin is a slave mark in the States. But we don't feel ashamed, at least not any longer."

"Are you treated differently than others?"

"Yes, but it's not just because we were once slaves," I replied. "Black skin made you a slave and now it makes you expendable." I'm not sure he understood what I was saying. "Are you treated differently? Do others know that your family is descended from slaves?" I asked.

"Yes, most definitely," he answered with a broad smile at my credulity. "The sons of slaves were generally the ones who were educated. Because when the English required the children to attend colonial schools, the chiefs didn't send their sons to be educated by the British, but the sons of slaves. They suffered that too." He sighed.

Idaissu shared all of this in a hushed tone, not to prevent Muhammad and Baba from hearing his story, since clearly they too knew it. But slavery was the kind of matter spoken of only in whispers or behind closed doors.

"The chief won't tell it all; it's to painful to discuss. He keeps secrets," explained Idaissu. It was not that the chief was being duplicitous, but rather that the pact of silence could not be violated without inflicting harm or exacerbating long-standing conflicts. For the chief, silence was the price of peace.

"Kwame Nkrumah forbade this pointing of the finger and labeling someone a slave," he added. Nkrumah systemically attacked forms of traditional privilege and caste. "But," Idaissu said with a laugh, "we all know who's who."

He was the first to descend the hill and cross Wankan-Baye. The Bath of Slaves—it sounded almost operatic, like the title of a dark, brooding drama in which love culminated in betrayal. It would be the kind of story with a bad beginning and an unhappy ending and filled with death and disappointment. What else was possible when slaves were the central players?

I followed down the hill after him. I asked Idaissu if I could photograph him by the dry streambed. He looked straight at me and smiled. I took his picture, then we traded places and he took mine. It was a moment of fleeting intimacy. This give-and-take was not a matter of blood or kinship, but of affiliation. We were the progeny of slaves. We were the children of commoners.

"WE HAVE STIRRED the dead by visiting these sites," Muhammed told us as we walked back to the town square. "A fetish priest has been called upon to set right what has been disturbed. The priest will pour libations at all the places we have been because the spirits have been roused."

The hunger of the dead was the debt we had to settle. What had not been sated or assuaged was our responsibility. Offering libations was a way of feeding the spirits and satisfying their need for recognition, all of which allowed the living to escape their wrath. The peace realized by this slaking of appetites had to be gained over and over again.

We made a small donation toward the priest's gargantuan labor. But I couldn't be persuaded, despite wanting to believe otherwise, that angry slaves could be put to rest. How could the dead be appeased? By not believing, did I consign them to a relentless state of misery? I would have preferred to imagine them resting in peace. Yet I didn't have faith in the serenity of dead slaves or trust that our offering could bring an end to their sorrow. I envisioned the dead raging and dispirited, like us, waiting for a future when all the slave marks would be gone. It was this mutual longing that bound our fate with theirs.

ELEVEN

Blood Cowries

AT FIRST GLANCE, the grassy flatland of the savanna doesn't appear like a landscape of relics. The clusters of baobabs don't seem like the signs of a history of destruction. Nor is it immediately evident that bare mounds of earth are the debris of scattered lives and that the sunken recesses where the soil has given way are the traces of the dead and the missing. "For those who can read the landscape," writes an anthropologist, "some natural features are as tragic as any scene of violent destruction." The straw and mud houses have returned to dust, the tutelary gods have vanished, and the brush has overtaken neglected shrines. Hollows and pocks scar the terrain. But who would ever have suspected that the symptoms of erosion were the text of a catastrophic history or guessed that the money yielded by centuries of slave trading lay hidden beneath the earth, like a buried secret or a corpse abandoned in an unmarked grave?

Pots of money safeguarded in caskets are all that remain of the wealth created by slavery. Kings, warriors, and merchants had intended to hoard their riches for eternity. Wooden boxes and leather chests and burlap bags filled with cowrie shells had been stockpiled in underground vaults and hidden away in shrines, but history took a different turn. The treasure became worthless before it could be exhumed. The underground banks of

the savanna became crypts for dead issue, resting places for obsolete currency. The yield of centuries of theft had vanished as readily as the slaves
sold in the marketplace. As an economist lamented, "The skeletons were
abandoned to their permanent graves."

Cowrie shells became the currency of West Africa in the era of the Atlantic slave trade. While North Africans had introduced them as early as
the eleventh century, they became ubiquitous in the seventeenth and eighteenth centuries when Europeans began exchanging them for slaves.
Traders alleged cowrie shells were the best goods for purchasing slaves,
because Africans so prized them. In *A Description of the Coasts of North
and South Guinea*, Jean Barbot wrote, "The trading nations of Europe
have for this trash [cowrie shells], to carry on their traffic at the coast of
Guinea and Angola; to purchase slaves or other goods of Africa, and are
only proper for that trade; no other people in the universe putting such
value on them as Guineans."

The shells were imported from the Maldives Islands. Women and men
waded waist-deep into the sea and detached the shells from stones, wood,
and palm leaves, which had been placed in shallows for easy collection.
One person could gather as many as twelve thousand shells in a day. The
shells were buried in sand for a few weeks until the mollusks died and the

smell of putrefaction vanished. They were then disinterred, washed, dried, and strung together for sale. The Dutch transported cowrie shells from the Indian Ocean via Ceylon to Amsterdam, the chief European entrepôt, and the English via the Bay of Bengal to London, and then shipped them to Africa as ballast in slave ships.

The English and the Dutch acquired the shells very cheaply and considered them worthless, except for their use as bulk in giving a ship weight and in the "Negro trade." European traders derisively called the shells "Negro money." To their eyes, Africans' esteem of these worthless pieces was yet another instance of fetishism—revering "mere trifles" as valued objects. In the eighteenth century alone, more than twenty-five million pounds of cowries were imported into West Africa. Of the six-million-plus captives transported to the Americas in the eighteenth century, anywhere from one-third to one-quarter of them had been exchanged for shells. Twelve to sixteen pounds of cowries were enough to purchase a strapping young man or two small children. That was about one pound of cowries for every thirteen pounds of human flesh.

Cowrie shells replaced the indigenous currencies of Africa. The advantages of cowrie shells, according to economists, were that they were "small in size, durable, readily divisible, impossible to counterfeit and augmentable." But why or how Africans came to place so much value in the shells has been the subject of much debate. The European traders simply attributed it to black stupidity and fetishism, which besides the obvious racism was ludicrous, as one historian noted, because such thinking was "based on the mistaken assumption that Africans and Europeans shared the same values. The existence of aspects of commodity exchange in a pre-capitalist [African] society did not make it a capitalist society." Prestige rather than utility largely motivated Africa's participation in the slave trade. Money, luxury items, and fancy goods were essential to defining and maintaining the hierarchy of class and status. And the love of extravagance was realized at the expense of human life.

Even now it is difficult to comprehend the scope of devastation wrought by the appetite for nonessential goods. This destruction of life gave birth to capitalism in the West, but what is staggering is that the enormous losses suffered in Africa were without any lasting gains.

African traders had no incentives to "maximize value," since the plundered societies bearing the losses were not the same societies profiting from the trade, which only serves to demonstrate the emptiness and irrelevance of an "African identity" in making sense of the Atlantic slave trade. Simply put, slaves were stolen from one group, exchanged by a second group, and then shipped across the Atlantic and exploited in the Americas by a third group. The violence and the wreckage necessary for the acquisition and circulation of money were borne by those who were not partners in the trade but its victims. From the perspective of the commodity, economic incentives, whether "rational" or "whimsical," effected the same disastrous end.

By the close of the eighteenth century, a male slave was sold on the coast for 176,000 cowries and upward. Cowries were more expensive in the savanna, so more slaves had to be exchanged per unit of money. In the Salaga market, slaves sold for between 20,000 and 40,000 cowries; the old and infirm sometimes sold for as little as 4,000 cowries. The literal piles and mountains of money must have made it seem as if this plentitude was without end and that the storehouse could never be exhausted. In the system for counting cowries, large units were referred to as "captives" and "bags of men."

However, the money Africans acquired by exporting people was inconvertible. The shells passed from white hands to black, but not back again, ensuring that they remained "Negro currency." Europeans would not accept the shells in payment for other imported goods and considered them of little more intrinsic value than stones or gravel.

The flow of cowries illuminated the unequal returns of the slave trade to its African and European partners. War and predation enabled Africa to produce slaves and purchase luxury goods, and permitted Europe to accumulate the capital necessary for economic development. As Marx wrote, the conversion of Africa into a preserve for captives was one of those idyllic moments "which characterize the dawn of the era of capitalist development" in the West. The consequences of this economy of theft were quite different in Africa. The money concentrated in the hands of merchants and royals created little new wealth, and the destructiveness of slave raiding and wars of capture disrupted farming, produced famine, and devastated social and political life.

◇ ◇ ◇

THE ARISTOCRATS AND NOBLES BELIEVED that cowrie shells were God's gift to the fortunate. So the story they told about how cowrie shells came into the world was bereft of the awful details of the slave trade. An elder in Gonja recited the story: "Before any cowry shell came into use, God sent a heavy rain, and this rain was to bring down the living things whose shells were to become currency for our use. The old people who had known the purpose of the rain defied the rain and gathered as much of the shells as possible, and they became the first rich men we have ever heard of. The rest of the creatures which nobody picked were washed into the sea." But even in the fairy tale, living things were sacrificed for the acquisition of wealth and money was entangled with death and putrefaction.

The commoners, not surprisingly, told a different story. They offered a grisly account of the origins of cowrie shells and how men came to acquire them. Blood money was what commoners called the shells because they fed upon the flesh of men. Looking at the cowries, the truth was plain to see. The shells possessed a long, slender orifice that resembled a vagina, and teeth lined the aperture. Like the *vagina dentata*, the shells conjured up images of procreation and destruction. But everyone knew the shells didn't bear life but instead devoured it. The teeth lining the aperture were clearly for eating. Few claimed ever to have heard the cowrie shells speak. But it would not be hard to imagine a ghoulish laugh or to discern the rumble of a full belly or to catch wind of a belch ripe with human flesh.

In every place ravaged by the slave trade, stories circulated about the human cost of money: cowrie shells feasted on the bodies of captives. Money multiplied if fed human blood. Rich men accrued their wealth through the labor of slaves slogging away in cities underneath the Atlantic. Others alleged that the cowrie shells washed back into the Atlantic were hoarded by witches or controlled by water spirits like Mami Wata, Mother of the Waters.

Popular lore held that the best places to harvest cowries were along the coast where slaves had been murdered or drowned. Nets were cast into the sea to dredge for treasure. The corpse of a slave would emerge from

the water encased by thousands of shells, which covered the figure from
head to toe. The fisherman who retrieved the bloated body of the human-
mollusk plucked off the money and returned home a wealthy man. Rich
men fished for cowries using the amputated limbs of slaves as bait. The
kind master waited for the slave to die a natural death before tossing the
body parts into a lagoon or river. Hovering at the edge of the water, guilt-
less and avaricious, the big men lingered until the money began to sprout
and welcomed it as a gift from God.

IT IS ALL DEAD MONEY now. The coffers of wealth accumulated by
the capture and sale of slaves had turned into rubbish. After the French
and British forces defeated Babatu and Samori, they took possession of
the savanna on a greater scale than the freebooters and warrior-princes
ever could have dreamed. Cowrie shells were demonetized and eventually
outlawed altogether by colonial governments, which had divided and
conquered Africa in the guise of emancipating it. The mortal anguish of
slaves had become apparent belatedly to European nations, and this nas-
cent abolitionist zeal provided the rationale for the conquest of Africa. In
the nineteenth century, the same nations responsible for the shipment of
millions of captives to the Americas declared themselves the antagonists
of slavery. Soon after colonial governments abolished Africa's internal
slave trade, the currency of the slave trade, at least what Africans had accumulated, was destroyed too. No similar effort to erase the past and start
anew was enacted in the West. The pounds and francs and marks that replaced cowrie shells were blood money too.

TWELVE

Fugitive Dreams

ON THE ROAD to Gwolu, the bus rippled with laughter. Our voices rushed from the windows and filled the vast expanse of unpopulated territory. Fomin, a historian from Cameroon, joked that he was going to sell the Kenyans at the next stop on the slave route. He was sure he could buy enough guinea fowls to feed the entire bus if he sold Hannington, M'Shai, Mumbi, and Richard. Richard shouted from the back of the bus, "I'm from Uganda, remember." Fomin's joke led to a spate of others about the vices of slaves from particular countries. With Jenks, the bus reached a consensus, we couldn't expect much for him. What could you do with a Nigerian? Who would have ever wanted to buy such a troublesome property? Jenks retorted, "a king of nothing, but a king all the same."

No one made any jokes about selling Sandra and me, the only African Americans in the research group, because it would have been in bad taste, like pointing out a missing limb or poking fun at a deformity or ridiculing the indigent, or about Jeffrey from South Africa, who evoked even more pity than we did. He had been made a slave in his own country. At least we had the excuse of having been abducted. When we crossed the border into Togo, the guys teased me, saying, "Saidiya, maybe this is where you're from." In Benin, they taunted, "Shouldn't you get off the bus and try to find your roots? We will conduct the interviews, while you try to figure out who you are."

Richard was the worst of the bunch because he knew I was fond of him. It was the combination of his sharp wit and easy manner that I liked. He loved to mock my Swahili name. The first day in the research seminar he had asked me if I knew what my name meant. I replied, "Of course, it means one who helps."

"But what you don't know," he said, "is that if you stand in the central market in Nairobi with your palms extended and say your name softly, Saidiya, Saidiya, people will think you are pleading for help and begging for alms." Hannington, who was the unrepentant Pan-Africanist of the group, looked at me with sympathy at such moments.

"His name was Karim Farrakhan Jones," Richard started out and the bus instantly erupted in laughter. "Now, Karim Jones," a few more chuckles, "was a slave in America who swam across the Atlantic because he wanted so badly to return home to Africa. As soon as he dragged himself onto the shore of Nigeria, he kissed the soil, but his homecoming was short-lived. He had only walked a few meters when he was captured by two bandits who, recognizing him as a stranger—the kiss had given him away—sold him into slavery. Karim Jones was sold so many times and passed through so many hands that eventually he landed on a clove plantation in Zanzibar. When he realized he would only ever be a slave in Africa, toiling away for a master who didn't call him a nigger but who treated him like one, he jumped into the Indian Ocean and tried to swim back to the States, but unfortunately he went down somewhere off the coast of South Africa."

I didn't want to laugh, but I couldn't help it.

Ibrahim, a graduate student from Senegal, readied to initiate the next round. He was a tall, lanky Wolof who had told me repeatedly that his family would never allow him to marry anyone of slave origins, although he would be permitted to have sex with me. He got as far as "there was once," when I piped up, "Enough already with the jokes about slaves." And to my surprise, the guys stopped.

◇ ◇ ◇

THIS WAS MY SECOND TRIP north, and it couldn't have been more unlike my first. If the first trip with Yaya, Lawrence, and Ayanna had been the tragedy of the slave route, then this was the burlesque version. Jokes and raucous laughter were a constant. My colleagues had turned into pranksters, leaving behind the sober academics they were at the university. Road trips have a way of doing that to people. Venturing out from the known world, wandering for days on end, and arriving at unheard-of places fueled the desire to leave our old selves behind and tricked us into believing it was possible. The more ground covered, the more liberated you became. All the moorings fell away.

The men got frisky and aroused, as wives and respectability fell behind in the distance. Fomin pinched my thigh and pressed his leg firmly against mine. After I tired of pushing his hand and leg away, I changed my seat and joined M'Shai. The women had become loquacious, building a wall of chatter between our randy male colleagues and us. Only Kofi Anyidoho, the director of the Institute of African Studies at the University of Ghana-Legon and the head of our research team, maintained his usual somber demeanor. Secretly I thought of him as the Patriarch, but I called him Prof as everyone else did.

The first day of the trip was uneventful. We made our way from Accra to Kumasi, the seat of the Asante Empire. Visiting the Asantehene's palace, I was reminded of the grandeur and barbarism of the great slave-trading civilization. "There is no document of civilization which is not at the same time a document of barbarism," writes Walter Benjamin. The spoils and cultural treasures of the victors could not be separated from the lives of the vanquished who were still lying prostrate. This was no less true of Asante than it was of Rome. In the nineteenth century, Asante was so rich that even the commoners owned slaves. It possessed one of the most developed and bureaucratic states in West Africa, and the wealth of the kingdom, which was exhibited in spectacular displays of gold and in royal pageantry, impressed all those who beheld it. The original stone palace of the king, which had been modeled after the European forts along the coast, was destroyed in the 1874 war with the British; the new palace was luxurious, but modest by comparison with the sprawling stone edifice. The gilded elegance of the court and the peacocks burdened by their beautiful plumage as they strutted on the palace grounds brought to mind an image of the Asantehene saddled with the heavy gold regalia that adorned his head, neck, forearms, wrists, ankles, and feet, which required him to navigate the courtyard with well-placed and careful steps so that he wouldn't be toppled by the weight of his gold. The ostentation also made me think of all of the lives sacrificed to produce such stateliness. The stool of the Asantehene, unlike that of the king of Dahomey, wasn't elevated on human skulls, but I could see them anyway.

As we made our way north, I entered a dark zone of private grief. Advancing slowly along the slave route, I began to feel increasingly alone in the group, which surprised me because I didn't think it was possible to feel any lonelier than I did already. Almost from the very first week of the research seminar, which had been assembled to investigate issues of slavery and memory in West Africa, I had felt my distance from the others. This wasn't an uncommon experience for me; I had been alienated from my peers as far back as I could remember. Even in first grade, I had played alone in the schoolyard, wrapping my head in my red sweater, pretending it was a nun's habit and that I was Sister Madonna. In whatever group I found myself, I usually felt like an outsider. What was different this time was that everyone else made it apparent that they considered me an outsider too.

The research group, which began meeting at the end of January and was scheduled to convene for eleven weeks, was composed of professors, lecturers, and graduate students from Benin, Cameroon, Gambia, Ghana, Kenya, Nigeria, South Africa, and Uganda. A pattern of collegial joking and teasing had developed over the course of our first weeks together. Ninety percent of the remarks began, "You South Africans," "You Nigerians," "You Ghanaians." But whenever I entered the circle I was greeted by an awkward silence, either because my colleagues didn't know what to say or because they feared that I would be insulted if they called attention to my difference, which was charged for all of us, especially in the context of our collective investigation of slavery. My presence tainted the glory of precolonial Africa. I was the disposable offspring of the "African family," the flesh-and-blood reminder of its shame and tragic mistakes. When behind my back my colleagues grumbled "those Americans," I didn't discern any tenderness or affection, only ridicule and envy.

"My friend from the diaspora," was how Akam addressed me, in contrast to the rest of the group whom he called his brothers and sisters from the continent. Diaspora was really just a euphemism for stranger, since for the most part none of my colleagues, with the exceptions of Prof and Hannington, gave much thought to the way their history was enmeshed with mine, nor did they entertain the idea that the Africa in my hyphenated African-American identity had anything to do with their Africa. They made it clear: Africa ended at the borders of the continent.

When I pressed my colleagues on this, they countered, "So will you stay in Ghana after the seminar?" They all knew that the answer was no. If I had decided to be a visitor, then why should they treat me as anything other than a stranger? And on this sour note our conversations most often ended.

I didn't ask Sandra if she felt the same loneliness I did. She had joined us at the end of the seminar for the two-week field trip. She and Anyidoho were the conveners of the two-part research seminar sponsored by CODESRIA, a social science research group based in Dakar, Senegal, and funded by the Ford Foundation. The first half of the seminar was on memory and slavery, which Prof directed at the University of Ghana, and the second half was on constructions of Africa in the Americas, which Sandra would convene at Northwestern University in the late spring. Sandra usually sat in the front of the bus with Anyidoho. Her senior status protected her from the group scuffles, which happened among the lower ranks at the back of the bus.

On the really bad days, I felt like a monster in a cage with a sign warning, "DANGER, SNARLING NEGRO. KEEP AWAY." And my colleagues did. The deeper into the heartland of slavery we entered, the greater the isolation I experienced. Most of my colleagues didn't experience slavery as a wound, at least they feigned that they didn't. A terrible history had not begun for them in 1492 that had yet to end. And if they believed this was the case, they refused to admit it.

For Baba, slavery was a scheme for generating revenue for his country. He had organized the International Roots Homecoming Festival to draw African-American tourists to Gambia. For Jeffery, it was a way of getting a fellowship to the States. He was an aspiring filmmaker eager to get to Hollywood and meet Denzel Washington. For Jenks, it was what Europe had done to Africa. And for me, slavery was the image of my great-great-grandmother on a dirt road in Alabama or marooned on a tiny island in the Caribbean Sea.

When we had started out on our journey, Anyidoho said he expected me to be the witness for the group, because I was the descendant of slaves. But I didn't believe I could act as witness for the collective. The witness required a listener, and everyone had grown weary of me.

AS THE BUS INCHED its way across Ghana toward the border of Burkina Faso, all the small disagreements kept piling up until we could barely see eye to eye about anything. Why had I expected anything different after weeks of arguing with my colleagues? Jenks and I were always in a deadlock. He was famous for saying things like, "Slavery was a benign institution in Africa." He drew an absolute line of division between African slavery and the Atlantic slave trade, as if one had nothing to do with the other. To my ears, his characterizations of slavery as a benign and paternal institution sounded too much like the justifications of Southern planters. Once he actually said that the taboo against mentioning a person's origin was equivalent to an act of abolition.

Richard believed it was incorrect to refer to involuntary servitude in Africa as slavery at all. For him, it was yet another example of the West defining African institutions, and inaccurately, at that. When I asked, "How then can we talk about exploitation in an African context?" he replied, "There are more pressing problems in Africa than that one."

Before leaving for the field trip, I had complained to John and Mary Ellen that I felt like a Martian in the group. I had given them a blow-by-blow account of the frequent clashes I had with my colleagues. I had expected sympathy, but instead Mary Ellen and John advised me to keep my mouth shut. "No one will listen to you," cautioned Mary Ellen, "and even if they did learn from what you said, the culture of saving face wouldn't allow them to admit it. There is no reason that you should be the voice of opposition. You will learn even more by simply taking it in and writing than by trying to do battle with what it is that they believe."

John nodded in agreement and added, "Certain things don't catch here. It doesn't matter whether it's a good idea or a bad one, but certain things won't catch." My way of thinking was clearly one of those things that wouldn't catch. I tried to heed their advice, but it had always been difficult for me to hold my tongue.

IN SALAGA, the rift began. Baba, the teacher whom I had met on my first visit there, had arranged for our group to meet Mama Demata. Her grandfather had been a slave trader, so she possessed a pair of shackles that her grandfather had used to transport slaves from Burkina Faso to Ghana. When Mama Demata showed us the shackles, Mumbi asked to try them on. After Mama Demata fastened them around Mumbi's sweatpants, the townspeople crowding around us burst out laughing. They pointed at her shackles and called her a slave. Was it the incongruity of her Nike baseball cap, auburn hair weave, athletic pants, and shackles? She was Kenyan, but she dressed like an American. Pretending to be a slave, Mumbi hobbled back and forth with tiny constricted steps in Mama Demata's front yard. The effort required to move her legs caused the rusty cuffs to scrape her ankles. After a few minutes she decided that she'd had enough and asked that they be removed. The shackles were cast off as easily as they had been locked in place. The crowd applauded when Mumbi became a free woman again. But I was seething.

The thicket of misunderstanding grew denser and more impassable as our journey continued. What had I expected of our little African union? I suppose I had wanted us to build a bridge across our differences. But nearly two months of working daily together had only made it more difficult for us to find a common vocabulary about slavery, or anything else for that matter. No matter how expansive the category "sister," I always fell outside its embrace. Whatever remained of Pan-Africanism, which had espoused solidarity among all African people, promoted the ideal of continental fraternity and sorority, and encouraged each and every one of us in the diaspora to dream of the continent as our home, no longer included the likes of me. For my colleagues, my self-proclaimed African identity, albeit hyphenated, was fanciful and my Swahili name an amusement. They could hardly manage to say it without snickering.

If there was any hope for Pan-Africanism, an essay by Anthony Appiah had concluded, "It is crucial that we recognize the independence of the Pan-Africanism of the diaspora and the Pan-Africanism of the continent." In the group, I constantly experienced this "independence," but it just felt like loneliness to me. No matter how hard I tried, I couldn't surmount the barricade that separated me from the others. Awkward interactions, strained conversations, and unspoken recriminations accompanied us along the slave route. And I was reluctant to admit that I was as much at fault as the others.

ON THE ROAD to Navrongo, Jeffrey and M'shai accused me of being self-centered. "You think that the story of those in the Americas is the most important," Jeffrey told me. "You're just another Alex Haley."

Jenks, siding with them, exclaimed, "My great-uncle disappeared. Everyone believed traders had kidnapped him. My grandfather traveled as far as Ghana trying to find him."

"I am not saying that my experience—"

Akam interrupted me, "My friend from the diaspora, you think you are the only one to suffer."

I made the countercharge, "You think Africa should get reparations for the slave trade, but not the descendants of the people actually stolen. So the elites who sold us the first time should now benefit by selling us out a second time."

"But we were coerced into the trade," Jenks shouted at me. "We were the losers, we received trinkets."

Prof intervened, "There are negative aspects of the trade we must own up to. We knew we were giving away our people, we were giving them away for things."

We returned to our separate corners and came out slugging again. It was a schoolyard brawl, so I was blind to my opponents' distress and humiliation but all too aware of my own. What I knew was that I hurt and I wanted them to hurt too. We each went for blood, increasing the distrust, deepening the silence, and widening a rift we couldn't hope to overcome.

My colleagues had pegged me as an arrogant, quick-to-get-angry, always having a bad attitude, acting like the world owes you something, well-heeled, pain-in-the-ass black American, the favorite target of everyone's disdain. Six months in Ghana had taught me I was in a lose-lose situation. So I settled for watching the countryside and looking out for the buried towns of the disappeared.

IT IS SAID that when you spot a cluster of baobab trees it's the sign a village once existed in that spot. I counted at least thirteen clusters on the way to Gwolu, but all the other signs of life had perished. These islands of baobab, shea butter, locust bean, and fig trees preserved the history of the stateless; they were the archive of the defeated.

Crossing the savanna, one came face-to-face with the violence of the slave trade. The vast stretches of empty space and the far-flung settlements testified to the long history of war and raiding. The desolate landscape and the great plain of uninhabited territory told the story of rout and pillage, and also the story of people running for safety. The deserted villages and ghostly towns were the traces of people in flight. And Gwolu was one of the places to which they fled, hoping to be safe.

In Gwolu, the first thing you noticed was the wall. It was the contrast between the wide-open spaces of the savanna and the piddling thing trying to contain it that solicited your attention. The defense wall looked stunted and ridiculous against the panoramic backdrop: rust, ocher, and cocoa-colored grasses covered the open field; granite outcrops punctuated the horizon; the spires of anthills reached toward the sky; and baobab trees loomed in the distance. Laterite dwellings the color of pumpkin and dung fanned out on either side of what remained of the wall. The austere beauty of the savanna was thrown into relief by the crumbling bulwark.

The wall was no longer the formidable barricade that had once protected the town against slave raiders. Time and weather had eroded it. The embankment extended anywhere from twelve to fifteen feet in length and dipped precipitously from twelve to four feet in height. It was about two or three feet wide. More exceeded its embrace than was contained by it, so it was difficult to believe that it once had encircled the entire town. The wall was no longer able to shut out anyone. When it had been built, the world beyond the village was a very dangerous place and the wall staved off the menace.

The rampart divided the world between friend and foe, ally and enemy. It separated the homestead and the bush and demarcated the zones of tenuous safety and great peril. Strangers, bandits, and raiders emerged from the bush. The ghosts, predatory spirits, and malevolent forces unleashed by the slave trade also occupied the terrain and threatened to transform every inch of the earth into a wild, uninhabitable realm. There was so much to fear: the bush, the night, the angry dead, the men on horses, the slavers' nets.

Like people elsewhere threatened by slave raiders, those in Gwolu defended themselves by building a wall. By the nineteenth century, fortified towns were commonplace throughout West Africa. High walls, sometimes as many as seven, protected the core of a city, and narrow passageways thwarted the entry of small armies and bands of raiders.

In response to the imminent dangers of threat and captivity, villages

became increasingly complex and elaborate in design and architecture endowed with military purpose. Town gates were built so low that adults had to crawl to cross the threshold, dwellings were designed with several exits that provided needed avenues of escape, and houses were arrayed along constricted and winding alleyways that obstructed the easy movement of enemies. Shelters were built under rocks, hidden in caves and caverns that were large enough to store food and cattle, nestled in impassable mountain ranges, or floated in lakes on stilts. Fences made of thorny trees and poisonous plants provided another level of defense. Centuries of war and raiding left their mark in walls and palisades throughout the savanna. Dwelling peacefully could no longer be taken for granted.

A DRUMMER PLAYED in the center of the square announcing our arrival and assembling the villagers. The whole town had gathered to meet us. The village regent and the elders were congregated under the thatched roof of the town's open-air hall. They had been waiting for us since eight o'clock in the morning. We arrived at nearly two o'clock in the afternoon. Since we were "important people from the south," they had swallowed their irritation and patiently waited for their audience.

Once we were settled properly on the benches before the elders, they offered us refreshment, and we accepted, pretending to drink the brackish water. The townspeople, who were packed behind the honored guests, laughed at those like me who brought the calabash to their mouths but were unwilling to drink. Anyidoho introduced himself, apologized for our tardiness, introduced each member of the group by name and country, and explained the purpose of our mission.

The elders seemed inattentive and disgruntled, probably because they had been waiting so long for us to arrive. They graciously accepted our apology, stating, "When you have a brother, you don't mind waiting for him because he is your brother. This is why we have waited so patiently. We have been waiting for you since morning." Each elder in the circle of men greeted us. None failed to mention that they had been waiting since morning, signifying on our lateness and lack of consideration. The regent said that we need not worry; they would give us the information for which we had come, stressing the mercenary character of our engagement and interest in Gwolu. They had grown accustomed to strangers coming, taking what they needed, and leaving without an afterthought.

The women stood outside the circle of elders, excluded from the precinct of historical knowledge. They were not represented in village or family councils, and, like us strangers, they listened to what they too should have rightfully claimed.

The grandparents of the men who were seated before us had built the wall to defend themselves against the raids of Babatu and his troops. Babatu, the infamous Zabarima warrior, ravaged the northern regions of Ghana in the last decades of the nineteenth century, pillaging settlements and cities, capturing women and children, slaughtering men, and seizing cattle and cowries. A few mentioned Samory Touré, the Malinke leader who battled French colonial forces and attempted to establish an independent state. To the communities raided by Babatu and Samory, the difference between a freebooter and an anticolonial hero made very little difference.

During the slave trade, "Every free man or woman was a captive on reprieve since at any moment he or she could end up in the slaver's nets." As the elders explained why they had built the wall, it was no longer just a blockade but a window onto the struggle between despots and commoners, and predatory states and small-scale societies. While the embankment had repelled raiders and protected the settlement, as well as the outlying farmlands and water sources, its importance exceeded these facts. The wall was a reminder that the relation between would-be masters and would-be slaves was achieved only at the cost of great violence.

"People didn't submit passively to raiders," one man said. "No one wanted to be made a slave." They had migrated to this remote area of the savanna to escape captivity. Flight was the language of freedom.

ON FOOT THEY HAD FLED from the slave raiders and traders from Asante, Gonja, Dagomba, and Mossi. The fugitives traveled for weeks not knowing where they were headed or what they'd find or how far away was safe. What they knew for sure was that they weren't safe where they were. On the journey, they dreamed of farms and watching their children grow up rather than disappear, they dreamed of toiling for themselves, and they dreamed of a place without royals and where they would never again hear the word "barbarian," "savage," or "slave." The pregnant women rubbed their bellies and comforted the unborn with stories about a land they had yet to see. And the elders overhearing these tales started to believe them also and to envision the clearing and to hear the rustle of trees. The place was still weeks away, but their hearts told them it was home. The men surveyed the landscape and anticipated the seeds to be planted in the new ground.

The unknown territory to which they were heading, as if freedom were a city waiting for them in the distance, acquired texture and detail in their imaginations, so a place they had never set their eyes on became tangible and then their own. At the end of one of these roads, the haven would be waiting. With each step taken it became more vivid. The crumbling blow-away soil cushioned the soles of their feet, their eyes traveled the length of the horizon, and all that vastness made them feel anchored in the world. They envisioned the houses they would build and tried to decide whether a dome or flat roof would be better, earth or straw.

As they walked, they thought of the stories about this journey they would tell the sons and daughters not yet born. Why they had made it and what it had cost them. They had consulted with the gods and trusted they had done the right thing. They believed there would be benefits to show and that no child with a blank face would ever need to ask why and put in doubt the whole adventure.

But what to say to the ones stumbling on the road with bruised feet and lips split from thirst and bodies caked in dirt was more difficult. No, they weren't lost, but they couldn't say exactly where they were going. It didn't keep the children from asking. The parents gave vague answers like a place near the bush, someplace nice, a great place alongside a spring, a safe place where anything can grow; if they were tired or feeling impatient, they'd just push the children forward with a shove and say keep walking. Don't dawdle. Don't stray from the path. Hold your brother's hand. And at night they didn't tell the children they were afraid and they didn't explain why they were hiding, just that they needed to be very quiet, and if the children were frightened too they'd hum a song with their lips pressed close to a son or daughter's ear, and the children would grow less anxious about sleeping in a cave and forget to ask why there weren't any stars.

The belongings they had dragged with them—calabashes and pots and mats and cloth and scythes and lances—were balanced on their heads or tied against their backs. There wasn't a donkey or a horse among them, so even the little ones had to carry things. The few objects they possessed were enough to make a start, but little more than that. They worried about the dead left behind and about who would attend them and they prayed they would be forgiven.

The spirits had directed them this far, and each day they looked for the signs of that guidance. But too many weeks spent heading toward nowhere in particular made them grow doubtful, and rather than live a day longer in uncertainty, every rock, bush, or stranger was the sign for which they had been looking. They trusted to the gods that they would know the place when they found it. Any place that put them out of reach of slave hunters was sacred to them. The new place would shelter their gods too. They had staked their lives on finding it.

On the journey, they cut new paths, fearing that the old ones might lead to capture and shackles and death. Even when they were faltering and clueless, they told themselves that any place was better than Gonja, the place from which they had come. It was something they repeated when they were afraid or hungry or thirsty or doubting why they had started out at all. They kept heading north, and when they had traveled so far they couldn't hope to find their way back and it seemed too far for anyone to come chasing after them, they said, We're almost there.

Finally, when the distance between them and the old world seemed unbridgeable, they began to feel safe. And even though the soil wasn't any good, it was more clay than dirt, and water would be a challenge, and they weren't used to living in such close proximity with other people, or acting as one large collective rather than as families, it would be worth it if they could survive.

When they saw a few houses huddled in the distance, after days of seeing none at all, they wondered whether they'd be welcomed, speculated about who these people were and if they could make a life among them.

The people already living in the place permitted them to share it, to build houses and to bury their dead as long as all agreed there would be no masters. So they put down their children, dropped their belongings, set up their ancestral shrines, and said, We're here.

If in exhaustion they had mistaken other places for the haven before realizing they were simply tired and said, "No, this wasn't it," or if others had turned them away before they arrived at "the place under the bush," it was soon forgotten. All they shared was the rift and the danger that had driven them. To remember what they had lost and what they became, what had been torn apart and what had come together, the fugitives and refugees and multitudes in flight were called the Sisala, which means "to come together, to become together, to weave together."

They had fled slave raiders, predatory states, drought, and exhausted land, and they desired never to know any of it again in this sequestered niche of the savanna. Each one had a different dream of what might be possible when you didn't have to look over your shoulder, or answer to the name "barbarian," or hand over your daughter or nephew as tribute, or forget your ancestors, or abandon your gods, and when you didn't have to wake each day worrying that you or someone you loved might disappear by dusk. For all this, they were willing to begin anew. Knowing that you don't ever regain what you've lost, they embraced becoming something other than who they had been and naming themselves again.

Newcomers were welcome. It didn't matter that they weren't kin or that they spoke a different language, because genealogy didn't matter (most of them couldn't go back more than three or four generations, anyway), building a community did. If the willingness to receive new arrivals and foreigners was what it took to make a world different from the one they had left, then so be it. So they put down their roots in foreign soil and adopted strangers as their kin and intermarried with other migrants and runaways, and shared their gods and totems, and blended their histories. "We" was the collectivity they built from the ground up, not one they had inherited, not one that others had imposed.

And the dreams of what might be possible were enshrined in the names of these towns and villages founded by fugitives: *safe at last, we have come together, here where no one can reach us anymore, the village of free people, here we speak of peace, a place of abundance, haven.* Like communities of maroons and fugitives and outliers elsewhere, their identity was defined as much by what they were running from as by what they were running toward.

Like other so-called tribes living in isolated and far-flung areas, their settlement was the result of the clash between military aristocracies and small societies, royals and commoners, owners and producers, and Muslims and animists. Flight was the most common response of threatened communities everywhere. Predatory states produced migrants and fugitives as well as slaves. Those on the run sought asylum in out-of-the-way places that offered suitable defense like rocky hillsides or they built walled towns or they hid in caves or they relocated to lagoons or mountainous terrain or anywhere else that appeared to be impervious to horsemen and raiding armies.

Refugees, fugitives, and wanderers flooded the savanna. New people were created and new societies constructed under the pressure of flight and rebellion. Defense was a priority, so they lived together in compact villages. Homesteads were clustered together for safety. Families were densely packed because greater numbers increased the chances for survival. Farms were situated close to the village rather than at great distances so that no one ever had to venture too far from home and shelter.

But the northwestern corner of Ghana was neither remote nor isolated enough to escape the pursuit of raiders. Aggressive and powerful states as well as freebooters, mercenaries, and would-be sovereigns followed on their trail, raiding, enslaving, and butchering the stateless. Staying free was difficult. The *ones who came together* were still the prey of the powerful, the raw material of the ruling groups, and harvested at will. The slave trade engulfed the northern savanna. The new terrors to be faced were part and parcel of the global trade in black cargo. An economy of theft joined this supposedly remote territory to the world at large. There was no place to run that was far enough away.

BY THE TIME they decided to build the wall, the dream of a safe place had vanished. The intruders had already entered the settlement, walked through its paths, memorized the lay of the land, counted the heads of cattle, targeted the women and children to be taken, decided which houses to burn and which of the men were to be killed. The enemy threatened the town, and then the town reacted. The worst enemies were those who had been friends.

Babatu first came to Gwolu as a friend, the kind you paid to enlist his help. He had been hired as a warrior of fortune to assist the Sisala in routing their enemies, the Pana, and he received cowries and slaves as payment for his services. An invitation extended to a freebooter had opened their house to the danger. Babatu resided in Gwolu, whether for a few weeks or a season no one recollected. But soon after his departure, Gwolu decided to construct the defense wall. Fearing the price of friendship or presaging the likelihood of Babatu's treachery, given his infamous reputation, they began building the fortification. Once they decided to build the wall, everyone understood they were involved in a struggle to survive. They learned that settlement in an outlying territory was not the guarantee of sovereignty and that flight was as near to freedom as they would come. And that the gap between what they had dreamed of and what they could have would never be bridged.

As soon as the shock had thawed and the breach had occurred, they waited for the intruders to approach the gate and they prepared to face Babatu. If they didn't act, they would disappear. To hand over enemies or unsuspecting strangers captured along the road as tribute to a powerful state or a freebooter was one thing, but delivering your brother, wife, and children was another matter altogether. Other pillaged and vulnerable societies had become raiders in order to survive. The Sisala hoped they wouldn't have to, but abducting strangers was the ugly truth of survival in the era of the slave trade. Powerful men as far away as Britain, France, the Netherlands, and Brazil and as close as Asante, Gonja, Dagomba, and Mossi had forced their hand, decided the rules of the game, and dictated the terms of continued existence. Out there beyond the wall were hostile states, a constant stream of raiders, and breakaway princes seeking to establish dominion in new lands. The bloodletting of the modern world allowed for no havens or safe places. The state of emergency was not the exception but the rule. The refuge became the hunting grounds for soldiers of fortune whose prizes were people.

Gwolu was not unique. It was a town like many others. It was "a common sample of humanity." It was filled with people who were passive and cowardly, kind and courageous, trustworthy and treacherous; mostly they were people trying to survive. They built the wall because they were required to do so; circumstance dictated their hand and they were desperate to live at all costs except being slaves. Like most people, they would have preferred a different set of circumstances, or the luxury of not having to act at all. They no doubt dreaded the thought of battling Babatu and his troops but had no choice in the matter. The thought of abandoning the settlement and taking flight again crossed their minds. Some did, but the others, perhaps tired of pulling up stakes, started digging the trenches. The wall might be enough of a deterrent to direct the marauder elsewhere; if not, they would have to take up arms. They couldn't contain the danger out there, so they contained themselves.

While they built the wall they preferred not to think of all the terrible things that might happen, only about keeping the danger on the outside. Neighboring clans assisted those in Gwolu in hollowing out the ditches, moving great barrows full of earth, hauling pails of water, mixing the clay with straw and dung, erecting sections of the walls, building the gates, designing the slots for arms, sharpening wood spikes and sinking them in the embankment, and then starting the process over again for the second wall. Other towns contributed their labor, knowing that if necessary, they too could find shelter behind the rampart. After four months of intensive labor, the wall was completed.

They hoped they were safe, but the wall's very presence reminded them that they were not. And even if they knew next to nothing about the world out there, and hadn't ever traveled beyond the settlements of neighboring clans, they knew in their gut that a wall wasn't enough to protect them. They suspected that the wall, like the ramparts and barricades erected in other beleaguered towns, could be mounted or toppled by a mighty enemy. When the news traveled that Sati, the fortified town on which they had modeled their wall, had fallen to Babatu, they knew they'd just have to wait and see. The town was here today but could be gone tomorrow like the thousand other towns that no one remembers ever existed. So all this hope and fear became a part of the wall, just like the water and straw and mud upon which they staked their lives. When the enemy arrived, they would find out if it had all been folly or if they had gambled correctly.

THE ELDERS BOASTED, "We trounced Babatu, the ruler of the world." The council of men guided us to the wall where the fighting battalions repelled Babatu. The fetish priest recounted the story. He wore a tattered and dirty trench coat that gave him the appearance of someone urbane and destitute. As he spoke, he extended his soiled beige arms and pointed toward the bulwark.

"We defended our village against raiders," said the priest. "If someone breached the outer wall, the inner fortification and the poisoned arrows of the warriors prevented further penetration." The enemy died in the trenches. In the heat of war, the besieged were unable to tend properly to their own dead, let alone that of the enemy, whose corpses were dragged to the bush and left for vultures to feed on.

The priest spread his arms to indicate the massive girth of the rampart, but with his arms spread wide he appeared frail and emaciated, not at all substantial like the immense wall he wanted us to imagine. There were two circular barricades, one enclosed by another at three hundred yards' distance. The inner wall surrounded the entirety of the town, and the outer wall protected the fields and crops as well as the water supply. The gates pointed toward the four corners of the earth, controlled the movement in and out of town, and allowed for multiple avenues of escape if all else failed. The trench increased the defensive capacity of the barricade and felled the combatants able to overcome the outer wall.

Another man, outfitted with the bow and arrow of his grandfather, joined the priest and assumed the position of the warrior. "Men would lie in the holes in the outer walls and shoot arrows," the priest continued. "The front of the hole was narrow and the back was wide. This way the men could enter the holes and not be seen from the outside."

The warriors positioned their bows through the narrow slots of the wall. Other men, waiting behind them, prepared to take their places when they became exhausted or if they fell. The fighters were ensconced in the triangular apertures of the barricade, so they were protected from the enemy's fire but were able to unleash their own. The aperture resembled a pyramid turned on its side, the opening successively narrowed to a thin strip at the exterior of the wall; the slit was large enough to allow for only the passage of arrows or the barrel of a musket. Cloistered within these burrows, they discharged lances and poisoned arrows. The men were outfitted in war clothes fashioned after those of their enemies, the soldiers of powerful states like Gonja, Dagomba, and the Mossi who enslaved them. By mimicking the victors, they intended to seize hold of their power. The war smocks were covered with leather and metal amulets to repel arrows and herbal sachets to offer spiritual protection.

Rigged and ready, the men of Gwolu established the line of defense. If women played a role in protecting the town, the elders failed to mention it. But a woman was the symbol of Babatu's defeat. When Kantanfugu, a Sisala warrior renowned for his bravery and military prowess, killed one of Babatu's warriors, he discovered to his surprise upon removing the war garments of his slain opponent that the brave man lying on the ground was a woman masquerading as a man. Adorned in trousers and a man's robe with a turban covering her head, she had waged war undiscovered. Although it was believed she was originally from Salaga, she was known only by the name she called herself, Mallam Muhamman. The news of this transvestite warrior who was nicknamed Ka Boye, which means "conceal yourself" in Hausa, spread quickly. The story passed from town to town and people began saying, "Look, Babatu's soldiers are women who mount horses and make war on us." Realizing that their enemies were only women, the Sisala rose in revolt.

"AFRICAN PEOPLE DIDN'T passively accept slavery," the priest told us in a voice resonant with pride. "We fought back."

I wondered why the priest had chosen the words "African people" to explain their resistance, since the Sisala had battled with other Africans who had intended to make them slaves. African people represented no unanimity of sentiment or common purpose or recognizable collectivity but rather heterogeneous and embattled social groups. The identity unraveled as it was projected back in time. What did Babatu or the warriors of Gonja and Asante know about the dreams of fugitives? How could they have envisioned the sacrifice required to name yourself anew?

Unlike *we come together* or *we who fled* or *we who were liberated, African people* crossed the lines of raider and captive, broker and commodity, master and slave, kin and stranger. The capaciousness of these words— African people—was as dangerous as it was promising. No doubt, for the priest, the longing that resided within them concerned *what we might become together* or *the possibility of solidarity*, which would enable us to defeat the enemy again, except that they described the enemy too.

In the eighteenth and nineteenth centuries, few people in West Africa had imagined themselves as African people or conceived of their histories as intertwined with a larger struggle against slavery being waged on the continent and in the Americas, or experienced the magnitude of the millions dead and exiled. Representing the fight against slavery waged by commoners and stateless societies did not engender a grand heroic narrative of Africans resisting slavery or the tragic one of betraying "their own people." It was a history that consisted of anecdotes, recollections, oral tales, rumors, folklore, and bits and fragments of narrative, which cohered not into one grand story but rather an assemblage of overlapping, disparate, and broken histories. Africa was never one identity, but plural and contested ones.

Listening to the priest, I came to realize that it mattered whether the "we" was called *we who become together* or *African people* or *slaves*, because these identities were tethered to conflicting narratives of *our* past, and, as well, these names conjured different futures.

GWOLU WAS MY LAST STOP on the slave route. There I had hoped to discover the signpost that pointed the way to those on the opposite shore of the Atlantic. While their ancestors were the *grunshi* sold in the market at Salaga and the captives on reprieve, the story they remembered best was the one in which they had eluded the net. I must admit I was disappointed not to have found any stories or songs or tales about the millions who had been unable to experience flight, evade terror, and taste victory.

I had come to the end of my journey, so if I didn't recover any traces of the captives here, in the heartland of slavery, then it was unlikely that I would ever find any. Theirs was an impossible chronicle, which no one had been willing or able to tell. Excepting for the baobabs, the enslaved had disappeared without leaving behind any witnesses.

I hadn't met anyone who spoke of the persons who were trampled by horses as they fled conquering armies, the towns that vanished overnight, the soldiers of the defeated army sold in the aftermath of a civil war, the nephew sold by his uncle for failing to present him with a female slave and three cows when his father died, the junior brother sold by his elder because of a squabble regarding their father's property, the girl sold by her guardian after her parents died, the niece seized when her uncle was away traveling, the fifteen-year-old boy sentenced to slavery because he had committed adultery with an important man's wife, the girls offered as gifts to mercenary soldiers, the young man kidnapped at the instigation of his brother-in-law, the two girls who, running away from freebooters, lost their way and ran into the territory of a hostile country where they were caught and made slaves, the prosperous trader seized trying to buy guinea corn in a faraway town, the band of children kidnapped while playing in the woods, the starving and impoverished who offered themselves as slaves, the migrants who fled to a strange country to escape raiders but were sold rather than sheltered, the sisters accused of witchcraft by the chief, the boy pawned by his uncle and sold to the Portuguese before his mother could redeem him, the infants abandoned along the trail, the father who offered himself as slave rather than allow his son to lose his liberty, the slaves sacrificed on the graves of kings, the infidels who resisted conversion to Islam, and all the millions and millions driven to the sea and carried away.

In Gwolu, it finally dawned on me that those who stayed behind told different stories than the children of the captives dragged across the sea. Theirs wasn't a memory of loss or of capitivity, but of survival and good fortune. After all, they had eluded the barracoon, unlike my ancestors. They had been able to reconstruct shattered communities. Despite their present destitution, they had fashioned a narrative of liberation in which the glory of the past was the entry to a redeemed future. My narrative was a history of defeat, which at best was the precondition for a victory, long-awaited, but that hadn't yet arrived. This was the story I had been trying to find. And in listening for my story I had almost missed theirs.

I had been waiting to hear a story with which I was already familiar. But things were different here; everyone spoke of fighting slavery, but no one spoke of slaves. Their story of slavery was a narrative of victory, a tale of resistance and overcoming, in which the captives had been banished. Even its sounds were strange to my ear, war chants and military songs rather than dirges, field hollers, and sorrow songs. I couldn't penetrate its idiom. In Gwolu, the history of slavery was a tale of fugitives and warriors, not of masters and slaves.

The language of the triumphant was as different from the language of the conquered, as that of the living from the dead. Although, like me, the Sisala were also the descendants of people who had been scattered, this event was not a source of pain but rather a source of pride. The past for them was a cause for hope, whereas I longed for a future that could be wrested from an irredeemable past. My present was the future that had been created by men and women in chains, by human commodities, by chattel persons. I tried hard to envision a future in which this past had ended, and most often I failed.

I DIDN'T FIND WHAT I had hoped to in Gwolu. And I wasn't sure how to make use of what I had learned. At the end of the journey, I knew that Africa wasn't dead to me, nor was it just a grave. My future was entangled with it, just as it was entangled with every other place on the globe where people were struggling to live and hoping to thrive.

The fugitive's dream exceeded the borders of the continent; it was a dream of the world house. If I learned anything in Gwolu, it was that old identities sometimes had to be jettisoned in order to invent new ones. Your life just might depend on this capacity for self-fashioning. Naming oneself anew was sometimes the price exacted by the practice of freedom. Maybe this was what the priest had intended to suggest by the words "African people," that is, they referred not to the past or to an extant collectivity but to a potential unleashed by struggles for autonomy and democracy. The priest as easily might have said *fugitives* or *migrants* or *commoners* or *dreamers*. As circumstances changed, so too did the ways we imagined ourselves.

The bridge between the people of Gwolu and me wasn't what we had suffered or what we had endured but the aspirations that fueled flight and the yearning for freedom. It was these shared dreams that might open a common road to a future in which the longings and disappointed hopes of captives, slaves, and fugitives might be realized. If an African identity was to be meaningful at all, at least to me, then what it meant or was to mean could be elaborated only in the fight against slavery, which, as John reminded me, was not about dead people or old forts built by white men but the power of others to determine whether you lived or died. A name was just a call for freedom, a rallying cry against the imperial states and their soldiers, an admonition to steer clear of the merchants of death and the rich men cannibals, a lament for your dead. And this loss and desire gave meaning to the words *we who become together*.

If after a year in Ghana I could still call myself an African American, it was because my Africa had its source in the commons created by fugitives and rebels, in the courage of suicidal girls aboard slave ships, and in the efforts, thwarted and realized, of revolutionaries intent upon stopping the clock and instituting a new order, even if it cost them their lives. For me, returning to the source didn't lead to the great courts and to the regalia of kings and queens. The legacy that I chose to claim was articulated in the ongoing struggle to escape, stand down, and defeat slavery in all of its myriad forms. It was the fugitive's legacy. It didn't require me to wait on bended knee for a great emancipator. It wasn't the dream of a White House, even if it was in Harlem, but of a free territory. It was a dream of autonomy rather than nationhood. It was the dream of an elsewhere, with all its promises and dangers, where the stateless might, at last, thrive.

IN THE SMALL CLEARING made by the ring of houses, four girls were playing a game of jump rope. Their mothers and grandmothers had been unable to speak about Gwolu's past, so the girls spoke for them. Two girls were at the center of the circle and the others surrounded them singing and clapping. Mumbi waited her turn and then jumped into the circle to the girls' delight, singing as she twirled round and round in the center. I stood at the outskirts of the circle, watching. My feet were not moving, but I felt as if I were dancing too. When Mumbi exited the circle, the girls resumed their song:

> Gwolu is a town of gold
> When you enter the circle
> You will be protected
> You will be safe

The young man standing next to me offered to translate. "Sister" was the first word out of his mouth. As soon as I heard it, I readied myself for what I was sure would follow. It was the lure, and I waited for him to reel me in. He said something that I couldn't hear because of the girls' song. I shook my head to indicate that I didn't understand what he had said. He moved a few inches closer to me and then shouted in my ear. The girls are singing about those taken from Gwolu and sold into slavery in the Americas. They are singing about the diaspora.

Here it was—my song, the song of the lost tribe. I closed my eyes and I listened.

NOTES

Prologue: The Path of Strangers

5 "white" slaves David Eltis, *The Rise of African Slavery in the Americas* (New York: Cambridge University Press, 2000), 57.

5 Iberians can be credited David Brion Davis, *Slavery and Human Progress* (New York: Oxford University Press, 1984), 30.

7 seven hundred thousand captives In the eighteenth century, nearly 700,000 captives were transported from the Gold Coast. We need to remember that the volume of trade was at least 20 percent higher than the export figures. Paul E. Lovejoy, *Transformations in Slavery: A History of Slavery in Africa* (Cambridge: Cambridge University Press, 1983), 56, 61.

7 the sprawling clans of Juffure Alex Haley, *Roots* (Garden City, NY: Doubleday, 1976). Henry Louis Gates, Jr., *Wonders of the African World* (New York: Knopf, 1999).

8 a stranger is like water running R. S. Rattray, *Ashanti Proverbs* (Oxford: Clarendon Press, 1916), 143.

8 scar between native and citizen Julia Kristeva, *Strangers to Ourselves* (New York: Columbia University Press, 1991), 98.

16 no record of their lives Michel Foucault describes these lives as "infamous in the strict sense: they no longer exist except through the terrible words that were destined to render them forever unworthy of the memory of men." "Lives of Infamous Men," in *The Essential Foucault*, edited by Paul Rabinow and Nikolas Rose (New York: New Press, 2003), 284.

ONE · *Afrotopia*

22 Christiansborg Castle At the end of the seventeenth century, the majority of slaves deported from the Gold Coast were shipped from Accra. Ludewig Ferdinand Roemer, *A Reliable Account of the Coast of Guinea*, trans. Selena Axelrod Winsnes (Oxford: Oxford University Press, 2000), 225–28; Per O. Hernaes, *Slaves, Danes and African Coast Society: The Danish Slave Trade from West Africa and Afro-Danish Relations on the Eighteenth-Century Gold Coast* (Trondheim: Trondheim Studies in History, 1995); Paul Erdmann Isert, *Letters on West Africa and the Slave Trade: Paul Erdmann Isert's Journey to Guinea and the Caribbean Islands in Columbia, 1788*, trans. and ed. Selena Axelrod Winsnes (Oxford: Oxford University Press, 1992); *The Writings of Jean Barbot on West Africa*, Vols. 1 and 2, edited by P.E.H. Hair, Adam Jones, and Robin Law (London: Hakluyt Society, 1992): Vol. 2, 435.

22 a fortress and a foreign entity Baffour Agyeman-Duah writes, "The government is still considered to be a foreign entity, and too many people feel no compunction or obligation to protect its property or services." "Ghana, 1982–6: The Politics of the P.N.D.C.," *Journal of Modern African Studies* 25, no. 4 (1987): 613–42.

22 "The old slave castle" Ayi Kwei Armah, *Fragments* (Boston: Houghton Mifflin, 1970), 44.

25 another path to Utopia had been blocked Frantz Fanon, *The Wretched of the Earth*, trans. Constance Farrington (New York: Grove Press, 1963), 164.

30 "There was in existence a fundamental class contradiction" Walter Rodney, "African Slavery and Other Forms of Social Oppression on the Upper Guinea Coast in the Context of the Atlantic Slave Trade," in *Forced Migration: The Import of the Export Slave Trade on African Societies*, edited by Joseph E. Inikori (London: Hutchinson, 1982), 64.

34 "We shall live among our equals" Charles H. Wesley, *Prince Hall: Life and Legacy* (Philadelphia: Afro-American Cultural and Historical Museum, 1977), 66–68.

34 the race would be redeemed Wilson Jeremiah Moses, *Afrotopia: The Roots of African American Popular History* (New York: Cambridge University Press, 1998), 55, 68. Moses notes that Africans in the diaspora "hoped to find within history some explanation of the contemporary African's 'barbarian' status (arrested development) and a vindication of their race from the charge of perpetual inferiority." What developed in response to this challenge was "a historiography of decline or narratives of defeat that could account for captivity of Africa's fallen-ness and at the same time proffer a vision of progress."

34 "not only unprotected" William L. Patterson, ed., *We Charge Genocide* (1951; repr., New York: International Publishers, 1971).

34 "The independence of Ghana" "Ghana Independence, Africa's Biggest Event," *Chicago Defender*, February 16, 1957; "Hail Ghana," *New York Amsterdam News*, March 9, 1957. Cited in Roger A. Davidson, "A Question of Freedom: African Americans and Ghanaian Independence," *Negro History Bulletin* 60, no. 3 (July–September 1997).

35 "I'll see Ghana yet" *Soledad Brother: The Prison Letters of George Jackson* (1970; repr., Chicago: Lawrence Hill Books, 1994), letters of April 18, 1965, and March 3, 1966.

35 had traveled to Ghana Penny M. Von Eschen, *Race Against Empire: Black Americans and Anticolonialism, 1937–1957* (Ithaca: Cornell University Press, 1997), 167–68. Norman Manley, the chief minister of Jamaica; Grantley Adams, the prime minister of Barbados; and Eric Williams, the chief minister of Trinidad, also attended.

35 began to weep *The Autobiography of Martin Luther King, Jr.*, ed. Clayborne Carson (New York: Warner Books, 1998), 112.

36 An apocryphal story Kevin K. Gaines, *American Africans in Ghana* (Chapel Hill: Univeristy of North Carolina Press, 2006), 5.

37 Sylvia Boone acted as a cutltural ambassador Sylvia Ardyn Boone, *West African Travels* (New York: Random House, 1974), 236.

37 the Revolutionist Returnees Maya Angelou, *All God's Children Need Traveling Shoes* (New York: Vintage, 1991), 18.

37 Independence was a short century Okwui Enwezor, ed., *The Short Century: Independence and Liberation Movements in Africa 1945–1994* (Munich: Prestel, 2001).

38 As Nkrumah tried to embrace the world Ali Mazrui, *Nkrumah's Legacy* (Accra: Ghana Universities Press, 2004). C.L.R. James, *Nkrumah and the Ghana Revolution* (Westport, CT: Lawrence Hill & Co., 1977), 182–84.

38 "We were tolerated" Leslie Alexander Lacy, *The Rise and Fall of a Proper Negro* (New York: Macmillan, 1970), 210.

39 "horizon of hope" David Scott, *Refashioning Futures: Criticism After Postcoloniality* (Princeton: Princeton University Press, 1999); *Conscripts of Modernity* (Durham, NC: Duke Univeristy Press, 2004); and David Scott, "The Dialectic of Defeat: An Interview with Rupert Lewis," *Small Axe*, 10 (September 2001) 86.

40 freedom dreams Robin Kelley, *Freedom Dreams* (Boston: Beacon Press, 2003).

40 Terror was "captivity without the possibility of flight" Louis Althusser, "The International of Decent Feelings," cited in Fred Moten, *The New International of Decent Feeling, Social Text*, 20.3 (Fall 2002), 194.

40 "conjured up the image of a New Jerusalem" B. Jewsiewicki and V. Y. Mudimbe, "Africans' Memories and Contemporary History of Africa," *History and Theory* 32, no. 4 (December 1993): 7; Ali Mazrui, "Nkrumah: The Leninist Czar," *Transition* 75/76 (1997): 106–26.

42 Whatever bridges I might build Brent Edwards, *The Practice of Diaspora* (Cambridge, MA: Harvard University Press, 2003), 15. Edwards employs the French word *décalage* to describe the gaps, discrepancy, and misunderstanding constitutive of diaspora. The joint, for him, best conveys the nature of this connection: "The joint is a curious place, as it is both the point of separation and the point of linkage."

42 "I didn't want to remember" Maya Angelou, *All God's Children Need Traveling Shoes* (New York: Vintage, 1991), 102–105.

45 Ghanaian citizenship In 2005, a measure had been passed to grant African Americans special life-long visas, which would enable them to have Ghanaian passports.

45 "it's the lonelist moment of your life" David Jenkins, *Black Zion* (London: Wildwood House, 1975), 165.

46 "the abstract nakedness of being nothing but human" Hannah Arendt, *The Origins of Totalitarianism* (San Diego: Harcourt, 1968), 299–300. Arendt provides a powerful description of the dangers of being "outside the pale of law," denied the protection of citizenship, and stripped of rights of equality.

46 disease of royalty Ayi Kwei Armah, *The Healers* (London: Heinemann, 1978).

47 "From gold and silver" Thomas More, *Utopia*, trans. Clarence H. Miller (New Haven: Yale University Press, 2001), 61, 75–76, 87. More turned the world of value on its head by denigrating the precious metal that was the ideal of the universal equivalent of money. But he did so by creating a set of dishonored persons who embodied the degrading effects of exchange. In the topsy-turvy world he depicted, some things remained the same.

47 We buy a slave Akosua Adoma Perbi, "A History of Indigenous Slavery in Ghana from the 15th to the 19th Centuries" (PhD diss., University of Ghana, Legon, 1997), 156.

47 mutability T. C. McCaskie speculates that the association between excrement and wealth has to do with their volatility as substances and "their capacity to transgress and to rupture categorical boundaries by conversion." "Accumulation, Wealth and Belief in Asante History," *Africa* 53, no. 1 (1983): 31.

47 The eye that sees gold O. Rytz, ed., *Gonja Proverbs* (Legon: Institute of African Studies, University of Ghana, 1966), 179.

TWO · *Markets and Martyrs*

51 European sailors and merchants The people "came to them naked and with many pieces of gold in their hands to exchange them for old clothes and for other things of little value, which the crew carried in the ship." Hernando del Pulgar, *Crónica de los señores reyes católicos don Fernando y doña Isabel de Castilla y de Aragon escrita por su cronista Hernando del Pulgar cotexada con antiguos manuscritos y aumentado de varias illustraciones ye enmendas* (1565; repr., Valencia: Imprenta de Benito Monfort, 1780); John W. Blake, *Europeans in West Africa, 1450–1560* (London: Hakluyt Society, 1942), 205.

51 "Mina de Ouro" "The origin of the modern English name Elmina is uncertain. The native name is Ednaa or Edinaa, but it would have been exceptional for the Portuguese to use a native name, and it seems more likely that Edinaa is a corruption of Elmina than vice versa." W.E.F. Ward, *A History of Ghana* (London: Allen & Unwin, 1958), 66.

51 The gold obtained The gold trade flourished at least until the 1530s. John Vogt, *Portuguese Rule on the Gold Coast 1469–1682* (Athens: University of Georgia Press, 1979), 201.

51 "there was no servile class" Walter Rodney notes: "There was in existence a fundamental class contradiction between the ruling nobility and the commoners; and the ruling class joined hands with the Europeans in exploiting the African masses. "African Slavery and Other Forms of Social Oppression," 64.

51 They kidnapped and purchased slaves Joseph Miller, *Way of Death: Merchant Capitalism and the Angolan Slave Trade* (Madison, WI: University of Wisconsin Press, 1988), 115.

51 For each slave sold For the period 1500–1535, it has been estimated that the Portuguese imported 10,000–12,000 slaves to Elmina. This figure doesn't take into account the numbers landed by smugglers. According to John Vogt in *Portuguese Rule*, "An adequate and continuous supply of slaves was indispensable for the success of the Portuguese trade at São Jorge da Mina . . . without such slaves much of the remainder of the trade goods would not have been sold." Slaves were sold for three to six ounces of gold. Also see *Chronicles of Gonja*, 10.

51 Slaves fetched better prices on the Gold Coast Hugh Thomas, *The Slave Trade: The Story of the Atlantic Slave Trade, 1440–1870* (New York: Simon and Schuster, 1997), 106; Robert Garfield, *A History of São Tome Island 1470–1655* (San Francisco: Mellen Research University Press, 1992), 45-61.

51 In the first century and a half Until 1650, the Portuguese transported virtually all of the slaves shipped from West Africa. John K. Thornton, *Africa and Africans in the Making of the Atlantic World, 1400–1680* (New York: Cambridge University Press, 1992), 155. The English surpassed them in the middle of the seventeenth century.

51 two million Africans Lovejoy, *Transformations in Slavery*, 38, 47.

52 sixty slave markets Herbert S. Klein, *The Atlantic Slave Trade* (New York: Cambridge University Press, 1999), 208–209; Perbi, "History of the Indigenous Slavery in Ghana," 70–76.

52 Elmina was a boomtown Harvey M. Feinberg, *Africans and Europeans in West Africa: Elminans and Dutchmen on the Gold Coast During the Eighteenth Century* (Philadelphia: The American Philosophical Association, 1989), 84–85. Christopher R. DeCorse, *An Archeology of Elmina* (Washington: Smithsonian Institution, 2001), 31–32. Ray Kea argues that shift from the trade in goods to the trade in captives resulted in a shift of settlement patterns and a "movement away from urbanization and town growth toward relatively widespread de-urbanization. This shift constituted a major economic and demographic upheaval." See Kea, *Settlement, Trade, and Polities in the Seventeenth-Century Gold Coast* (Baltimore: Johns Hopkins University Press, 1982), 11.

58 The Portuguese built Elmina Castle P.E.H. Hair, *The Founding of the Castelo de São Jorge da Mina: An Analysis of the Sources* (Madison: University of Wisconsin-Madison African Studies Program, 1994), 15. According to Hair, in 1471, a respected citizen of Lisbon and agent of the Portuguese king Dom Afonso V "discovered gold at the place we now call the Mina." Fernao Gomes established the first trading post at Elmina in 1472. He held the contract for the exploration of the Guinea Coast. For the riches extracted from Mina, he was ennobled and given a coat of arms—a shield with a crest and three heads of Negroes on a field of silver, each with golden rings in ears and nose, and a collar of gold around the neck, and "da Mina" as a surname in memory of its discovery (109-10).

59 Portuguese to become the masters The Portuguese transported 150,000 slaves to the Atlantic islands and Portugal in little over a decade and virtually all of the enslaved Africans who reached the Americas by 1620. See Blackburn, *Making of New World Slavery*, 112; Thornton, *Africa and Africans*, 155.

59 the encounter between Europe and Africa Christopher Miller, *Blank Darkness: Africanist Discourse in French* (Chicago: University of Chicago Press, 1985); V. Y.

Mudimbe, *The Invention of Africa: Gnosis, Philosophy and the Order of Knowledge* (Bloomington: Indiana University Press, 1988).

60 "land of the negroes" Gomes Eanes de Zurara, *The Chronicle of the Discovery and Conquest of Guinea*, ed. and trans. Charles Raymond Beazley and Edgar Prestage (London: Hakluyt Society, 1896–99), I: xxx.

60 Cartographers drew the imaginary places Robert W. Harms observes that Guinea was "one of those imaginary geographical constructions of European cartographers that kept showing up in different places on different maps." *The Diligent: A Voyage Through the Worlds of the Slave Trade* (New York: Basic Books, 2002), 114. V. Y. Mudimbe tracks its first appearance to a fifteenth-century papal document. *The Idea of Africa* (Bloomington: Indiana University Press, 1994), 32. According to the OED, Guinea's exact origins are unknown.

61 symbols of their sovereign and God A.C. de C.M. Saunders, *A Social History of Black Slaves and Freedmen in Portugal, 1441–1555* (New York: Cambridge University Press, 1982), 13; Robin Blackburn, *The Making of New World Slavery: From the Baroque to the Modern, 1492–1800* (New York: Verso, 1997), 112; Thornton, *Africa and Africans*, 155.

61 *terra nullius* The Romanus Pontifex (1454) established the political and theological authority for Europeans to seize the lands of non-Christian people, who were required to pledge their submission to the king of Portugal and to convert to Christianity. Submission or subjugation was the outcome of this military philosophy of conversion. Mudimbe, *Idea of Africa*, 30–37.

61 *Fala de preto* Portuguese seamen and traders employed a simple trade pidgin to attend to matters sexual and alimentary, but diplomatic relations relied on black interpreters. Slave interpreters were essential to Portuguese expansion in Africa and, for this reason, all voyages to Guinea included black translators. The royal ordinances or *regimentos* issued by the Crown to ships on exploratory voyages to Guinea included a routine instruction directing seamen to kidnap natives, male and female alike, so that they could be trained as translators. P. E. Russell, "Some Socio-Linguistic Problems Concerning the Fifteenth-Century Portuguese Discoveries in the African Atlantic," in P. E. Russell, comp., *Portugal, Spain and the African Atlantic, 1343–1490: Chivalry and Crusade from John of Gaunt to Henry the Navigator* (Brookfield, VT: Variorum, 1995), 4.

61 "repay them with love" "E que por esas cousas de amor, el-Rei lhas queria pagar com amor." João de Barros, "Décadas da Ásia (excerptos das quarto décadas) Ensaio biográfico e histórico-crítico, selecção, notas e indices remissivos, por Mário Gonçalves Viana" (Pôrto: Editôra Educação Nacional, 1944), 118, excerpted in Hair, *Founding of the Castelo*, 105; Duarte Pacheco Pereira, *Esmeraldo de Situ Orbis*, trans. George H. T. Kimble (London: Hakluyt Society, 1937).

62 Portugal's rights of occupation Herman Bennett, "Sons of Adam," *Representations* 92 (Winter 2006).

62 Even the king's scribes disagreed J. D. Fage, "A Comment on Duarte Pacheco Pereira's Account of the Lower Guinea Coastlands in his Esmeraldo de Situ Orbis and Some Other Early Accounts," *History in Africa* 7 (1980): 47–80. Hair concludes, "It is unlikely that any further evidence will ever be found to clarify this aspect of the history, hence varying interpretations will flourish and varying significances be conse-

quently given to the whole event of the founding of the fort." Ballong-Wen-Mewuda contends that the Akan did not give permission to build the castle; if so, traditional ceremonies of libation would have been conducted. *Founding of the Castelo*, 38, 87n172.

62 **love had many expressions** José Rabasa, *Inventing America: Spanish Historiography and the Formation of Eurocentrism* (Norman: University of Oklahoma Press, 1993), 6. Love was the language of dominion; it required nothing less than Caramansa's submission to the Christian God and his earthly representatives; it demanded the viceroy's self-abnegation.

63 **ferried the captives from the Slave Rivers** The Portuguese established trade relations in Benin in the 1470s and settled the islands of São Tomé and Fernando Po in the 1470s and '80s. Blackburn, *Making of New World Slavery*, 106; A.F.C. Ryder, *Benin and the Europeans, 1485–1897* (New York: Humanities Press, 1969), 26.

63 **seared with the cross** Ryder, *Benin and the Europeans*, 26, 55–57.

64 **the royal converts** Basil Davidson, *The African Slave Trade* (Boston: Back Bay Books, 1961), 142; Harms, *The Diligent*; Michael A. Gomez, *Exchanging Our Country Marks: African Identity in the Colonial and Antebellum South* (Chapel Hill: University of North Carolina Press, 1998), 142.

64 *ad propagandam fidem* Vogt, *Portuguese Rule*, 52. The Romanus Pontifex was one in a series of papal bulls issued by Nicholas V granting and ensuring the Portuguese monopoly over the slave trade, as well as granting them dominion over Guinea and its inhabitants. The first slaves were kidnapped in 1441. See Mudimbe, *Invention of Africa*, 30–37; Blackburn, *Making of New World Slavery*, 107; Thornton, *Africa and Africans*, 45, 51; Anselm Guezo, "The Other Side of the Story: Essays on the Atlantic Slave Trade" (manuscript), 26.

64 **The Portuguese attacked the villagers** Blackburn, *Making of New World Slavery*, 104; Gomes Eanes de Zurara, *Chronicle of the Discovery and Conquest of Guinea*, 63–83.

64 **Saint George had many faces** Samantha Riches, *St. George: Hero, Martyr, and Myth* (Stroud: Sutton, 2000).

66 **an emblem for the suffering of slaves** This description of Saint George's trials is culled from Eduardo Galeano, *Memory of Fire*, trans. Cedric Belfrage, 3 vols. (New York: Pantheon, 1985–1988), Vol. 2.

67 **In the horrible trials endured by saints** Carole Walker Bynum, *The Resurrection of the Body* (New York: Columbia University Press, 1995).

67 **"commodities in the hands of merchants"** Claude Meillassoux, *The Anthropology of Slavery: The Womb of Iron and Gold* (Chicago: University of Chicago Press, 1991), 109.

68 **The dead were reborn** Ibid., 106, 107–108, 138–40.

68 **"neither death nor rebirth was glorious"** Aharon Appelfeld, *The Iron Tracks*, trans. Jeffrey M. Green (New York: Schocken Books, 1998), 13. On reincarnation, see J. B. Danquah, *The Akan Doctrine of God* (London: Lutterworth Press, 1944), 158–61.

68 **toiling away in Lisbon** See Saunders, *Social History of Black Slaves and Freedmen in Portugal*, 59. By the mid-sixteenth century, 10 percent of the population of Lisbon was black. By 1551, there were 9,950 slaves within the city's population.

68 The Portuguese referred to them as *braços* Stephan Palmié, "A Taste for Human Commodities," in *Slave Cultures and the Cultures of Slavery*, edited by Stephan Palmié (Knoxville: University of Tennessee Press, 1995), 46.

68 The Spanish called them *pieza de India* Hugh Thomas, *The Slave Trade: The Story of the Atlantic Slave Trade, 1440–1870* (New York: Simon and Schuster, 1997), 212fn; *A Historical Guide to World Slavery*, edited by Seymour Drescher and Stanley L. Engerman (New York: Oxford University Press, 1998), 88.

69 "whitewashed the black man's history" Imahkhus Vienna Robinson, "Is the Black Man's History Being Whitewashed?" *Uburu*, 9: 48–50.

70 The family loves the corpse Kwame Arhin, "The Economic Implications of Transformations in Akan Funeral Rites," *Africa: Journal of International African Institute* 64.3 (1994) 307–22. Sjaak van der Geest, "Funerals for the Living Conversations with Elderly People in Kwahu, Ghana," *African Studies Review*, 43.3 (December 2000): 103–29.

70 "Africa was a land of graves without bodies" Kwadwo Opoku-Agyeman, *Cape Coast Castle* (Ghana: Afram Publications, 1996).

72 "People pride themselves" Emmanuel Akyeampong, "History, Memory, Slave-Trade and Slavery in Anlo (Ghana)," *Slavery and Abolition*, 22.3 (December 2001), 19.

72 "but now we're poor" Bayo Holsey, "Routes of Remembrance: The Transatlantic Slave Trade in the Ghanian Imagination" (PhD diss., Columbia University, 2003), 105.

75 shattered any illusions of a unanimity of sentiment David Scott and Brent Edwards suggest that these forms of misunderstanding, bad faith, unhappy translation, and extended disputes define the character of diaspora. See David Scott, *Refashioning Futures: Criticism After Postcolonialism* (Princeton: Princeton University Press, 1999), 123–24; Brent Hayes Edwards, *The Practice of Diaspora* (Cambridge, MA: Harvard University Press, 2003), 14.

THREE · *The Family Romance*

77 "rope of captivity" Paul Riesman, *First Find Your Child a Good Mother: The Construction of Self in Two African Communities* (New Brunswick, NJ: Rutgers University Press, 1992), 205.

77 "lays herself low to his lust" W.E.B. DuBois, *The Souls of Black Folk* (1903; New York: Penguin Classics, 1989).

78 the Dutch slave trade The Dutch exported only a few hundred slaves from the Gold Coast in the seventeenth century. This number would increase exponentially by the first decade of the eighteenth century. Johannes Postma estimates that 136 slaves were exported from the Gold Coast in the years 1675–1699, but the volume of trade increased to almost 3,000 in the years 1700–1709. See "The Origin of African Slaves: The Dutch Activities on the Guinea Coast, 1675–1795," in *Race and Slavery in the Western Hemisphere: Quantitative Studies*, edited by Stanley L. Engerman and Eugene B. Genovese (Princeton: Princeton University Press, 1975); Postma, *The Dutch in the Atlantic Slave Trade, 1600–1815* (New York: Cambridge University Press, 1990), 299.

79 For tracking purposes Postma, *The Dutch in the Atlantic Trade*, 52.

79 Curaçao, which was the way station Sometime after 1648, Curaçao emerged as a slave port. See J. Hartog, *Curaçao, from Colonial Dependence to Autonomy* (Aruba: De Wit, 1968).

79 The numbers identified Ibid., 37.

79 officers traveled with instructions for branding Ibid., Appendix 8, 368.

79 picture of the purchase and branding of property William Bosman, *A New and Accurate Description of the Coast of Guinea, Divided into the Gold, the Slave and the Ivory Coasts* (London: Cass, 1967), 363–64.

80 The mother's mark See Fred Moten, *In the Break* (Minneapolis: University of Minnesota Press, 2003), 17. Racism is another way of describing the marks passed from one generation to the next.

80 "a blank parody" Hortense J. Spillers, "Mama's Baby, Papa's Maybe" and "The Permanent Obliquity of an In(pha)llibly Straight: In the Time of the Daughters and the Fathers," in *Black, White, and in Color* (Chicago: University of Chicago Press, 2003).

FOUR · *Come, Go Back, Child*

86 The comings and goings of the spirit child Ben Okri writes that the spirit child "enters the world weighted with strange gifts of the soul" and "inextinguishable sense of exile." See *The Famished Road* (New York: Doubleday, 1993). His description of the spirit child echoes DuBois's description of the Negro as "gifted with a second sight" and a "stranger in his home." See *Souls of Black Folk*.

87 The origins of the word *odonkor* This etymology of *odonkor* is indebted to Mrs. Kofi Anyidoho. The word for "poor" shares the same root. *Odofu* means "loved one." See Wilhelm Muller, "Description of the Fetu Country," in Adam Jones, ed., *German Sources for West African History* (Wiesbaden: Franz Steiner, 1983), 325.

87 the words of the master R. S. Rattray, *Ashanti Law and Constitution* (1929; repr., New York: Negro Universities Press, 1969), 46; Rattray, *Ashanti Proverbs*, 123.

87 Being an outsider Moses Finley, "Slavery," *International Encyclopedia of the Social Sciences* (New York: Macmillan, 1967).

87 "The insistent, maddening, claustrophic pounding" James Baldwin, *Notes of a Native Son* (1955; repr., Boston: Beacon Press, 1983), 57, 111.

88 the need to "destroy tirelessly" C.L.R. James, *The Black Jacobins: Toussaint L'Ouverture and the San Domingo Revolution* (New York: Vintage Books, 1963), 88.

90 DNA tests And who were you after having discovered that your ancestors were Konkomba or Dagarti or Yoruba? Many of these identities were little more than the inventions of colonial administrators imposing their own fanciful taxonomies onto Africa. Could the fiction of origins resolve the stranger's dilemma? "Blacks Pin Hope on DNA to Fill in Slavery's Gaps in Family Trees," *New York Times*, July 25, 2005, A1, A17.

91 the word "revolution" Hannah Arendt, *On Revolution* (1963; repr., New York: Penguin Books, 1990), 47, 45.

92 Amina or Elmina slaves The identity assigned to the captives by Europeans was often the port or region from which they had been exported.

92 Akwamu was one of the principal states The majority of the slaves taken from the Gold Coast during this period had been shipped from Akwamu and the Fanti coast. Lovejoy, *Transformations in Slavery*, 95–97.

93 "*donkor* work" C.G.A. Oldendorp, *C.G.A. Oldendorp's History of the Mission of the Evangelical Brethren on the Caribbean Islands of St. Thomas, St. Croix, and St. John*, ed. Johann Jakob Bossard; ed. and trans. Arnold R. Highfield and Vladimir Barac (Ann Arbor: Karoma, 1987), 226. Oldendorp interpreted *donkor* work as night work because the chores were performed after laboring in the field. I believe it was called *donkor* work because the chores were considered especially onerous and degrading.

93 The rebels decided Pierre Pannet, *Report on the Execrable Conspiracy Carried Out by Amina Negroes on the Danish Island of St. Jan in America 1733*, trans. Aimery Caron and Arnold R. Highfield (St. Croix: Antilles Press, 1984); Oldendorp, *History of the Evangelical Brethren*, 220; Aimery P. Caron and Arnold R. Highfield, *The French Intervention in the St. John Slave Revolt of 1733–1734* (Virgin Islands: Bureau of Libraries, Museums and Archaeological Services, Department of Conservation and Cultural Affairs, 1981), 10.

94 An Akan-style polity Michael Craton, *Testing the Chains* (Ithaca: Cornell University Press, 1982), 99.

94 the gun-slave cycle The commodification of life in the context of the slave trade, according to Patrick Manning, resulted in a zero-sum game in which "one could gain only at the expense of one's neighbors." Patrick Manning, *Slavery and African Life* (New York: Cambridge University Press, 1990), 124.

95 the idea of revolving back to former times Arendt, *On Revolution*, 47, 45.

96 "murder the memory" Caryl Phillips, *Higher Ground* (New York: Vintage, 1995).

97 shattered a mother's image Frederick Douglass, *My Bondage and My Freedom* (1855; repr., New York: Dover, 1969), 42; Frederick Douglass, *Narrative of the Life of Frederick Douglass, An American Slave, Written by Himself* (1845; repr., New York: New American Library, 1968).

97 "Possessing nothing" Wilson Harris, "Continuity and Discontinuity," in *Selected Essays of Wilson Harris: The Unfinished Genesis of the Imagination*, edited by A. J. M. Bundy (New York: Routledge, 1999), 179.

98 Cleavage The journey from the Old World to the Americas, as Wilson Harris observes, was a "limbo gateway between Africa and the Caribbean." The dislocation that began as slavers crossed the miles of the Atlantic, he reminds us, entailed not only dispossession but also the promise of a new architecture of cultures and the remaking of dismembered men and gods. See "History, Fable and Myth in the Caribbean and Guianas," *Selected Essays*, 157–58. Paul Gilroy writes, "The modern world represents a break with the past, not in the sense that premodern, 'traditional' Africanisms don't survive its institution, but because the significance and meaning of these survivals get irrevocably sundered from their origins. The history of slavery and the history of its imaginative recovery through expressive, vernacular cultures challenge us to delve into the specific dynamics of this severance." *The Black Atlantic:*

Modernity and Double Consciousness (Cambridge, MA: Harvard University Press, 1993), 222–23.

99 "summon filial love" Derek Walcott, *What the Twilight Says* (New York: Farrar, Straus and Giroux, 1998), 64.

100 Strivings and failures David Scott, *Conscripts of Modernity* (Durham, NC: Duke University Press, 2005).

100 an overture Was the rebirth of Toussaint Breda as Toussaint L'Ouverture the symptom of transformation as much as its precondition? At the news of another victory against the French, the word spread that Toussaint made an opening everywhere. As C.L.R. James notes, "L'Ouverture means the opening." *Black Jacobins*, 126.

100 to see beyond the end of the world James describes this process of resurrection by which the wild hordes and debased men become revolutionary masses. Ibid.

100 Loss remakes you Judith Butler, *Subjection: The Psychic Life of Power* (Palo Alto, CA: Stanford University Press, 1997); Anne Cheng, *The Melancholy of Race* (New York: Oxford University Press, 2003). This "ongoing loss or impossible recovery of the maternal," according to Fred Moten, animates the practices of freedom. *In the Break*, 228. Eduoard Glissant, *Caribbean Discourse* (Charlotteville: University of Virginia, 1989).

FIVE · *The Tribe of the Middle Passage*

103 The slave was as an orphan Douglass, *My Bondage and My Freedom*.

103 The Middle Passage was the birth canal Gomez, *Exchanging Our Country Marks*.

107 "time had faded nothing" George Jackson wrote from his prison cell in Soledad: "My recall is nearly perfect, time has faded nothing. I recall the very first kidnap. I've lived through the passage, died on the passage, lain in the unmarked, shallow graves of the millions who fertilized the Amerikan soil with their corpses; cotton and corn growing out of my chest 'until the third and fourth generation,' the tenth, the hundredth." *Soledad Brother*, 233.

SIX · *So Many Dungeons*

110 Adam and Eve *Board of Trade: Report of the Lords of the Committee of Council Appointed for the Consideration of All Matters Relating to Trade and Foreign Plantations* (1789), Part I, James Arnold's testimony.

111 the Royal Africa Company From its incorporation in 1672 to its dissolution in 1752, the Royal Africa Company owned those who were held here. James A. Rawley, *The Transatlantic Slave Trade: A History* (New York: Norton, 1981), 161.

111 "The castle looks very fine from the sea" *Writings of Jean Barbot*, 392, 404n11.

111 they called it a factory Peter Linebaugh and Marcus Rediker, *The Many-Headed Hydra: Sailors, Slaves, Commoners, and the Hidden History of the Revolutionary Atlantic* (Boston: Beacon Press, 2000), 150. The word has its origins in the Portuguese *feitoria*, a merchant company's trade outpost. Joseph E. Inikori, *Africans and the Industrial Revolution in England* (New York: Cambridge University Press, 2002).

111 "the refuse and offscourings" *Board of Trade Reports*, Part I, 80; George Francis Dow, *Slave Ships and Slaving* (Mineola, NY: Dover Publications, 2002), 83.

112 Nana Taabiri watched over all the creatures When the British built the fort, the shrine was moved outside the castle, but it was returned in 1977.

113 Olaudah Equiano believed Olaudah Equiano, *The Interesting Narrative* (1789; repr., New York: Penguin, 1995), 55.

113 On the slaving voyage of the *Albion Frigate* See *Churchill's Collection of Voyages* (London, 1746), Vol. 5; Dow, *Slave Ships and Slaving*, 83.

114 Sengbe Pieh, the leader of the slave revolt Matthew Christensen, "Cannibals in the Postcolony," *Research in African Literatures* 36, no. 1 (2005).

114 "In their own country" Isert, *Letters on West Africa and the Slave Trade*, eleventh letter, 175.

114 Excrement was the material residue Elias Canetti, *Crowds and Power*, trans. Carol Stewart (New York: Farrar, Straus and Giroux, 1984), 211.

115 a team of archaeologists Doig Simmonds, "A Note on the Excavations in Cape Coast Castle," *Transactions of the Historical Society of Ghana* 14, no. 2 (1973): 267–69. Also see Bayo Holsey, "Routes of Remembrance: The Transatlantic Slave Trade in the Ghanaian Imagination" (PhD diss., Columbia University, 2003).

115 Waste is the interface of life and death My own line of argument is much informed by Marcel Hénaff's reading of waste in *Sade*. "Bodily wastes remain truly irredeemable, unspeakable . . . They evoke dull, ordinary horror of what is vile, worthless and contemptible—a pile of shit, in the vulgar phrase that indicates an act of foreclosure. Of all the foreclosures on which culture is founded, this one is the most violent, and therefore the most necessary. It must leave behind no traces and of memory. It is outside history, dissolved in utter amnesia." *Sade, The Invention of the Libertine Body*, trans. Xavier Callahan (Minneapolis: University of Minnesota Press, 1999), 196.

119 a thousand or more men and boys This is based on a 15.5 percent mortality rate in the first decades of the eighteenth century; prior to the eighteenth century, the mortality rate was 21.6 percent. A. W. Lawrence, *Trade Castles and Forts of West Africa* (London: Jonathan Cape, 1969), 189; David Eltis and David Richardson, eds., *Routes to Slavery: Direction, Ethnicity, and Mortality in the Transatlantic Slave Trade* (London: Cass, 1997), 45; Lovejoy, *Transformations in Slavery*, 61. The mortality rate in the dungeon sometimes exceeded that of the Middle Passage. Most of the captives died from dysentery.

119 arrived at the castle in small lots For the most part, the trade was characterized by exchanges of small groups of slaves. For example, between 1772 and 1780, Richard Miles, the governor of Cape Coast, made 1,308 purchases in order to obtain 2,218 slaves. Herbert S. Klein, *The Atlantic Slave Trade* (New York: Cambridge University Press, 1999), 122–23.

119 The coffles traveled hundreds of miles By the eighteenth century, the journey averaged two hundred miles. Gomez, *Exchanging Our Country Marks*, 155; Manning, *Slavery and African Life*, 58, 62, 64–72; Van Dantzig, *Records of Dutch West India Company*.

119 women and children usually were not chained Governor Robert Miles noted that in the years 1765 to 1784, "they have generally sores from travelling through the woods, by paths which admit but one at a time, and are much emaciated. The men are

brought down with a sort of log on their arms; the women and children are at liberty." *Board of Trade Reports*, Part I, 41.

120 irons were attached *Minutes of the Evidence taken before a committee of the Whole House to whom it was referred to consider of the Slave Trade*, Part I, 58, 1789.

120 The double irons Colin Palmer, *Human Cargoes: The British Slave Trade to Spanish America, 1700–1739* (Urbana: University of Illinois Press, 1981), 43; PRO, T70/5, p. 40. When the forts were poorly supplied and lacking the necessary irons, captives were unfettered. See Stephanie Smallwood, "Salt-Water Slaves: African Enslavement, Forced Migration, and Settlement in the Anglo-Atlantic World" (PhD diss., Duke University, 1999).

120 The number of prisoners fluctuated Lawrence, *Trade Castles and Forts*, 189. A decade after it lost its monopoly in the trade, the Royal Africa Company delivered as few as 395 slaves in 1711. Rawley, *Transatlantic Slave Trade*, 161.

120 Each slave was confined to his own place Simmonds, "Note on the Excavations," 267; Palmer, *Human Cargoes*, 43.

120 made dysentery commonplace These subterranean conditions proved fatal for many slaves, although the trading company considered it "a good security to the garrison against any insurrection." *Writings of Jean Barbot*, 404n11. Richard B. Sheridan, *Doctors and Slaves: A Medical and Demographic History of Slavery in the British West Indies, 1680–1834* (New York: Cambridge University Press, 1985), 116; Wendell Leon Hicks, *The Bloody Flux* (Pittsburgh: Azaka Publications, 1982), x.

120 the bloody flux Sheridan, *Doctors and Slavery*, 116.

121 None of these recommendations There was no archaeological evidence of bunks arranged along the walls for slaves to sleep on. Simmonds, "Notes on the Excavations."

123 His name was Kwabena This account is based upon Cugoano's *Thoughts and Sentiments on the Evil of Slavery*.

127 too awful to describe? In a letter written to Reverend E. Bass of Massachusetts in July 1775, Quaque described slavery as an "iniquitous practice methinks seems to set Religion aside and only making Room for the height of Ambition and Grandeur, the pride of Monarchs &c. to enter." Paul Edwards and David Dabydeen, eds., *Black Writers in Britain 1760–1890* (Edinburgh: Edinburgh University Press, 1991), 110.

128 the black chaplain at Elmina F. L. Bartels, "Jacobus Eliza Johannes Capitein," *Transactions of the Historical Society of Ghana* 4, part 1 (1959): 3–13.

130 each generation felt anew Fred Moten, "Uplift and Criminality" (manuscript, 2004); Cedric Robinson, *Black Marxism* (London: Zed Press, 1995).

132 "no human involved" Sylvia Wynter observes that the Western discourse of Man created an Other, the deselected "Nigger," with the latter being made to function as the signifier of the symbolic death to our present conception of the human being. This other, called an alien, a stranger, if not entirely of a different species, was "plac[ed] outside the 'sanctified universe of obligation,'" and thus deemed disposable. "Forum N.H.I. Knowledge for the 21st Century," *Knowledge on Trial*, 1.1 (Fall 1994) 5–6, 45. See also "Unsettling the Coloniality of Being/Power/Truth/Freedom," *CR: The New Centennial Review*, 3.3 (2003), 257–337.

133 "the sublime ideal of freedom" Petition of Boston Committee of Slaves 1773, in Dorothy Porter, ed., *Early Negro Writing, 1760–1837* (Boston: Beacon Press, 1971).

133 "without providence or final cause" Michel Foucault, "Nietzsche, Genealogy and History," in *Language, Counter-Memory, Practice*, trans. Donald F. Bouchard and Sherry Simon (Ithaca, NY: Cornell University Press, 1977), 155.

134 I wondered how the children Manning, *Slavery and African Life*, 99.

SEVEN · The Dead Book

136 if you look at the sea long enough Fernand Braudel, *Memory and the Mediter-ranean*, trans. Siân Reynolds (New York: Vintage, 2001).

136 "the sea is history" Derek Walcott, "The Sea Is History," *Collected Poems* (New York: Farrar, Straus and Giroux, 1986), 364–67.

136 "well excavated grave" Marianne Moore, "The Grave," *The Collected Poems of Marianne Moore* (New York: Penguin Books, 1994), 49.

137 "the precarious domicile of words" Michel Foucault describes these lives as "infamous in the strict sense: they no longer exist except through the terrible words that were destined to render them forever unworthy of the memory of men." "Lives of Infamous Men," in *The Essential Foucault*, edited by Paul Rabinow and Nikolas Rose (New York: New Press, 2003), 284.

138 a musty trial transcript *Trial of Captain John Kimber for the Murder of a Negro Girl on Board the Ship Recovery* (London: H. D. Symonds, 1792), 8. The other versions of the trial I have consulted are *The Supposed Murder of an African Girl at the Admiralty Sessions* (London, 1792); *The Whole of the Proceedings and Trial of Captain John Kimber for the Willful Murder of a Negro Girl* (London, 1792); *The Trial of Captain Kimber for the Murder of Two Female Negro Slaves, on Board the Recovery, African Slave Ship* (London, 1792).

140 The girl was sick It is possible that the girl was infected with a sexually transmitted disease—such diseases spread in Africa, Europe, and the Americas as a result of the transatlantic trade—or that her yaws was mistaken for a venereal disease. Gonorrhea and syphilis too formed a bridge connecting the worlds of the Atlantic—diseased emissions, fluxes, and discharges. See Philip Curtin, "Epidemiology and the Slave Trade," *Political Science Quarterly* 83 (1968). At this point, Europeans believed yaws was a venereal disease, which it is not; it is an infectious tropical disease caused by dermal contact. This would also explain why the other women isolated the girl. Because of racist notions about the "sexual proclivity of Africans," venereal disease was believed to be common among them. John Hippisley, *Essays on the Populousness of Africa* (London, 1764); Thomas Phillips, *A Journal of a Voyage Made in the Hannibal of London, ann. 1693, 1694, from England, to Cape Monseradoe in Africa; and Thence Along the Coast of Guiney to Whidaw, the island of St. Thomas, and So Forward to Barbadoes. With a Cursory Account of the Country, the People, their Manners, Forts, Trade, &c.* (London, 1752).

140 resembled a slaughterhouse Alexander Falconbridge, *An Account of the Slave Trade on the Coast of Africa* (London, 1788), 25.

140 The venereal distemper was common among the blacks James Barbot, the captain of the *Albion Frigate*, advised: "The venereal distemper is very common, the blacks seeming to be little concerned at it as they have a way to cure with mercury; but few Europeans who get it escape dying miserably. I cannot therefore but seriously recommend to all such as happen to go thither, to forebear having to do with any black women as they value their own lives." Despite this warning, he remarked on the difficulty of restraint, because of the "young sprightly maidens, full of jollity and good humor, afforded us abundance of recreation." *An Abstract of a Voyage in the Albion Frigate*," in *Churchill's Voyages*, Vol. 5, reprinted in Dow, *Slavers and Slave Trading*, 81.

141 murder was part of "work at sea" Marcus Rediker writes, "Calculated viciousness was often a foundation of authority, a stellar part of a large economy of discipline . . . Murder was clearly a part of the social relations of work at sea." *Between the Devil and the Deep Blue Sea: Merchant Seamen, Pirates, and the Anglo-American Maritime World, 1700–1750* (New York: Cambridge University Press, 1987), 219.

141 "Outrages of that nature" *Trial of Captain Kimber for the Murder of Two Female Negro Slaves*, 18.

141 "The prey was divided" John Newton, *The Journal of a Slave Trader* (London: Epworth Press, 1962), 104.

143 "A young girl of fifteen" *Parliamentary Debates (Hansard)* (1792), 30: 1070.

143 132 live slaves dumped into the sea When the captain of the *Zong* jettisoned 132 slaves into the Atlantic to minimize his losses and collect the insurance, (£30 for each slave lost to the "perils of the sea"), the court of King's Bench decided in his favor. The response to this atrocity was new laws restricting the kinds of losses insured at sea. Mr. Piggot, counsel for the insurers in the *Zong* trial, also defended Captain Kimber. An act of 1788 "rendered void all insurances on slaves against any risk other than 'the perils of the sea, piracy, insurrection, or capture by the king's enemies, barratry of the master and crew and destruction by fire.'" An act of 1799 provided that "no loss or damage shall be recoverable on account of the mortality of slaves by natural death or ill treatment, or against loss by throwing overboard of slaves on any account whatsoever." J. P. Van Niekerk, *The Development of the Principles of Insurance Law in the Netherlands from 1500–1800* (Cape Town: Juta & Co., 1998), 433n88. See also Rawley, *Transatlantic Slave Trade*, 299; Prince Hoare, *Memoirs of Granville Sharp, Esq. Composed from His Own Manuscripts, and Other Authentic Documents in the Possession of His Family and of the African Institution* (London: H. Colburn, 1828), viii, xvii–xviii; Henry Roscoe, *Reports of Cases Argued and Determined in the Court of King's Bench* (1782–1785), III: 232–35.

144 none of the surgeon's rememdies improved her lethargy or sulkiness *Extracts of such journals of the surgeons employed in ships trading to the coast of Africa . . . 18th June 1789*, the Sheffield copy, 3. Vague disorders like sulkiness and decline transformed grief into an illness or complaint to be treated and eliminated. In the extracts of the journals he presented to the Customs House of London, Joseph Buckhman, a surgeon, recorded sulkiness as the cause of death of a woman who died on board the ship *James*. Two slaves on board the *Lively* died of decline. These were common forms of curing melancholy according to Alexander Falconbridge, "Upon the negroes refusing to take sustenance, I have seen coals of fire, glowing hot, put on a shovel, and placed so near their lips as to scorch and burn them. And this has been accompanied with threats, of forcing them to swallow the coals, if they any longer persisted in refusing to eat. These

means have generally had the desired effect. I have also been credibly informed, that a certain captain in the slave trade, poured melted lead on such of the negroes as obstinately refused their food." *Account of the Slave Trade on the Coast of Africa.*

144 "No one who had the melancholy was ever cured" Dr. Thomas Trotter of the *Brookes* advised dancing as a therapeutic measure against suicidal melancholy. However, he admitted that despite such efforts to exercise the body and improve the spirits, melancholy still prevailed. "Minutes of the Evidence (1790) Part II," *House of Commons Sessional Papers*, 86. The surgeon on board the *Elizabeth* estimated that the death of at least two-thirds of those lost in Atlantic passage was due to melancholy: "He heard them say in their language that they wished to die . . . The symptoms are lowness of spirits and despondency. Hence they refuse food. This only increases the symptoms. The stomach afterwards got weak. Hence the belly ached, fluxes ensued and they were carried off." "Minutes of the Evidence, Volume II, Part II," *House of Commons Sessional Papers* 562 (219).

144 a reputation for destroying themselves Philip D. Morgan, *Slave Counterpoint: Black Culture in the Eighteenth-Century Chesapeake and Lowcountry* (Chapel Hill: University of North Carolina Press, 1998); Postma, *Dutch in the Atlantic Slave Trade.* Henry Coor noted that when driven to despair, Gold Coast Negroes cut their throats, while those from the interior hung themselves. "Minutes of the Evidence IV," *House of Commons Sessional Papers*, 71. Slaves shipped from Elmina had a propensity for suicide by hanging. See William Piersen, "White Cannibals, Black Martyrs," *Journal of Negro History* 62 (April 1979): 153.

144 Mild means were used "Part II, Minutes of the Evidence," *House of Commons Sessional Papers* 569 (222).

145 the relation between the loins and the buttocks Abbé Boileau, *Historia Flagellantium, de recto et perverso flagrorum usu apud Christianos* (Paris, 1700), 294–95, cited in Ian Gibson, *The English Vice: Beating, Sex, and Shame in Victorian England and After* (London: Duckworth, 1978), 7. Sex and punishment were linked inextricably in the economy of slavery and, as well, because the story of a naked fourteen-year-old being flogged was all too easily confused with the erotic articles of *Gentleman's Magazine*. See G. S. Rousseau and Roy Porter, eds., *Sexual Underworlds of the Enlightenment* (Chapel Hill: University of North Carolina Press, 1988), 52.

146 similarly attired sailors The sailors probably were outfitted in overcoats and vests and hats and silver buckled shoes rather than attired in the standard baggy, wide breeches of heavy nap, which were tar-smeared to protect from cold and dampness, checkered shirts of coarse linen, and Monmouth caps. Marcus Rediker, *Between the Devil and the Deep Blue Sea*, 11.

147 the picaresque proletarian Peter Linebaugh, *The London Hanged: Crime and Civil Society in the Eighteenth Century* (New York: Cambridge University Press, 1992).

147 "No difference, no-one at night" "The Sable Venus, An Ode," 1781.

147 "death from natural causes" Van Niekerk, *Development of the Principles of Insurance Law*, 433–34.

147 The London Assurance Company Policy on slaves Ibid., 434. Also see H.A.L. Cockerell and Edwin Green, *The British Insurance Business 1547–1970: An Introduction and Guide to Historical Records in the United Kingdom* (London: Heinemann, 1976), 14;

Bernard Drew, *The London Assurance: A Second Chronicle* (London: London Assurance, 1949), 36–38; A. H. John, "The London Assurance and the Marine Insurance Market of the Eighteenth Century," *Economica* 25 (1958): 126–41; Frederic R. Sanborn, *Origins of the Early English Maritime and Commercial Law* (New York: Century Company, 1930).

148 "The insurer takes upon him the risk John Weskett, *A Complete Digest of the Theory, Laws and Practice of Insurance* (London, 1781), 525.

149 "where all life is violence" *The Whole of the Proceedings and Trial of Captain John Kimber, for the Wilful Murder of a Negro Girl.*

150 "Before men can benefit" Hansard, *Parliamentary Debates*, 29: 1061.

150 *it afforded a salutary lesson Trial of Captain Kimber for the Murder of Two Female Negro Slaves*, vi.

152 "I am going to meet my friends" A woman on board the *Pegase* refused all sustenance and declined even to speak. As a consequence, "she was then ordered the thumb screws and suspended in the mizzen rigging, and every attempt made with the cat [o' nine-tails] and those instruments they have generally on board; but all to no purpose. She died three or four days afterwards." The night before she died, she confided to the other women that "she was going to her friends." "Part III, Minutes of the Evidence," *House Sessional Papers*, 887.

EIGHT · *Lose Your Mother*

156 European traders, too, employed occultists Sylviane A. Diouf, ed., *Fighting the Slave Trade* (Athens: Ohio University Press, 2003), xviii.

156 A famous slave trader on the Rio Pongo Djibril Tamsir Niane, "Africa's Understanding of the Slave Trade, Oral Accounts," *Diogenes* 179, 45.3 (Autumn 1997): 75–89.

156 In Ewe country Anne Bailey, *African Voices of the Atlantic Slave Trade* (Boston: Beacon Press, 2005), 160.

157 in the household of the owner Patterson, *Slavery and Social Death*, 52.

157 soulless men, and walking corpses Joan Dayan, *Haiti, History, and the Gods* (Berkeley: University of California Press, 1995), 36–37.

157 "they soon forgot" Zurara, *Chronicle of the Discovery and Conquest of Guinea*, I: 85.

158 Like the term "nigger" Sterling Stuckey, *Slave Culture: Nationalist Theory and the Foundations of Black America* (New York: Oxford University Press, 1987), 198–99; Winthrop D. Jordan, *White Over Black: American Attitudes Toward the Negro, 1550–1812* (Chapel Hill: University of North Carolina Press, 1968), 74, 95–96. Cedric Robinson writes, "The 'Negro,' that is the color black, was both a negation of Africa and a unity of opposition to white. The construct of Negro, unlike the terms 'African,' 'Moor,' or 'Ethiope,' suggested no situatedness in time, that is history, or space, that is ethno- or politico-geography. The Negro had no civilization, no cultures, no religions, no history, no place, and finally no humanity that might command consideration." *Black Marxism: The Making of the Black Radical Tradition* (Chapel Hill: University of North Carolina Press, 2000), 81.

158 "the human pulse stops at the gate of the barracoon" Aimé Césaire, *Notebook of a Return to the Native Land*, trans. and ed. Clayton Eshleman and Annette Smith (Middletown, CT: Wesleyan University Press, 2001), 28.

158 "applied strictly to any man or woman" Rattray, *Asante Law*, 35; T. Edward Bowditch, *Mission from Cape Coast Castle to Ashantee, with a Statistical Account of the Kingdom, and Geographical Notices of Other Parts of the Interior of Africa* (1819; repr., London: Cass, 1966), 182–83. *Donkor* referred to a captive from the northern regions of Guinea, which included areas of Mossi and Hausaland and Dagomba and Gonja.

158 "they were middle size" Captain John Adams, *Sketches Taken During Ten Voyages to Africa Between the Years 1786 and 1800* (1822; repr., New York: Johnson Reprint Corp., 1970), 9.

158 "One could hardly call them human" Roemer, *A Reliable Account of the Coast of Guinea*, 28, 182.

159 " 'It is you, Whites' " Ibid., 35.

160 population decline Manning, *Slavery and African Life*, 55, 58, 82.

160 Lemba Miller, *Way of Death*, 201–202; John M. Janzen, *Lemba 1650–1930: A Drum of Affliction in Africa and the New World* (New York: Garland Publishing, 1982).

160 the Diola built altars to their captives Robert M. Baum, *Shrines of the Slave Trade: Diola Religion and Society in Precolonial Senegambia* (New York: Oxford University Press, 1999), 116–18.

161 By honoring slave spirits Judy Rosenthal, *Possession, Ecstasy and Law in Ewe Voodoo* (Charlottesville: University of Virginia Press, 1998), 48, 95, 153.

161 King Buzzard Edward C. L. Adams, *Tales of the Congaree*, ed. Robert G. O'Meally (Chapel Hill: University of North Carolina Press, 1987), 120–21. The tale Adams recorded was in his version of Negro dialect: "An' when he dead, dere were no place in heaven for him an' he were not desired in hell. An' de Great Master decide dat he were lower dan all other men or beasts; he punishment were to wander for eternal time over de face er de earth. Dat as he had kilt sperrits of mens an' womens as well as dere bodies, he must wander on an' on. Dat his sperrit should always travel in de form of a great buzzad, an dat' carrion must be he food."

163 old-style blackface performance Catherine Cole, "Reading Blackface in West Africa," *Critical Inquiry*, v. 23.1 (Autumn 1996).

164 the Ministry of Tourism launched an advertising campaign "Ghana's Uneasy Embrace of Slavery's Diaspora," *New York Times*, December 27, 2005, A1, A8.

164 "the abuse of human beings and things" Armah, *The Healers*, 94.

167 "a privilege so dangerous" Douglass, *My Bondage and My Freedom*. See Stephen Best and Saidiya Hartman, "Fugitive Justice," *Representations* 92 (Winter 2006).

167 "Am I not a man and a brother?" "The apologetic density of the assertion 'we are human beings like any others,' " writes Achille Mbembe, "can be gauged only with respect to the violence that precedes it and makes it not only possible but necessary." "African Modes of Self-Writing," *Public Culture* 14, no. 1 (Winter 2002).

170 two Ghanaian boys were found dead *Guardian*, December 6, 2002.

172 better than that of brothers Amilcar Cabral, *Return to the Source: Selected Speeches by Amikar Cabral* (New York: Monthly Review Press, 1973), 76.

NINE · *The Dark Days*

174 The mind has been described as an inner eye Richard Rorty, *Philosophy and the Mirror of Nature* (Princeton: Princeton University Press, 1981).

177 "Electricity in abundance" Kwame Nkrumah, *The Autobiography of Kwame Nkrumah* (London: Panaf, 1973); Kwame Nkrumah, "African Prospect," *Foreign Affairs* 37, no. 1 (October 1958): 45.

177 most of Ghana was still in darkness Fanon, *Wretched of the Earth*, 311.

TEN · *The Famished Road*

179 A woman named Thiamba Gwendolyn Midlo Hall, ed., *Databases for the Study of Afro-Louisiana History and Genealogy 1699–1860* (Baton Rouge: Louisiana State University Press, 2000). The information about Thiamba was found in the inventory of belongings of Alexandre Baure, dated 1790, in the courthouse of St. Charles Parish.

180 The largest caravans R. la T. Lonsdale, *Blue Book 1882*, in Marion Johnson, ed., *Salaga Papers* (Legon: Institute of African Studies, University of Ghana, 1965); Paul E. Lovejoy, *Caravans of Kola: The Hausa Kola Trade, 1700–1900* (Zaria, Nigeria: Ahmadu Bello University Press, 1980), 124–25, 103.

181 a road of torment and devastation My description of the road is borrowed from Ben Okri's *The Famished Road* (New York: Anchor Books, 2001), 114–15, 326–27.

183 *"Zaa ni gun ja goro"* See Hahdi Adamu, *The Hausa Factor in West African History* (Zaria, Nigeria: Ahmadu Bello University Press, 1978). At least 70 to 140 metric tons of kola passed through the market. Lovejoy, *Caravans of Kola*, 114–15.

183 the Islamic reform movement "The extension of Islam into the savanna and the sahel was closely related to the export of slaves in this region." Henry A. Gemery and Jan S. Hogendorn, eds., *The Uncommon Market: Essays in the Economic History of the Atlantic Slave Trade* (New York: Academic Press, 1979), 201, 205. Lovejoy, *Transformations in Slavery*, 155.

184 ten thousand people entered the market This figure is from M. J. Bonnat, *Liverpool Mercury*, June 12, 1876, in Johnson, *Salaga Papers*. Gouldsbury cites the same figure in his report.

184 And then there were the slaves Marion Johnson, "The Slaves of Salaga," *Journal of African History* 27 (1986): 343. In the opening decades of the nineteenth century, a slave cost one basket of kola or 5,000 cowries; by the 1870s and 1880s, a slave sold for anywhere between 36,000 and 70,000 cowries, or four baskets of kola. Friedrich August Ramseyer, *Four Years in Ashantee* (New York: R. Carter & Brothers, 1875); *UNESCO Research into Oral Traditions: Oral Traditions of Gonja* (Legon: Institute of African Studies, University of Ghana, 1969), 34.

185 the Reverend Theophil Opoku Johnson, *Salaga Papers* (Legon: Institute of African Studies, University of Ghana, 1965).

186 the volume of slave trading increased According to David Eltis, about 310,000 slaves were exported each decade in the period from 1821 to 1830 and 1831 to 1840. Eltis cited in Jan S. Hogendorn and Henry A. Gemery, "Abolition and Its Impact on Monies Imported to West Africa," in *The Abolition of the Atlantic Slave Trade: Origins and Effects in Europe, Africa, and the Americas*, edited by David Eltis and James Walvin (Madison: University of Wisconsin Press, 1981), 108. See also Frederick Cooper, Thomas C. Holt, and Rebecca J. Scott, eds., *Beyond Slavery: Explorations of Race, Labor, and Citizenship in Post-emancipation Societies* (Chapel Hill: University of North Carolina Press, 2000), 113. On *The Spade*, see Thomas, *Slave Trade*; Lovejoy, *Transformations in Slavery*, 19.

186 The greater demand for slaves Meillassoux, *Anthropology of Slavery*, 62–63.

187 more slaves in Africa Martin Klein and Paul Lovejoy, "Slavery in West Africa," in *The Uncommon Market*, edited by Henry A. Gemery and Jan S. Hogendorn (New York: Academic Press, 1979).

189 No chain of common ancestors The Gonjas attacked only strangers and their enemies. *UNESCO Research into Oral Traditions*, 137.

190 "a way of establishing a place for the living" Michel de Certeau, *The Writing of History*, trans. Tom Conley (New York: Columbia University Press, 1988).

191 the words of the *ngbanya UNESCO Research into Oral Traditions*.

192 "sumptuous memories of plundering kings" Martin Klein, "Studying the History of Those Who Would Rather Forget," *History in Africa* 16 (1989): 209–17.

193 without either a history or an inheritance Patterson, *Slavery and Social Death*, 5.

194 "'Give her to me and I will give you mine'" *UNESCO Research into Oral Traditions*, 95.

201 Ruins were the only monuments to slavery in Salaga This line of thinking is indebted to David Lloyd's essay "Ruins/Runes," in *Cities Without Citizens*, edited by Eduardo Cadava and Aaron Levy (Philadelphia: Slought Books/Rosenbach Museum and Library, 2005).

ELEVEN · *Blood Cowries*

205 "For those who can read the landscape" Mariane C. Ferme, *The Underneath of Things* (Berkeley: University of California Press, 2001), 25.

206 Cowrie shells Jan Hogendorn and Marion Johnson, eds., *The Shell Money of the Slave Trade* (New York: Cambridge University Press, 1986), 104.

207 shipped them to Africa as ballast Hogendorn and Johnson, *Shell Money*, 46.

207 more than twenty-five million pounds of cowries Ibid., 62.

207 "based on the mistaken assumption" Anselm Guezo, "The Other Side of the Story: Essays on the Atlantic Slave Trade" (manuscript), 19, 26; Thornton, *Africa and Africans*, 45, 51.

208 "Negro currency" Bosman, *New and Accurate Description*, 362–64. Europeans did believe that better care was taken of the slaves exchanged for cowries than for other goods.

TWELVE · *Fugitive Dreams*

219 they were the archive of the defeated Carola Lentz and Hans-Jürgen Sturm, "Of Trees and Earth Shrines: An Interdisciplinary Approach to Settlement Histories in the West African Savanna," *History in Africa* 28 (2001): 139–68.

219 Laterite dwellings This relation between earth and dwelling, between land and house, is at the heart of the Sisala cosmology. The land is revered and "conceived as a personal being, capable of feelings and also able to enter into relationship." Edward Tengan, *The Land as Being and Cosmos* (Frankfurt: Peter Lang, 1991), 38.

220 There was so much to fear Ibid., 57; Rosalind Shaw, *Memories of the Slave Trade: Ritual and the Historical Imagination in Sierra Leone* (Chicago: University of Chicago Press, 2002), 50–68.

222 The women stood outside the circle of elders Tengan, *Land as Being and Cosmos*, 66.

222 "a captive on reprieve" Adama Guèye, "The Impact of the Slave Trade on Cayor and Baol: Mutations in Habitat and Land Occupancy," in *Fighting the Slave Trade: West African Strategies*, edited by Sylviane A. Diouf (Athens: Ohio University Press, 2003), 53.

225 the Sisala The migration stories of stateless groups are dense poetic constructions rather than literal accounts of migration routes and dates. I have replicated the poetics of the historical imagination of the stateless in my own telling. See Carola Lentz, "Of Hunters, Goats and Earth Shrines: Settlement Histories and the Politics of the Oral Tradition in Northern Ghana," *History in Africa* 27 (2000): 193–214; Tengan, *Land as Being and Cosmos*, 21.

225 blended their histories R. S. Rattray writes: "The only traces of the former origin, in some cases being clan totems and sometimes the retention of certain distinctive customs which mark them out as different from the tribes in which they have been absorbed."

226 tribes See Morton H. Fried, *The Notion of the Tribe* (Menlo Park, CA: Benjamin Cummings, 1975); Eugene L. Mendonsa, *Continuity and Change in a West African Society: Globalization's Impact on the Sisala of Ghana* (Durham, NC: Carolina Academic Press, 2001), 25; Charles Piot, *Remotely Global: Village Modernity in West Africa* (Chicago: University of Chicago Press, 1999); Emmanuel Forster Tamakloe, *A Brief History of the Dagbamba People* (Gold Coast: Government Printing Office, 1931).

226 Refugees, fugitives, and wanderers These new migrants "greatly increas[ed] the population over the autochthons who dotted the area." However, "immigrants and original inhabitants alike continued to be pursued and raided even after taking refuge in this relatively isolated area." Aggressive and powerful states like Gonja, Mamprusi, Dagomba, Wala, and Mossi, as well as raiders and mercenaries continued to follow them, raiding, enslaving, and butchering them. Mendonsa, *Continuity and Change*, 27.

226 *ones who came together* Eugene Mendonsa has described the *grunshi* as the raw material of the ruling groups, "not unlike a field of grain, to be harvested at will." Ibid.

229 corpses were dragged to the bush In Ulu , so many died combating the Zabarimas that they were unable to maintain their customary funeral practice that entailed a second ceremony months after interment in which beer was brewed, "and the bow, quiver, mats and stool of the deceased was taken to the cross-roads and burned and the fire quenched with beer and the widows shaved." When a belated funeral was finally held for all those killed by Babatu, not all the names of the dead were called, and the neglected dead became angry. Rather than risk the opprobrium of the dead, the practice of the second funeral ceased. Rattray, 536. In neighboring towns, Babatu slaughtered so many people that funeral practices were transformed. The *tindana* (earth priest) could no longer call all the names of those who died.

230 the Sisala rose in revolt Stanislaw Pilaszewicz, *Hausa Prose Writings in Ajami* (Berlin: Dietrich Reimer, 2000), 289–90.

232 persons who were trampled The raiding armies that blazed through towns and villages across the savanna kidnapping people, destroying crops, burying men in anthills, slaughtering the elderly, abandoning infants to die, raping women, and branding and selling slaves were African too. See S. W. Koelle, *Polyglotta Africana, or a Comparative Vocabulary of Nearly 300 Words and Phrases in More Than 100 Distinct African Languages* (London, 1854), 13.

233 no one spoke of slaves The word for "slave" is *yomo*. Slaves in Sisalaland like those elsewhere were defined as people without kin or ancestors. For this reason slaves could not own ancestral shrines or perform the ritual duties connected with them. According to Eugene Mendosa, "The slave child (*yomobie*) remained a jural minor all of his life and passed this inferior position on to his children, much like a bastard (*mengmouribie*)."

ACKNOWLEDGMENTS

On this journey, I have accrued many debts to persons known and unknown. The easiest obligations to acknowledge are to those I can name and the greatest to those I cannot. Mary Ellen and John Ray opened their house and made a place for me. They taught me far more than is reflected in these pages and for that I will be ever grateful. Anna Bannerman-Richter, Mary Dillard, Geneva Moore, Margaret Musgrove, and Doris Awunor offered friendship and attenuated the loneliness. Kofi Anyidoho encouraged me to write a history of slavery that was a personal story. Joseph Nkrumah supported this project in its infancy. Laura Hartman and Maria Vargas-Pile shared family stories that they told far better than I ever have. Zonya Johnson and Julia Lowe provided wise counsel. Lindon Barrett, Stephen Best, Judith Butler, Eduardo Cadava, Joan Dayan, Tina Campt, Hazel Carby, Anne Cheng, Donna Daniels, Farah Griffin, Tera Hunter, Anthony and Maria Grahn-Farley, Judith Jackson Fossett, Oliver Jackson, Abdul JanMohamed, Donna Jones, David Lloyd, Sharon Marcus, June Miller, Fred Moten, Kaja Silverman, Ula Taylor, Robyn Wiegman, and Frank Wilderson read the manuscript and made many helpful suggestions for revisions. Marina Benjamin, Tobe Correal, Greg Klerx, Tom Jenks, Vijaya Nagarajan, Paul Rogers, and Ethel Smith have guided me along the way. Marisa Fuentes has been my devoted research assistant. Her labor has made my own so much easier. Lisa

Ze provided much assistance in the last stages of the project. This book has benefited greatly from the comments of my editors, John Glusman and Paul Elie. My agent, Joe Spieler, has believed in this project from the very beginning and supported it with rigorous criticism and generous praise.

I owe everything to Samuel, who has been unstinting in his love and support. He has read these pages again and again and his enthusiasm has been constant during the long life of this project. Kasia never fails to remind me of beauty, especially during those moments when it is hardest for me to see.

The enduring debt is to strangers.

INDEX

Page numbers in *italics* refer to illustrations.